LAWYERS IN BUSINESS

Lawyers in Business:

And The Law Business

Karl J. Mackie

Lecturer in Law and Social Psychology
University of Nottingham

M

MACMILLAN
PRESS

First published 1989

Published by
THE MACMILLAN PRESS LTD
Houndsmills, Basingstoke, Hampshire RG21 2XS
and London
Companies and representatives
throughout the world

Phototypeset by Input Typesetting Ltd, London SW19 8DR
Printed in Hong Kong

British Library Cataloguing in Publication Data
Mackie, Karl J.
Lawyers in business: and the law business.
1. Corporation lawyers
I. Title
342.6′66   K118.15
ISBN 0–333–41908–1

Contents

List of Tables

Acknowledgments

Many individuals and organisations have helped in the research which led to this work. I should like to thank the professional associations and their officers for their support — the Commerce and Industry Group of The Law Society, the Bar Association for Commerce, Finance and Industry, the New South Wales Corporate Lawyers' Association and the Victoria Corporate Lawyers' Association. Other organisations which have assisted are the Confederation of British Industry, the Nottinghamshire Chamber of Commerce, the Chartered Institute of Arbitrators, the Institute of Arbitrators (Australia), the Australian Centre for Commercial Disputes and the General Municipal and Boiler-makers' Allied Trades Union. In particular, of course, I owe a great debt to the many individuals who gave me their time for often lengthy interviews, and especially the in-house lawyers who participated and who helped frame many of the ideas in this work although, of course, the responsibility for the views expressed and the accuracy of comments is entirely my own. Amongst the companies and legal organisations who took part (and agreed to be named) were Aaron & Partners, Air Products Ltd, Baker & McKenzie, BAT Industries, The Boots Company plc, Bates Wells & Braithwaite, Clifford Chance, CPC (United Kingdom) Ltd, D. J. Freeman, Freshfields, Hunt Dickins, Lloyds Bank plc, John Player & Sons, the Prudential Group, J. Sainsbury plc, The Wellcome Foundation Ltd, Australian Trade Commission, ICI Australia, Mahlab Group, Minter Ellison, Morris Fletcher & Cross, Shell Australia, and Peko-Wallsend Ltd. The project would also not have been possible without the financial assistance provided by the Economic and Social Research Council, the British Academy and the Australian Studies Centre, who funded various of its aspects.

I should also like to thank Ann Mackie, Dr Brian Harvey and Professors Alan Paterson and Paul Fordham for their comments and advice, at different stages of the book's development from idea through thesis; Sue Alvey and Judy Rose for their dedicated support until they were overtaken by new technology; and Ray Dennerstein for his very patient editing. Last but not least my thanks to Ann, Karen and Alan for their

support through a period when they must have wondered about
the concept of the 'integrated father'.

Part I
Lawyers in Business

1 Introduction: New Directions in Lawyering

Lawyers are not business people; however large a lawyer's experience may be, in the conduct of business he is absolutely useless.

Sir Henry Deterding, 1916

'Let's kill all the lawyers',[1] has probably been uttered more often by lawyers in their own defence than by generations of budding Thespians. The profession's fondness for the quote, of course, derives from its neat forensic value in demonstrating that there is nothing new in public antagonism towards its members — aversion to lawyers is a timeless social habit, an unfortunate side effect of the essential social role of the profession, part of the ritual and mystery at the heart of the practice of lawyering. Nevertheless, in the climate of the 1980s, there is now a more real fear in the profession than at any previous period that the suggestion of Jack Cade's comrade may be in the process of enactment in the real world. But, this time round, the danger appears in the more subtle economic and organisational forms of the 20th century rather than those envisaged by Shakespeare's rough character. It demands a more adequate response than forensic skill. Ever talented, the legal profession is beginning to respond to the challenge, to talk more explicitly than it once did of 'business' matters, of the economic structure of the legal profession, of the organisational constraints on the profession in meeting the challenges and opportunities of the 20th-century marketplace. Advertising, once an 'unethical' practice amongst solicitors, is now becoming widespread; the Bar discusses the possibility of allowing the public direct access to its members; the Lord Chancellor calls in management consultants to investigate court practices. The need to come to terms with the demands of the modern world is recognised, although the details of the restructuring required are hotly debated.

This book is concerned with a relatively modern branch of the legal profession, one which is by its very nature involved

3

deeply in economic and organisational issues — the salaried lawyer in business organisations. It is a branch which only emerged in the last quarter of the last century and only attained significant size and recognition within the last 25 years. It has passed without a great deal of attention in studies of lawyers,[2] usually being treated as a marginal element in the legal profession where mentioned — 'the forgotten men of the profession' (Maddock, 1968). This has partly reflected the attitude of the bulk of lawyers in private practice, in turn echoed not only by researchers but also by legal educators, legal writers and legal critics. Yet there is some interest in asking; what is the nature of legal practice inside a business organisation? How does it relate to and affect the wider legal profession and the world of business? What lessons are there for the modernisation of the law business?

There has been equally little interest shown in this group by social scientists,[3] a surprising omission given the central theme in public policy debates of the legal regulation of business[4] and amongst organisation theorists of the importance of the environment to explain organisation behaviour.[5] One might expect *a priori* that lawyers working in business would play an important part in defining and managing the business environment, but what part? And in whose interest? Finally, one could also say that 'in-house' legal departments have 'the somewhat dubious distinction of presiding over one of the few mystery religions left in modern business.' (Choka, 1970: 1011) They have not occupied much space in business and management journals, nor do business schools show great interest in law as an important theme for management courses. Yet law and lawyers play an increasingly significant role in business activities, and in-house lawyers are 'in the woodwork' in the largest business organisations.

It is part of the argument of this book that the emergence of the 'in-house lawyer' is not only deserving of study in its own right, but that it has lessons also both for business practice and for the legal profession as a whole in terms of more general concerns such as the delivery of legal services, and the structure and functions of the legal profession. Also, the rise of the in-house lawyer reflects important trends in the role of law in society and in turn, in-house lawyers are coming to play an important role in influencing processes of law-making and the reform of litigation.

The case for making these assertions is set out in the chapters to follow. However, it may be worthwhile at this stage to set out four important themes which run through the rest of this work. First, it draws new attention to the importance of the organisational structure and context, the institutional basis, of legal services in determining the nature, and therefore perhaps quality, of these services. The in-house lawyer is organisationally linked to his or her client in a way that is different from the traditional lawyer in private practice. What are the effects of this on the legal service received by the client, on professional identification, on relations with the outside profession, on career options? Within this argument there is also a need to recognise and analyse the influence of organisational *purpose* in the law/society mix. How well do the ends of the professional organisation that is the legal system match with the purposes of the business world?

Second, as a case study this work offers insights into some of the processes of structural change that are taking place within the legal profession, into some of the causes and consequences of changing legal specialisms and lawyer functions. Probably the majority of lawyers now accept that the 'law business' in England and Wales is in the process of a major transformation to make it more responsive to the 'consumer' of its services. A 'consumer-led' profession will perhaps necessarily divide into different 'businesses', but of what kinds, and in what way effective, in what way regulated, in what way in harmony? This study of in-house lawyers highlights some important elements of one example of such a process, and offers some thoughts on the implications for the profession at large.

Third, as a study of the psychology of lawyers, of the 'occupational life-space' of one branch of the profession, the research discussed can be seen as a case study of the professional's search for 'competence', an example of a more universal psychological need and ability of individuals effectively to cope with the challenges of their working lives. The 'drive' for competence, in the context of the social role of a lawyer, is expressed in the way the in-house lawyers studied are concerned to articulate the nature of effective professional legal service in a new institutional setting. This book is partly intended as a contribution to that search for competence amongst in-house lawyers, in trying to help define a new type of legal practice (or perhaps merely re-emphasise the traditional ideal of professional practice), one I have described as the 'integrated lawyer'.

Finally, accompanying this search for competence and springing from it, the processes of 'professionalisation' *within* a profession underlie this case study — an example of a new branch of a profession emerging and searching for its own distinctive self-identity. The practice of law is, of course, one of the 'ancient' professions, a profession characterised by tradition-alism and conservatism, and a profession in which, perhaps more than any other profession, the concept of 'independence' is asserted as central to its vocation. What is the standing in such a profession of a new breed of lawyer, a lawyer employed full-time by the client? How is professional identity sustained?

While this work emphasises the role of the in-house lawyer in business, many of its suggestions as to the distinguishing features of this branch of the profession will also hold true for, and be of interest to, the many other lawyers working inside client organisations, be they local or national government, trade unions or charities. However, the business lawyer is also of especial interest in being at the heart of the commercial world, a central force of innovation and social change in society, for better or worse. The study therefore has some interest, too, I hope for those who shape public policy on business and business regulation as well as for those who find the world of business merely an object of intellectual curiosity. Finally, it would be remiss of me not to mention the need for businessmen to read about lawyers in business. It had obviously never occurred to some of the managers I have spoken to that they could 'manage' their lawyers to their mutual benefit. I hope this study will give them food for thought, as much as it is intended to give lawyers something to consider.

Signs of the birth of in-house legal services, however, were greeted with similar expressions of dismay to that which have clung to the traditional lawyer. The Chairman of Shell, Sir Henry Deterding, wrote in the following terms to the Managing Director of Shell's New York office in 1916:

You gave me rather a start with your letter, because I gather from it that you employ solicitors much oftener than we would ever dream of doing. Although we have an emormous business here, we very rarely consult lawyers. We only do so when there is really a legal difference or legal difficulty, whilst it seems to me that you employ them in practically every instance.

Lawyers are not business people; however large a lawyer's experience may be, in the conduct of business he is absolutely useless. A lawyer placed at the head of a concern, would soon bring the business to rack and ruin. He is not a creative genius, he is able to give his opinion, if a case is laid before him, but to ask a lawyer to draw up a contract for you is a most foolish thing to do, and this is bound to lead to trouble. Our custom here is to draw up a contract before having seen the lawyer and then to ask him to put it in a more legal shape. Such a contract is more likely to embody the spirit of what has been agreed upon than one drawn up by the lawyer; to ask his opinion as to what you should do or not do is the worst possible way of conducting business, which should be kept as far as possible from the lawyers. . . . A lawyer is absolutely unfit as a business man, he is to give us advice if trouble arises and if you employ him, say 6 times a year, this can be considered the average maximum. I do not think we employ a lawyer many more times . . . I hate to see a lawyer in our office, if I want him I go to *his* office and limit the conversation to the shortest possible period. Allowing a lawyer to be practically in daily touch with me would certainly take 90% of my time which ought to be devoted to money making and not to discussing legal squabbles or legal phraseologies.[6]

History has judged Sir Henry Deterding's remarks as inappropriate, even in the context of his own company, which now houses respectable-sized legal departments in each of its national branches, running into several hundred legal staff in total. (In another slight irony of history, a major survey of the legal profession in the United States and England in the 1960s described the Shell Legal Department as 'one of the best in the United States' — Johnstone and Hopson, 1967: 211.)

Most articles on lawyers in business have been written by in-house lawyers, usually for comsumption by others in the same branch of the profession, although occasionally to waken management to the fact that they have a significant service sector in their midst which they may not be making full use of. This book explores some of the reasons for the growth of this new sector of the legal profession and analyses the role of lawyers in it. The major part of the book provides a detailed outline of the world of the in-house lawyer — reasons for their growth, the nature of their work, methods of practice management, their career attitudes and aspirations, their relations with outside lawyers and with management. The latter part of the book uses some of the evidence presented to comment on some of the broader issues raised concerning the legal profession and the legal system, and on questions of business regulation and litigation.

The study is based on the author's research into in-house legal departments in Britain and Australia, as well as on a survey of the literature on in-house lawyers. The remainder of this introductory chapter is concerned with the origins of the study, the approach taken to the research, its place in the academic literature, and the methods employed. But first a word on terminology.

IN-HOUSE AND OUT-HOUSE LAWYERS AND THE LAW BUSINESS

One of the Australian lawyers I interviewed found the term 'in-house lawyers' slightly offensive, a reminder of the era when lawyers in private practice regarded employed lawyers as an inferior branch of the profession. (Vestiges of this attitude still remain.) 'In-house lawyer', however, is a widely accepted term in the UK when lawyers are describing their own role.[7] Within a business they will normally have a more official title such as Company Lawyer or Legal Adviser or Company Solicitor or may combine their in-house legal role with the post of Company Secretary, or are referred to in the company as the 'Legal Department'. In the United States 'House Counsel' or 'Inside Counsel' or 'Corporate Counsel' or 'General Counsel' (a more senior post) are more common. Australia follows the American rather than the British pattern in its preference for 'corporate lawyer'.[8]

Although I considered using the terms 'business lawyer', 'commercial lawyer' or 'company lawyer' as a compromise, in the end I have opted to keep to the expression of 'in-house' lawyer as the most apt, given that the study is primarily set in the UK, and that the alternatives may be confused with specialisation in private practice. However, to avoid monotony I use the expression 'in-house' interchangeably with 'lawyers working in business', 'salaried lawyers' or similar expressions. It is important to note that the study is concerned with lawyers working *as* lawyers in a company, not with lawyers performing other roles in, for example, personnel or sales departments of companies, who are for some purposes sometimes also referred to as 'employed lawyers'.

The expression 'out-house lawyer' is never used by in-house lawyers, although 'outside lawyer' is common. I have therefore used the latter or refer to 'lawyers in private practice' as being readily understandable alternatives to the in-house lawyer branch of the profession. 'Solicitor' and 'barrister' refer to the divided legal profession in England and Wales, a division based largely around separate training and the restriction of rights of audience in the higher courts to the Bar. The expressions apply also in Australia, although not necessarily with the same implications for training or professional practice in that country (where practice differs even from state to state). The expressions are also used to refer to the professional qualifications of in-house lawyers. Some of the complexities of these matters for in-house lawyers are outlined later in this work, but I have restricted my comments to England, where the distinction remains sharply drawn in training and professional matters, rather than stretch the patience of the reader too far by detailing the position in the six Australian states where the distinction between the two branches is less sharply drawn overall.

Although such points may seem pedantic, there are deeper issues underlying them as the objector to the expression 'in-house' pointed out. Also, some of the possibilities for change in the legal profession which are discussed later in the book, may have repercussions in the terminology of future legal roles, for example, if there are moves to a fused profession[9] or if lawyers in private practice come to merge with other businesses, form mixed-profession partnerships, limited companies, or are employed by businesses to offer legal services to the public[10] — to whose 'house' will one be referring?

The expression in the title of this book, 'the law business', was used as a concise way to encapsulate what seemed to me one of the critical issues now facing the legal profession, namely how to balance its professional ethos with the commercial requirements being placed upon it by a consumerist society and a society which increasingly rejects restrictive practices in all spheres of service. It can be argued in any case that law always has been a business but was too status conscious to admit it. (This point is considered further in chapter 12.) Now that lawyers are being forced to talk openly about commercial needs, it is time to bring out more clearly the different options for running this 'service industry' and their implications for the profession and for public access to legal services. This issue is closely bound up with questions about the in-house lawyer, client access and services. The mere fact that the in-house lawyer has already accommodated to being 'in business' itself carries a message for the profession at large. Finally I have used the expression to indicate that this book deals also with the business of law in its broader senses — questions of law-making and regulation (chapter 10), of litigation and dispute-resolution processes (chapter 11).

THE WORLD OF THE IN-HOUSE LAWYER

In a sense, of course, it is misleading to talk of 'the world' of the lawyer in business, just as it is unlikely one could find a 'typical' lawyer as such, although one can find degrees of approximation. There are many such worlds, both on a literal and on a psychological level of discourse. Lawyers work for a great variety of business and non-business organisations, each situation making different demands on their personal, organisational and lawyering skills. This study concentrates on lawyers who work in a general legal department of a large business corporation. It should be remembered that many others work not only in other types of organisation but also in other specialist departments of companies such as patents, tax, pensions, insurance as well as in non-legal capacities in personnel, sales and general management.

The world of the in-house lawyer is also intangible at a deeper conceptual level, in that all human activity is subject to a range of interpretations and perceptions. New interpretations can feed into an activity and cause it to be redefined in such a way as to alter how those carrying it out, and those affected by it, perceive it and act on it. Indeed, one example of such a process, the growth of 'consciousness of themselves as a class' amongst in-house lawyers, forms a significant element in what I have to say about the business lawyer 'movement' in the legal profession. Similarly, processes of education can be seen as concerned primarily with developing new models for understanding and acting on the world, as can books on the legal profession! Another example of the use of 'interpretative frameworks' is evident in considering the way critics of in-house lawyers have responded to the role. Some of the advantages claimed for in-house legal work can be seen from other perspectives as eroding the independence of lawyers or creating imbalance in legal services in favour of the wealthy and powerful sectors of society.[11] These criticisms are discussed later (chapter 12 and 13), but certainly one reply to them, and one favoured in this work, would turn some of the criticisms around to assert that the in-house model offers a radical and positive alternative to traditional private practice.

Finally it would be absurd to pretend that there is one world of the lawyer in business in an era when processes of rapid business and social change ensure that all occupations are in a state of instability and continuing change.[12] The legal profession has more than most been readily charged with traditionalism and conservatism, yet it has undergone and is undergoing major changes, while the lawyer in business is caught up in forces of change and transition which are inescapable in a competitive business environment.

Despite all these provisos, one is still left with certain fundamental similarities in occupational roles, with sufficient stability in social systems to say that there can be found underlying characteristics both in occupational roles and in trends of social change. It is these unifying features which are emphasised in this book. Nevertheless, the flaws inherent in this assumption allow me to justify a personal preference for approaching this piece of research in an 'illuminative' rather than statistical mode — using in-depth interviews to search for the common critical factors in the life-space of the lawyers studied as I could gradually unravel them, rather than seeking to survey and present opinions in the form of itemised percentages, which

Lawyers in Business

would provide what I regard as spurious statistical certainty to inevitably complex issues and judgements. I have instead set out what I assess to be the critical issues and questions, noting where necessary if the views were expressed by a majority or minority of those interviewed, or are my own. One might say therefore that the analysis set out in the book is closer to the conclusions one might draw from a cross-examination of witnesses than a sample survey of the field, or that it is in the 'interpretive' research tradition (Cohen and Manion, 1980). However, the range of companies studied in England and Australia, together with my other contacts with in-house lawyers' professional associations and training, give me some confidence in the conclusions reached.

FRAMEWORK OF THE STUDY

The author's interests in law, psychology and adult learning processes have all helped influence the content and approach of this study. It is, however, first and foremost a legal inquiry in the sense that it surveys a relatively neglected branch of the legal profession, seeking to understand its working methods, client relations and place within the legal system. It is not primarily about substantive law — that is being left for a later inquiry. In particular it derives from an interest in employment law and industrial relations. It was from these areas that the author's first interest in the study of in-house legal work emerged, from questions as to how companies coped with increased legal regulation of their activities in the sphere of labour relations. However, I quickly grew more interested in the world of the in-house lawyer as an occupation which was in transition, moving towards greater definition and confidence in its competence and needs as a branch of legal services. Thus, it is also an inquiry rooted in social psychology and sociology; social psychology because it seeks to understand human behaviour and human goals within their particular social and organisational setting; sociology because this subject area has had most to say about the nature of the professions and their place within the wider occupational and social system.[13]

Most importantly perhaps, this work is about adult learning and development. The primary approach of the adult education movement has always been motivated, unlike the world of psychologists, by a concern for human self-determination and development, by a recognition of a need for the learner to participate as an equal in any educational endeavour.[14] In a similar vein, some voices have called for lawyer-client relations to be collaborative rather than a relationship of domination, participative rather than directed by the status and expertise of the professional.[15] It seemed to me that the predominant approach of the in-house lawyer reflected this philosophy, and it is therefore a theme which recurs in many areas of the discussion to follow. Equally, one can as researcher choose a method of approach and report which emphasises either distance or involvement with the concerns of those researched. I have attempted in this research to stay closer to the latter, a commitment which grew into an involvement with the continuing education of in-house lawyers.[16]

The difficulty about using several disciplines as background, however, is not only that one may end up pleasing nobody, but that one is acutely aware of a failure to pursue some of the avenues of theoretical debates which excite most academic specialists. Nevertheless, specialisation has its own dangers of irrelevance and unreality which I have sought to avoid:

> Even the dogs may eat of the crumbs which fall from the rich man's table; and in these days, when the rich in knowledge eat such specialized food at such separate tables, only the dogs have the chance of a balanced diet. (Vickers, 1980: 11)

SOURCES OF MATERIAL

The material for the book comes from several sources. Much of it was collected from in-depth interviews[17] over three years (1983–86) with in-house with lawyers in England and Australia, 23 lawyers in 15 English companies, and later a further 11 lawyers from 11 Australian companies. Access was obtained through three routes — recommendations from the professional bodies representing in-house lawyers (barristers and solicitors in England), and from personal approach to around a third of the companies involved. A diversity of industries was chosen insofar as this was feasible — in the UK two oil companies, two

pharmaceutical, two manufacturing, two food production/distri-
bution, and one in each of mining/construction, newspaper
publishing, banking, insurance, retailing, tobacco, consumer
goods; in Australia, from financial services, consumer products,
security systems, transportation, oil, chemicals, metal industry,
newspaper publishing, insurance, mining, accountancy. (This
classification refers to the dominant business operation of the
company. The fact of diversification of company operations
meant many lawyers dealt also with other areas of business
operated by the parent or holding company.) Diversity was also
obtained in the capacity of the interviewees — seven heads of
department, six sole advisers, the others acting as one of a
number of staff lawyers in a legal department. The interviews
were supplemented by access to written documentation or
company analysis of the in-house function, made available to
me in over half the cases — newsletters or circulars from the
legal department, input into company management manuals,
or reports analysing the work of the legal function for senior
management evaluation of the service. In addition I attended
two professional conferences for in-house lawyers and have had
some feedback on my views from over a hundred in-house
lawyers who have so far attended the continuing education
courses developed out of this research.

To provide supplementary insights on the in-house legal role,
30 additional interviews were carried out (mainly in the UK)
with: two lawyers working for the in-house professional legal
bodies (one a part-time Secretary of a Trade Association); one
lawyer working for a major trade union; a legal academic who
had spent some sabbatical leave in a company legal department;
two lawyers working for a major employers' association; one
lawyer in a lawyer-recruitment consultancy firm; and 16 lawyers
in private practice. (The lawyers in private practice all practised
in commercial law, all but two from City firms in London or
their Australian equivalent in three Australian cities. These
firms were thought most likely to have had regular dealings
with in-house lawyers. Eleven of the 14 City firm lawyers were
partners, the other three salaried associates. The two lawyers
interviewed outside the City firms were partners in UK provincial firms, and both had practised as in-house lawyers at an
earlier stage of their careers.) Seven managers were also interviewed for their views on lawyers, three in companies with in-

house lawyers, three in a medium-sized manufacturing company with no in-house lawyers, and one the secretary of a small employers' association.[18]

It was apparent that lawyers in Australia were fairly equivalent to the UK lawyers in attitudes and approach; therefore the comments made in this book can be taken to refer also to Australian in-house lawyers, with one proviso. I found the Australian lawyers to be more outspoken in their criticisms of the legal profession and legal system. Therefore where I use in this book a quote made by an Australian interviewee, I make that explicit in fairness to the reader. However, it is my own view that this is more indicative of differences of cultural expression between the two countries than of underlying attitudes. While in Australia I particularly studied the issue of arbitration, a process undergoing significant developments during the period I was there, 1985–86.[19] Chapter 11 touches on aspects of this in relation to lawyers' views on litigation. To avoid the confusion and repetitiveness inherent in constantly referring to Australia, however, the rest of the discussion with regard to the wider issues facing the legal profession refers solely to the position in England and Wales. I apologise to Australian readers for having to provide their own translation. Most of the literature on the topic is American, since the US is where the largest concentrations of in-house lawyers can be found.[20] Again, however, this literature indicates, and itself helps contribute to, a similar search for self-identity and professionalism within this modern branch of the profession, a challenge to in-house lawyers which forms the major theme of the chapters to follow.

NOTES

1 William Shakespeare, *Henry VI*, Part II, iv.
2 For some important exceptions, see Levy (1967), Donnell (1970), Podmore (1980), Tomasic and Bullard (1978), Sexton and Maher (1982), Kolvenbach (1979), Rosen (1984), Spangler (1986), Levy concentrated, by means of biographical sketches, on the traditional question in the US of how the development of the corporate lawyer (in private practice and in-house) was influencing the character of lawyering in the United States. (Writers in the United States have tended to write of 'corporation lawyers'

with an emphasis on the development of the large law practice serving corporate clients — see, for example, Smigel (1969) — in a way that British writers talk of 'City firms', so that articles on corporation lawyers are not always about in-house lawyers). Podmore's study is a survey of solicitors and their community contacts, which includes useful data on the in-house lawyer's degree of participation in the professional bodies and in the community. It is also, in this author's view, an example of the slightly negative approach to in-house lawyers which has at times been evident in the attitudes of outside lawyers, and gives only limited attention to the fact that in-house lawyering may be a separate branch of the profession, with distinctive professional concerns. Donnell's *The Corporate Counsel* is one of the pioneer academic studies in the field, concentrating on what was, for sociologists at the time, a prominent issue of the role conflict experienced by professional workers in organisations, based on the dominant paradigm that 'bureaucracy' and 'profession' were incompatible. (The present work disputes that stance, an approach consistent with Donnell's finding of little role strain amongst in-house lawyers.) Tomasic and Bullard's book is an attitude survey amongst different branches of lawyers in New South Wales, Australia, which includes references to lawyers in commerce and industry. A more recent Australian commentary on lawyers and the corporate community can be found in chapter 5 of Sexton and Maher's survey of the legal profession in Australian society. Kolvenbach, himself a corporate lawyer in West Germany, has written probably the most encyclopaedic account to date of the in-house lawyer's work on an international scale, an excellent introduction to the subject, concentrating on the administrative arrangements of in-house legal work. Rosen's recent dissertation is a stimulating account of the 'style' which lawyers can choose to adopt in their professional approach — a limited 'risk-taking' defensive professional stance, or a more influential approach of 'decision-consultant'. His model of the 'influential lawyer' is close to my own concept of the 'integrated lawyer' but Rosen puts less stress on how the situation of the in-house lawyer facilitates this choice, though he uses in-house lawyers as his prime example. *Lawyers for Hire* by Spangler came to my attention too late for its arguments to be explored in this work but it provides an excellent complementary account of lawyers in business and other employed lawyers in American society. Spangler's theoretical approach to the area is heavily influenced by a longstanding sociological debate over the increasing 'incorporation' of lawyers into public and private bureaucracies although her presentation of the interview material allows her respondents to speak more directly of their occupational concerns. One of the best sources for regular articles on the work of the in-house lawyers in the US is *The Business Lawyer*, the journal of the Section of Corporation, Banking and Business Law of the American Bar Association.

3   See Abel (1980).
4   See Utton (1986) for a useful discussion of the extent and nature of regulation in Britain.
5   See, for example, Pfeffer and Salancik (1978).
6   Quoted in Bentham (1978).

7   See, for example, the definition used in the evidence of the Commerce and Industry Group of the Law Society to the Benson Royal Commission on Legal Services. 'An 'in-house' lawyer is a lawyer who is exclusively employed as a salaried employee by an employer who is not himself a lawyer' (Law Society, 1977: para. 2.1).

8   See Kolvenbach (op. cit.: 10, 11) for a more international list of terminology. One might also add to the catalogue for the sake of comprehensiveness the more disparaging expression used in the film *Tootsie* — 'wall-to-wall lawyers'!

9   For a recent call for fusion, see Reeves (1986).

10 See the Report from the Director of the Office of Fair Trading (1986).

11 See, for example, Smyser (1976).

12 See Mackie (1983).

13 See, for example, Dingwall and Lewis (1983).

14 See, for example, Knowles (1978).

15 One of the most important statements of this position with regard to the legal profession is Rosenthal (1974).

16 Discussed in chapter 8.

17 A comprehensive, structured interview schedule was devised to be used as the framework for the interview. However, it was used only as a framework rather than as a set list of questions. The exact course of the interviews varied according to the particular interests of the interviewee or according to the interviewer's assessment of the areas in which the interviewee would provide greatest insights into the issues at which the project was directed. This research method was felt most appropriate for an exploratory project of this kind. Detailed notes were taken during the interviews and typed out soon afterwards. Similarly, once it became apparent that the Australian interviews were covering similar ground to the English ones, the interview questions dwelt more fully on the issues of dispute resolution in Australia. Interviews normally took between 1½–2½ hours to complete, and were restricted in every case to a single session to avoid repeated demands on the interviewee's time. Despite the length of the sessions, there was little sign of interview fatigue in the lawyers interviewed! Indeed, several commented at the end of the interviews that they found the opportunity to talk and reflect on their work to be both valuable and enjoyable. Interview material was supplemented informally in a number of cases by an invitation to a lunch following the interview, and by observation of telephone calls or other brief interruptions of the meeting. The interviews conducted with those individuals outside the company legal functions were more varied in form because of the variety of perspectives involved, but naturally were directed at throwing most light on the role of the in-house lawyer.

18 The question of managers' perceptions of lawyers was an intriguing issue which needs fuller study than the present one was able to give, managers' responses taking a fairly stereotyped pattern. The small size of the managers' sample was partly dictated by constraints on research time, partly by the assumption that I was reasonably cognisant with managers' views of lawyers, having taught law on a number of management courses. However, there is clearly a need for a more detailed study of the type

which Rosen (1984) has begun. The author hopes to develop the research
in this direction in a later project.

19   The research was funded by the Australian Studies Centre of the Institute
of Commonwealth Studies and by the British Academy.

20   See chapter 2 for the figures on US in-house lawyers.

2 The Rise of the Company Legal Department

> We're part of an international movement.
>
> *Australian lawyer*

There is no statutory requirement on companies to employ an in-house lawyer as such[1] nor to maintain a legal department of any size. So there is no official starting date for this institution, nor an official history. The in-house lawyer 'just growed'. A company can choose to rely entirely on external legal advice, and many of course do. The rise of the in-house lawyer represents, therefore, a product of *business* decisions on the means by which companies should obtain legal services.

Most commentators have attributed the growth of the company legal department to the response of business to the post-war boom in government legal regulation of industry and commerce.[2] The reasons for this expansion of government intervention derive from several sources — the increasing size of business economic units with consequent extension of the impact of business on day-to-day society; increasing international economic competition precipitating increased state intervention in the economic sphere; an increasing recognition of the rights of employees and consumers in business activities; recognition of the environmental hazards of unregulated business activity; identification of business as a major source of national income and tax revenue; the formation of new political structures, such as the European Economic Community (EEC), an outcome of the effects of the new global economy on national alliances — all of these have conjoined to create a 'tangled thicket' of business regulation of various kinds.

> There is no such thing now as a major unregulated business, particularly if it is diversified ... And, a substantial part of today's applicable regulations require affirmative business action of very specific kinds. This means, of course, that the daily business activity is not just limited by law, but is

dictated precisely by law (and thus by the counsel who interpret these requirements). (Johnson, 1978: 827)

. . . few companies can go as long as six months without some
change in their operating procedures caused by a change in
the law. (Choka, 1970: 1021)

Certainly the era of the 1960s and 1970s, noted for its social
reformism, saw the most rapid expansion in the employment of
salaried lawyers by business. There are no exact statistics on
the numbers of in-house lawyers in England and Wales, but it
is possible to gauge the trend from the figures available on the
number of solicitors seeking practising certificates each year. It
should be remembered that these figures considerably *underestimate* the numbers of in-house lawyers, since they exclude
company legal advisers who do not require or take out practising
certificates. In some companies, for example, only the Head of
the legal department might take out such a certificate (which
provides the right to act for the company as a solicitor and is
necessary for executing court documents or appearing in court
or handling client accounts, and so on).[3] Also they exclude the
figures on barristers working in business. Although the Bar is a
much smaller part of the profession than the solicitors' branch,
its training and recruitment procedures make it likely that there
will be a much larger *proportion* of barristers who leave private
practice for in-house lawyering.[4] These points only serve to
further emphasise an unmistakeable trend evident in the statistics. (The starting date of 1956/57 was chosen because that
was the first year for which the Law Society Annual Reports
give a separate breakdown of solicitors employed in 'commerce,
industry and nationalised undertakings'.)
   The figures bear out an international trend, not only towards
increasing absolute numbers of lawyers, but a trend to in-house
lawyers as an increasing, if still small, *proportion* of lawyers in
practice. While the number of solicitors outside commerce and
industry grew just under two-and-a-half times between 1956
and 1984, *the number of in-house lawyers increased nearly fivefold* (and
this is probably an underestimate for the reasons mentioned
earlier). It is noteworthy that the decade of the 1970s saw
particularly striking growth, numbers doubling over that period.
The argument for government regulation as the major factor in

Table 1   *Practising certificates issued by the Law Society*

Year	Solicitors in business sector	Solicitors outside business sector[5]	Solicitors in business as percentage of solicitors outside
1956/57	430	17 914	2.4%
1961/62	523	19 267	2.7%
1966/67	732	21 501	3.4%
1971/72	851	25 476	3.3%
1976/77	1029	32 812	3.2%
1981/82	1799	39 939	4.5%
1984/85	1989	44 501	4.5%

in-house lawyer growth is confirmed in that the largest increase in numbers took place during the second half of the 1970s, a period when a Labour government was in office with a major programme of reform of business practice in employment law and other spheres.

Bearing in mind the underestimate element in the figures above, and the fact that barristers employed in business are not included in the statistics, it seems reasonable to conclude that lawyers employed in business in the UK therefore constitute probably something between five and ten per cent of the total population of lawyers. (There are almost a thousand members of the Bar Association for Commerce, Finance and Industry. Not all of these are in-house lawyers but nor is there any requirement for in-house barristers to join this association.)

Nor is the 'in-house lawyer movement' limited to the UK. The picture from around the industrialised, capitalist world is similar, indicating that the phenomenon is international in its causes. Professional associations of in-house lawyers have been set up, for example, in the US (1951), Belgium (1968), France (1969), Italy (1976), The Netherlands (1930), Sweden (1954), West Germany (1978) (Kolvenbach, 1979), and Australia (where the first all-Australian Corporate Lawyers' Association was set up in 1986, although several states had their own associations at an earlier date, the earliest (1955) being that of Victoria). In Britain, the Commerce and Industry Group of the Law Society (solicitors) was established in 1960, the Bar

Association for Commerce, Finance and Industry (barristers) in 1965.

The largest concentration of in-house lawyers can be found not unexpectedly in the United States, which, as well as being a major base for business activities, also has one of the largest concentrations in the world of lawyers relative to population. There are again no completely accurate records of the numbers of in-house lawyers but such records as there are indicate a similar massive growth in the number of in-house lawyers between 1950 and 1980, doubling between 1970 and 1980. Some estimates now put the proportion of in-house lawyers at nearly one in five of the over 600 000 lawyers in the United States, and again in the context of a faster rate of growth than the profession at large (Coombe, 1985; *Business Week* 1984), although a more conservative estimate would be one in ten (Curran *et al.* 1985).[6] As with the British figures, the US figures suggest a levelling off of the *rate of increase* in the 1980s although absolute numbers continue to rise, confirming a deregulation, or possibly recession, impact in both countries.

While it may be accurate to pinpoint increased legal regulation of companies as the main spur to the spread of the in-house lawyer service (and hence any decline in regulation as likely to impede in-house lawyer growth), it should not by any means be treated as the whole story. First, in-house lawyers could be found long before this period. The letter from the Chairman of Shell referred to in the Introduction was, after all, written in the early years of the century, and an association of company lawyers formed in the Netherlands as early as 1930. One of the companies in my own research, a major insurance company, had established an in-house lawyer as early as the 1870–80s. Similarly, lawyers were employed in the 19th and early 20th century in major oil companies and public utilities (Kolvenbach, 1979).

It is possible, of course, to argue that the major sources of early in-house lawyer appointments were located in industries which were also the earliest to be regulated by government — oil, public utilities, insurance. Nevertheless, the example of the insurance company points to a more general factor, namely the amount of business activity involving relatively complex legal transactions, or at least the relationship between sales and legal costs. Although this may not account entirely for the rise of in-house lawyers, it seems a more accurate ground for forecasting in-house lawyer growth. To attribute the increase in numbers as purely a factor of government regulation ignores the fact that the impact of regulation is not uniform, either in its demands on the need for legal services (which may be a short-term need requiring merely clarification for the company as to the changes in company routines to be adopted in response to regulation) or in its impact on particular industrial sectors. Certain industrial sectors, such as oil, incur greater legal costs in proportion to sales than other sectors (Carney, 1982), and hence would be expected to perceive earlier a need for increased legal services. The exact correlation, however, between such a factor and in-house lawyer growth would require a sophisticated economic analysis.[7]

Only a minority of the lawyers I interviewed were able to tell me when their department had been formed, or why. Where they could, it was normally because the department had been formed within the last 20 years. The reasons given covered the following cases: 'I think it grew out of the Company Secretary function' (a pre-war formation); 'This company was bought at that time by the present US parent which brought in a lawyer' (1960s); 'I moved in from the holding company when it bought this group' (1970s); 'The company were having employment law problems at the time; they knew I had a legal background and asked me to write a paper on the new legislation. Then I was asked to set up a Legal Department'. (1970s); 'I don't really know why — I suppose they had received such a poor service from private practice. No, I didn't really mean that' (pre-war).

While it is true to say that there is no statutory requirement to employ an in-house lawyer as such, there is a statutory requirement for companies to have a company secretary and, in the case of a public company, the Companies Acts require certain qualifications for this office holder, lawyers being one of the prescribed categories. This requirement, together with various other statutory reporting requirements and powers (for example, to sign administrative contracts), ensures that many companies will find it useful to use a lawyer as Company Secretary and such an in-house lawyer may combine that function, either formally or in practice, with other in-house legal or administrative matters. Where thereafter there is an increase in legal aspects of the business it is not unlikely that a legally-qualified Company Secretary would seek to employ further in-house legal assistance.

A further point which argues against regulation as the *sole* causal factor, is the fact that, as we shall see, in-house lawyers also carry out many functions which are not strictly related to, or predominantly to do with modern regulatory control. For example, many of them spend much of their time on convey-ancing and other property transactions while work with commercial contracts is also an important item in the work of most legal departments.

Similarly, although the argument for regulation as the sole cause of in-house lawyer growth would lead one to a predict a levelling off of such growth in the 1980s, given the political backlash in this era against regulation (and given the fact that this is what one finds in the figures to date), a more detailed analysis might not present such a clear case. First, the prediction is complicated by the fact that the same period has been accompanied by economic recession and unemployment, which would also affect the numbers of lawyers employed in business. In any case, it is not entirely clear that regulation has slowed down despite the political rhetoric. (See chapter 10.) Most significantly, however, despite the attempts to reduce regulation, and despite major staff cutbacks caused by the recession of the 1980s, the number of in-house lawyers in the UK and US continues to rise, although in both countries not with the same rate of increase as was evident in the 1970s.

The theory that recent government regulation has *caused* the growth of the in-house legal department must therefore be quali-fied. It would perhaps be more apt to adopt an explanation based on a broader dimension of 'business need' or 'economic activity' which will reflect external regulatory pressures but may also reflect other important aspects of business activity — the increased formalisation of company actions (both inside and outside the corporation),[8] increased concentrations of owner-ship, increased frequency of property transactions, contractual matters, acquisitions, company restructuring and so on. Nor should one rule out the simple notion of business 'fashion' as an additional contributory factor. The legal upheavals of the 1960s and 1970s may have drawn business attention to legal issues or highlighted a possibility that few had given attention to. Once the trend to in-house lawyering began, many would pick this up by example or see an in-house legal function as a 'necessary' accompaniment to doing business without the calculated analyses of the founding fathers of the in-house legal department. At a more basic level, one may suggest that lawyers are capable of creating their own competitive momentum, as witness the growth in the ratio of lawyers to the population at large:

> The ability of the legal profession to absorb increased supplies of lawyers is truly remarkable, suggesting that in this profession supply creates its own demand and lending credence to the claim that the first lawyer in town prospers only after the second arrives. (Kafoglis, in Carney, 1982: 54)

Therefore, while an explanation based on a broader dimension of business need, rather than regulation as such, seems more appropriate to account for the growth of in-house legal departments, even that cannot suffice as an all-embracing explanation. One can find companies in what seem to be similar business circumstances adopting different approaches to the type of legal service they adopt, a point made very explicit in one of my interviews with a clearing bank lawyer, who pointed out the significantly different ratios of in-house to outside legal service adopted by the four major clearing banks, despite their apparently common business circumstances, from one having no such department (though working very closely with one firm of solicitors) to a department of over one hundred staff.

The reason for a particular company choosing to go in-house for some or all of its legal requirements may, therefore, relate to any combination of a number of relevant factors, such as amount of legal business, types of regulatory control, managerial attitudes, assessment of the quality and/or cost of existing legal services, and business fashions. Only a more detailed analysis of the history of particular departments could unravel the relative importance of the various elements in any particular case.

Clearly company size and profitability are intrinsically related to the employment of in-house lawyers, and to the numbers of lawyers employed. (One should bear in mind, however, the role in-house lawyers play in smaller companies which are part of a larger business structure and serviced by parent company service departments.) Beyond a certain size, measured by the

number of employees, or the scale of legal costs to sales transactions, or merely based on a direct audit of existing legal costs
incurred by the company, it may be appropriate to employ one's
own lawyer(s).[9] In-house lawyers are therefore concentrated in
the largest companies, and more likely to be found in particular
sectors. For example, according to 1980 figures (Curran *et al.*,
1985), almost half the business lawyers in the US were employed
in companies which were listed in the Fortune 500 or the
Fortune 50 for special sectors. Of the remaining 51 per cent, 15
per cent were in insurance and banking companies. The number
of lawyers employed by a single company ranged from one to
over 700 (not necessarily the size of the legal department),[10]
although 55 per cent worked in companies with 25 or fewer
lawyers, 31 per cent in companies with one to three lawyers on
staff. Naturally the greater the number of lawyers employed,
the more likely it is that there will be a formal legal department
as such. While there are no equivalent statistics available in
Britain on the correlation between the size of companies and
the employment of in-house lawyers, a glance at the membership
list of the professional associations of in-house lawyers in the
UK again confirms the predominance of major companies, the
larger companies tending to have the largest legal departments.[11]

The reasons for *establishing* a legal department are, of course,
not necessarily equivalent to the reasons for *maintaining* or
expanding it. Once an internal legal service is created it may well
create a dynamic of its own. This will not only occur in the
rather basic sense expressed by the Managing Director of a
medium-sized company without an in-house department: 'Of
course it would be useful to have a lawyer here, but I'll tell you
this, once they were here you would never get them out again'.
More fundamentally, the presence on site of a lawyer may act
in important ways to *alter the nature of the legal service itself.* An
in-house lawyer may serve to educate management into a more
sophisticated appraisal and understanding of legal risks and
opportunities. This point is developed later in this work, but an
initial insight into how it occurs can be obtained by considering
a fundamental question with regard to the growth of in-house
legal departments. Namely, if the use of in-house legal departments has grown extensively, *what are the advantages of legal services
provided by the in-house lawyer compared to those provided by the outside
lawyer* which would justify a business decision to employ one?

After all, the main reasons we have considered so far — increased regulation of business, and increased business activities — might lead one to expect a growth in the demand for legal services *in general*. But why should a company choose to go in-house, to 'privatise' legal services when they are already freely available in the marketplace? This issue is considered in the next chapter.

NOTES

1 There is, however, a 'facilitating' section in the Companies Acts which lists lawyers as one of the prescribed categories of qualification for appointment as a Company Secretary.

2 See, for example, *Business Week* (1974); Galuccio (1978).

3 The Commerce and Industry Group of the Law Society noted this in their evidence to the Royal Commission on Legal Services: 'It is . . . certain that a considerable number of commerce and industry solicitors do not hold practising certificates' (Law Society, 1977: para. 2.11).

4 The number of barristers in the Bar Association for Commerce, Finance and Industry is almost a fifth of the numbers practising at the Bar (just under 1000 members compared to over 5000 in practice); the Commerce and Industry Group of the Law Society has around 2000 members as against almost 45 000 solicitors in private practice.

5 These figures include solicitors working for local and national government. The number of 'in-house' lawyers in these sectors has also increased. The numbers working in national government are relatively small but have shown a substantial increase in the last 25 years, from 54 in 1961/62 to 163 in 1984/85. The numbers in local government have increased in line with the profession as a whole, from 1544 in 1961/62 to 2896 in 1984/85.

6 Some of the estimates of in-house lawyer growth seem to be based on the numbers of salaried lawyers (outside private practice) rather than lawyers working in business. Figures published by the American Bar Foundation (Curran, 1985) confirm that the largest single group of lawyers working outside private practice in the US in 1985 were lawyers in private industry, but the proportion is closer to ten per cent of the lawyer population (of 655 000) compared to over eight per cent working in various branches of government and 70 per cent in private practice. The proportion in private practice had declined from 72 per cent in 1960, although it was up slightly from the 1980 figure of 68 per cent, while there was a slight decline in the proportion of business lawyers over that period. Thus the American figures also suggest that the *rate* of growth of in-house lawyers as a proportion of the profession at large may have levelled off although, like the profession at large, actual numbers continue

to grow rapidly. For example, the total number of American lawyers between 1980 and 1985 went up from 542 205 to 655 191 over the five years, an increase which included around 9000 *additional* business lawyers on the 1980 total of 54 626. An additional complication in interpreting the statistics is that the figures cited by Curran *et al.* like the Law Society figures, do not automatically equate with lawyers working in corporate legal departments (Curran *et al.*: 21). They refer to lawyers licensed to practice who are *employed* in a business. The figures also indicate incidentally that business lawyers have overtaken government lawyers who once clearly outranked them in numbers — see the figures reported in Blaustein and Porter (1954: 8–10).

7 For an interesting but ultimately inconclusive discussion of whether industry characteristics are more important than regulation in explaining the growth of in-house lawyers, see Pashiagnis in Carney, 1982: chapter 1.

8 It should not be forgotten that the growth of the legal profession generally was linked to the development of the business world. With the rise of market relations and law as a form of social control, social relations in general become more differentiated and conflict between independent parties is increasingly seen as a legitimate phase of social life for which traditional social and informal means of resolution become inappropriate (Rueschemeyer, 1973).

9 Pashiagnis (in Carney, 1982) suggests one cannot assume a constant ratio of legal department growth to company growth. His figures suggest that there may well be a growth plateau for a company in the size of its legal department.

10 Cohen, 1984, 143f., suggests that the highest number is now 900 lawyers in one company, A.T. & T. (See footnote 6 for the difficulties in interpreting such figures.)

11 A figure of just over 90 lawyers has been quoted as the largest UK legal department number attained, for the National Coal Board.

3 Advantages and Disadvantages of In-house Lawyers

ADVANTAGES OF THE IN-HOUSE LAWYER

Bald assertions that the number of in-house lawyers has grown because of increased government regulation or increased and more complex economic activity conceal the real question concerning in-house lawyer growth — why have not outside legal services expanded to meet these demands? Of course, part of the answer to this question is that they have expanded — the number of lawyers in general has risen in all industrialised societies. But the other part of the answer must deal with the fact that in-house legal services have also grown, and grown at a more rapid rate than the general population of lawyers. Why is this? What prompts companies to take the 'legal leap' and employ their own lawyers?

I have identified, from my interviews and from the literature on in-house lawyers, six significant reasons to justify the employment of an in-house lawyer — costs, familiarity with the client, accessibility, preventive role, administrative/problem-solving skills, and outside-lawyer management. Caution is always necessary with data based on interviews with any occupational group as there is a danger of self-justifying pronouncements. However, these advantages were derived not only from answers to an explicit question on 'why have an in-house lawyer?' but also from the implications of general statements about their role,[1] and indeed most of the points, once stated, are fairly self-evident. Also the statements of outside lawyers tended to corroborate these points from a different angle. Several expressed appreciation of the opportunity of working with in-house lawyers because this tended to speed the process of familiarisation with the background to a problem and helped in the 'translation process' between lawyers and managers. (See Managing outside lawyers, below.) Most importantly, the fact

29

of the rise of the in-house lawyer position, of the privatisation of legal services, in itself testifies to business recognition and appreciation of these advantages, whether singly or in combination.[2] However, as a balance to possible bias, I have also set out possible disadvantages of employing an in-house lawyer. Of course, the advantages depend on the assumption of other things being equal, and in particular that the lawyer employed is reasonably competent and that he or she is given an appropriate role within the corporation. The lawyers interviewed, both in-house and outside, were quick to point out that 'one can't generalise', a feature perhaps of their occupational training as lawyers rather than social scientists. The nature of the individual lawyer, his role, the type of industry — all of these factors could influence the balance of advantages and disadvantages to a company in employing an in-house lawyer. In this respect it is also important to stress that in discussing the advantages of the in-house lawyer, one must be careful to note that it is not easy to make an exact comparison with outside lawyers who are themselves segmented into various kinds of practice structures, from small provincial firms dealing mainly with individual clients to major City firms dealing regularly with multinational clients. The type of companies which employ in-house lawyers tend to be those which use the larger commercial firms, particularly City firms. However, the argument of this book is that in-house lawyers may form a distinct branch of lawyering. While they often liaised with City firms over major transactions or specialist issues, and larger departments would themselves conduct such work, much of their work (see chapter 4) was of a more general character, making them perhaps more akin to lawyers in a major provincial commercial practice, or to the more generalist roles in City firms.

We are really general commercial practitioners. We soak everything up, then turn it round. We have to range over a whole variety of topics and have got to be good and general enough to recognise where problems are, and try to be pre-emptive about them, and make sure we have resources available for them when we need them. We use City firms almost in the way counsel was traditionally used but we use them because they've developed 'niches'. And part of my job is to find out where those niches are. (Consumer products industry lawyer)

It is equally possible to argue that more attention in legal training to the specialist needs of in-house lawyers would further increase the advantages and reduce possible disadvantages (see chapter 8 on training and development). Also, the debate within the in-house lawyer movement about what I have called 'integrated' lawyering (chapter 5) is an attempt to build a model of professional practice which seeks to articulate these advantages even more clearly. The essential product of the advantages is that a company can hope to move *from the position of being managed by its legal environment to one where it manages its legal environment.*

Costs

A necessary condition for creating the position of in-house lawyer is that a company is earning sufficient income to pay for someone not directly involved in production or selling,[3] a fact which explains the absence of in-house lawyers in smaller companies. However, there is a clear case also for stating that, at a certain point, many organisations will find they can save on existing legal costs by hiring their own lawyer. With the greater impact of the legal environment and the inflation-driven increases in legal fees in the 1960s and 1970s, increasing legal costs have been a matter of more and more concern to companies and have heralded, together with a changed business climate, an era of more active management of these costs.[4] 'When I met business executives on airplanes, I used to talk about the weather, because that's one of the few things we had in common. Now . . . we talk about outside legal fees' corporate critic Ralph Nader is quoted as saying (*Business Week*, 1984). 'My company opted for a legal department when they found their annual expenditure on legal costs was £100 000' (lawyer in a manufacturing concern). 'I'm unique. None of the other major accountancy firms here have an in-house lawyer. How do they do without one? Frankly, I'm mystified by it. I can only assume they're paying a fortune for it. No, it's not a case that I create work — I've so much work, I've no time for it all.' (Australian lawyer who had received Law Society approval to become a partner in the firm.)[5]

Where a business is likely to carry out legal transactions on a regular basis, clear economies may be made by bringing the transactions inside. They will avoid by this some of the additional overheads normally built into an outside solicitor's fee to pay for his practice, as well as the additional cost elements in the outside lawyer's fee of, first, familiarisation with the business background and problem (although a solicitor in private practice who is in regular contact with a client will also avoid this aspect, but probably never to the same extent as the in-house lawyer), and second, of the fee perhaps reflecting the value of the transaction to the organisation rather than the cost of the legal effort.

The clearest case of such economies is in the field of conveyancing where in-house lawyers can do all of the work in property transactions for a fixed salary. Thus, an in-house lawyer specialising in property transactions may well be handling conveyances of property running into several millions of pounds annually at a fixed salary of, say, £20 000.[6] It is unlikely that any firm of outside lawyers, particularly the City firms that tend to be used by large companies (with minimum hourly fees of £100 upwards), could match this in fee levels, even allowing for the indirect costs additional to a salary which companies incur for an employee.

The same argument applies to other areas where regular legal work is carried out on a salaried basis, whether commercial contracts, insurance, tax or patents work. However, in-house lawyers recognised that there were areas of regular work, litigation in particular, which were too time-consuming for the in-house lawyer to take on while retaining other responsibilities. In a large department a litigation specialist was more common but even in those cases their greatest involvement and contribution to cost-saving was in preparatory work, most of the actual work in court going to outside lawyers (and had to, in the case of those courts where only barristers had rights of appearance). However, a few legal departments also conducted their own litigation up to the point where they had to use counsel.

Another, less obvious, source of cost-saving is the work of the in-house lawyer of a *preventive* or *advisory* nature, where a transaction would not necessarily have led the company to consult a lawyer, for example, in drawing up employment contracts or disciplinary procedures, advising on health and safety or industry regulations. The advantages of the in-house lawyer in these areas is discussed more fully below. However, the interviewees clearly saw their role in these areas as making potentially large savings for companies by way of avoiding litigation or ensuring effective legal procedures to achieve and protect company objectives. One instance, quoted by an oil company lawyer, involved intervention by the legal department at a point where company managers had been on the verge of altering the price signs on all their petrol stations throughout Britain, in the belief that this was required by new regulations governing the industry. The legal department advised management that their interpretation of the regulations did not lead to such a conclusion, thus saving the company many thousands in alteration work. Similar significant cost savings, of up to several million dollars, by in-house lawyers in the banking sector have been reported (Chan and Wilson, 1983) arising from a legal department absorbing the work of formerly separate risk, insurance and corporate compliance departments, or from in-house lawyers' speed of response to new business opportunities in the context of financial deregulation.

Other cases have been reported where legal departments have employed additional staff (or sometimes absorbed private firms which were largely dependent on a particular company's work) in order to reduce overall costs, particularly where litigation costs have been high or previously uncontrolled. Fischer (1984) describes a successful productivity exercise in the Alcoa legal department where, litigation costs being a large proportion of the legal department's budget, substantial savings were made by hiring two additional in-house litigation specialists to reduce dependence on outside lawyers. Similarly, Standard Oil were reported to have employed a lawyer on $50 000 a year when they realised the costs of an outside firm on an anti-trust case would run to $500 000 (*Business Week*, 1984). The same report refers to a company which did not know how many product liability suits it faced at any one time until it employed an in-house lawyer — 'The difference was like night and day'. (Also, the company's success rate on cases rose from 50 per cent to 80 per cent, a difference one might predict from the other advantages outlined below.)

In addition to *reducing* costs, a few legal departments argued that in-house lawyers brought in additional *income* for the company by way of handling property investments or by effectively pursuing insurance and litigation claims that might not otherwise have been as effectively conducted, if carried out at all, or by more effective structuring of business or tax arrangements. One in-house lawyer who was particularly commercially-minded pointed out that 'if you see yourself as an item of cost for the company, then a line can be drawn through you when they're looking around for savings'.

Finally, where outside legal assistance was going to continue to be used rather than replaced, the in-house lawyer could also more effectively control such expenditure. This issue of controlling outside legal costs is dealt with in more detail below.

As to exactly when a company should consider going in-house on cost grounds, clearly one could not specify an exact point, as much would depend on the type of legal questions which face the company. However, it is obviously important to make the calculations involved. Companies in the past tended to treat legal costs as an unalterable feature of their environment, like the weather, so it would be safe to predict that many managers would not have considered an audit of their legal costs and legal involvement. Such attitudes are apparently changing,[7] making such an audit advisable. It has been suggested (as I found in the case quoted earlier) that a company should be ready to invest in its own in-house lawyer once it finds its legal costs exceeding £100 000 per annum, although some might find this a generous threshold for outside lawyers![8] It should also be borne in mind that the assessment of existing legal costs may not properly take into account the savings an in-house lawyer could make by *improving* aspects of business practice, for example, instituting new credit control systems, or monitoring and acting on sources of legal actions against the company. Such improvements, however, might depend on the company finding itself the 'right type' of lawyer, on which more is said later in this work.

How much could a company expect to save? In the literature on in-house lawyers, consultancy estimates are quoted to the effect that an in-house lawyer costs less than half of what would be incurred in hiring outside lawyers, even taking into account employee overheads. Others have suggested even greater savings have been made, for example, that an in-house lawyer costs as little as a third of outside legal advice (Chambers, 1986), or even, in one department's economic estimate of its cost, a quarter or a fifth of the cost of using outside lawyers (Cohen, 1984, 135, citing the example of London Transport).

However, any such figures can be little more than intelligent estimates of average cost savings; the equation in any specific case is likely to depend on the level of outside legal costs, the type of legal advice needed, the nature of the individuals used, and so on. However, whatever the level of savings, few have contested that for companies with regular legal transactions, there is a cost-reduction potential for a company in hiring its own lawyers.

Familiarity with the client

In-house lawyers reported gains on a number of fronts arising out of their acting for a single client, in terms of specialisation, knowledge of client policies, procedures and objectives, and in terms of knowledge of the facts of any legal problem. First, they had the opportunity to specialise, to gain in-depth knowledge of the legal issues arising for their organisation, specialism which was not normally attainable (nor necessarily desirable in terms of income to be gained) for those working in private practice. Industrial sectors, such as oil, food or chemicals, are subjected to batteries of detailed regulations, arising from the British legislature and, more and more frequently, from the European Economic Community (in an oil company, for example, with respect to North Sea oil licences, oil platform safety legislation, oil-pipe regulations and planning permissions, distributorships, licensing agreements, and so forth; in the foods sector, there are regulations and codes dealing with ingredients and ingredients listing, nutritional claims, date-marking, advertising, labelling and packaging, and others). Lawyers working in these sectors had the incentive and the opportunity to develop detailed knowledge of this extensive field of law as well as to keep up to date with it. At the same time they were working regularly with technical specialists in the area and so had a better grasp of the factual background to the legal provisions.

Procedures as well as substantive law may reflect the specialist environment within a company. A conveyancer reported this effect in his own field merely from having moved from a senior partnership in a West End firm into an industrial environment with scope to specialise — 'One's instructions are, how shall I put it, "more ordered" . . . In the last six years I have probably only used counsel six times compared to dozens of occasions in the same period in private practice.'

Also seen as important was the in-house lawyers' familiarity with the commercial objectives of the company. This gave them opportunities to appreciate the value to the company in terms of its business strategy of, for example, a request for planning permission for a particular property development. This evaluation helped them to assess how important the background preparation might be or what alternative legal avenues might be open. This aspect of familiarity was particularly relevant to cost-saving. In-house lawyers are more likely to be able to judge the priority rating of a problem, and to assess whether the cost of working on it will be repaid in savings for the company, where an outside lawyer might see it as a self-contained legal question to do all the work on it it requires. They would know, for example, whether the business was more interested in getting a long-term effective legal form worked out for its contracts or was more interested in immediate cash flow and defaulting customer problems.

Similarly, in-house lawyers have a better knowledge of *timing* needs:

> legal assignments, artificially isolated from a current commercial struggle, take their place on the general practitioner's desk in competition with pending assignments, commonly for other clients. (Hickman, 1964: 476)

The in-house lawyer is more likely to be aware of the degree of urgency of the problem as well as being aware of the relevant case-law if it is a typical problem area for the company, and will often have been involved with the project from an early stage and so know the background to it.

Equally valuable is the knowledge acquired of company attitudes or culture, reflected in personnel and public relations policies as well as in knowledge of communication and decision-making styles, down to matters as simple as just being at home with company jargon or acronyms through day-to-day contact with managers. Thus, for example, advice on dismissals could be given in the knowledge of the standards of procedure and enquiry into individual cases required by the company as well as at law. This could work in an employee's favour in certain instances but equally against if it was a practice the company felt particularly sensitive to (for example, theft cases in the retail environment). It particularly affected the question of out-of-court settlements, the grounds on which companies would fight on principle as against cases where they would wish to avoid bad publicity or avoid upsetting local authorities, regulatory officials or residents living near company premises. (As in one instance where a company paid to instal double-glazing in all local residents' houses because of complaints arising from early and late lorry-loading hours.)

A final interesting facet of this familiarity was the lawyers' approach to 'client trust'. Familiarity with personnel in the company led, with experience, to knowledge of who might be trusted or who was unreliable or what motivations might be involved in presenting information (in terms of taking instructions or evidence or assessing risk in advising on whether to pursue a legal action). Insofar as the in-house lawyer represented the company to outside regulatory or other agencies, he or she could also ensure a better *consistency* of approach by the company than if the cases were channelled through outside legal firms.

All of these factors — awareness of personalities, case background, commercial objectives, priorities and time factors, company policies and specialist technical matters of fact and law — give the in-house lawyer an undoubted advantage over the average outside lawyer. In addition, the in-house lawyer's experience in the company will provide a better base for knowing or finding out the facts of a case, perhaps the essential source of legal effectiveness.

Most legal problems find their origin and their answer in the facts. One of the great values of corporate counsel is his ability to get the facts of a situation, not only promptly but accurately and fully.

. . . The very existence of factual investigations by outside counsel may arouse rumors, fears and occasionally an effort to cover up mistakes. With rare exceptions, the outside counsel considers only those problems which are brought to him and

builds his factual background by a cross-examination of the
corporate employee who consults him. . . . The files of Alcoa
are replete with brilliantly reasoned opinions of general practitioners which have little or no value because of the incom-
pleteness or the distorted emphasis of their factual assumptions. (Hickman, 1964: 477–8)

Where outside lawyers had regular dealings with a client they
could, of course, also claim a degree of familiarity with a business. However, their comments on the advantages of working
with in-house lawyers showed an acceptance that they rarely
could match the in-house lawyer's familiarity. However, this
was not viewed in any competitive sense. There was no shortage
of work for commercial lawyers and those working in the City
firms tended to be used for their role as specialists or in major
transactions or overflows of work from in-house legal
departments.

We tend to know [clients] not as well, but in a different sort
of way. (Commercial lawyer in City firm)

The in-house lawyer can be slightly more sensitive to the
company's concerns. He can be less brutal in considering
litigation for example. He may know if emotionally it may be
a bad thing for the company. Hopefully if you work for a
company long enough you would also know. (Litigation
partner in City firm)

It's one of our weaknesses [as a smaller firm], not being able
to provide continuity of attention. If you want the same chap,
there's no assurance he can do the job when you want it done.
You have a straight clash between continuity and speed. But
it's a hell of a drawback for clients, particularly as they have
their own problems of continuity internally. If you have a
continuous relationship, you don't have to tell me the background and history. That's an aspect of efficiency that's rarely
mentioned but very important. (Partner in smaller City firm)

Continuity of service? One does what one can but it's an
extremely difficult thing. One of the problems is that you start
at one level. Two years later you're above that level and it's

not cost-effective to do that kind of work. But they're big organisations. They don't find it too difficult to deal with different people doing the transactions. The partners are really the people who do the cuddling. They provide the continuity. In theory. (Commercial lawyer in City practice)

One of the differences in private practice is that you're much more at arm's length than when in-house. I tend, because I've been an in-house lawyer, to try to find out about the client first to know the context. For example, leasing offices, you have to know the commercial context. . . . In many ways it's more difficult to know how to handle priorities as an outside lawyer. In-house you can point to the man above the department wanting the work done. . . . It's an advantage in some ways that you can keep your distance from clients but a disadvantage that you know less of the background. For example, even if you do want to find out the background, there's always a clock running if you're talking to them about their work and they may not understand later why they are being charged for that time just talking generally. (Commercial partner in provincial firm who had two years earlier moved out of in-house lawyer work)

Accessibility

An indirect economic benefit to companies is the fact that the presence of an in-house lawyer ensures a ready response to problems which often demand (or are not tackled until they do demand) a prompt legal action or opinion if they are to influence company decision-making. The convenience of a lawyer being only a telephone call (or memo or a few doors) away, cannot be overstressed in a discussion on the advantages of employing an in-house lawyer. Added to this, the service is effectively 'free' for individual managers in most companies, since the cost comes out of general expenditure rather than departmental budgets (although this is not always the case, some companies working on a cost allocation system).

. . . nine-tenths of the matters that occupy the attention of a corporate legal department would simply be decided without

the advice of lawyers if such counsel were not given cooperat-
ively, promptly and competently. (Hickman, 1964: 476)

. . . most active companies now require — or are best served
by — the constant availability of counsel who is informed, on
a day-to-day basis of the company's activities and directions,
including sensitive contingency plans never publicly disclosed.
The busy corporate executive needs more service — continu-
ously at hand, and fully loyal to corporate objectives. Thus,
the trend is increasing towards a choice of inside counsel,
more talented and better paid — motivated by corporate
incentive plans and positioned in the company more closely
to a policy level. This is particularly true of diversified holding
companies. (Johnson, 1978: 827)

The theme of accessibility cropped up time and again in the
research, although more often from the point of view of the
objectives an effective in-house lawyer had to meet. Accessibility,
in other words, did not come automatically by mere presence
inside the company but had to be worked at. Interviewees
emphasised the importance they placed on *being known* to
company personnel and being *known as approachable* in fulfilling
an effective in-house role. (The managers I spoke to on this
stressed the need for a lawyer who 'makes sense' to them, a
similar concept to that valued by in-house lawyers but one
which reflects the problems of communication many managers
find when faced by lawyers.) This stress on being seen as
approachable was linked to the emphasis placed by in-house
lawyers on the preventive role performed by them on the
company's behalf (see below) as well as on their evaluation of
the qualities required of the in-house lawyer, in particular the
need for a *positive* approach. They could effectively prevent the
company getting into legal difficulties through its operations if
company employees knew both that legal advice was there and
that it would be given both sympathetically, not in a 'policing'
sense, and constructively, rather than in terms of prohibitions.
New regulations and other legislation could be monitored and
communicated to company personnel but equally there had to
be a flow in reverse — employees who actively consulted with
lawyers would discover legally effective working practices in
areas affected by new legislation, or would avoid more readily

breaches of existing legislation arising out of the natural development and change of company working practices. The overall result would be to provide more effective and efficient legal means to support company practice and initiatives. Thus, liaison with appropriate levels of management was required as well as adopting practices by which the legal department could become 'known', for example, by means of a company newsletter, and generally by acquiring the status of a 'valued adviser'.

The stress they placed on being accessible, however, testifies equally to one of the difficulties faced by in-house lawyers (and correspondingly to a greater extent by outside lawyers), namely that they recognised that 'lawyers' were seen in a negative light by some managers or sections of the company and that this had to be overcome. Thus, one lawyer said to me he preferred to use the term 'politics' for what I called 'accessibility' (although I see the two as separate, albeit related). This negativity from some sections of management arose partly from a general public image of lawyers as nit-picking and obstructive (particularly recognised in contract situations), partly from managers' wariness of being 'pulled up' or 'told off' for illicit operations. However, the latter phenomenon was not seen as particularly prevalent, most in-house lawyers regarding accessibility as a question of merely becoming known. That is, once managers knew a face or had made an initial contact, they would frequently approach the same person again. By this means a 'client group' was built up. One of the lawyers interviewed who was new to her company adopted a deliberate policy along these lines, using her trips round the country on industrial tribunal cases also as a means of becoming acquainted with management at the different company plants.

Preventive role

In much of the literature this has been identified as the pre-eminent virtue of in-house lawyers, sometimes referred to as their 'proactive' rather than 'reactive' role. This partly derives from the greater accessibility of in-house lawyers. Most companies will be less prone to approach outside lawyers to discuss what is legally feasible or desirable, or to ascertain whether there is a potential legal point in a decision they are taking, than to tackle a pressing and obvious legal problem that has arisen. In turn, it is argued that most outside lawyers are better equipped at advising on whether there has been a breach of law, and on how to respond to this, than on turning their knowledge of legal requirements into healthy company practice which will forestall legal difficulties. The in-house lawyer can prevent difficulties and litigation by advising on company practice from the point where a new law is introduced or by pointing out potential difficulties from existing legal rules if company policies or practices are altering. Even in the obvious cases, in-house lawyers may have a more effective preventive role because they know the urgency of the decision and can avoid the delay sometimes associated with outside lawyers. 'My company had reached the point where they were wondering whether they were getting advice when they needed it, whether it was correct advice, and what to do with it. Many lawyers are not very good at the last part.' (Australian lawyer in a media business.)

It would not be possible to map out the exact extent of this difference between the two groups of lawyers from the data collected in this research, and to some extent outside law firms are attempting to become more 'proactive' in their dealings with clients by means of brochures, newsletters, guidebooks and seminars. Nevertheless, the potential for legal 'prevention rather than cure' is heightened by the presence of the in-house lawyer. This would be particularly true of lesser legal changes than of the major ones. A sweeping legal reform is perhaps likely to lead most major companies to consult lawyers but minor reforms are likely to be ignored. Equally, the day-to-day actions of management — drafting an early retirement letter, agreeing on new advertising wording — are unlikely to lead managers to reach for their outside lawyers. The in-house lawyer on the other hand may be down the corridor, or certainly at the end of an internal telephone or memo with no difficulty of contact, arrangements to meet, or fees to consider.

In-house lawyers can act as a contraceptive, stopping problems becoming pregnant. Outside lawyers can do that too but they have less opportunity; for example, over initial flurries of correspondence in a business dispute. A company might not think to give them to an outside lawyer but it's remarkable how many cases are won on that sort of correspondence. In most cases, it comes down to a construction of letters, trying to infer motives from the words used. (Litigation partner in City firm)

I had a recent example of where I think an in-house lawyer would have had a preventive role. I was presented with a whole pile of paper by a company and asked to advise on a legal problem. Inevitably there was a lot of time just going through it, and of course I have to bill them at £150 an hour for that time. In the end there was a very simple contractual point which prevented them making the claim they wanted to make. It would be simpler for an in-house lawyer to sift through a bundle of documents than have me do it at £150 an hour. (Partner in City firm)

The preventive role adopted by lawyers in a broader sense in relation to the development of law and the passage of legislation, that is, the role of in-house lawyers as a 'business pressure group', is discussed in chapter 5 in the context of a fuller analysis of preventive legal practice.

The good administrator/problem-solver

Legal training, it is often suggested, is recognised as developing qualities of objectivity, ability to handle complex information and paperwork, and to marshall facts and arguments for decision-making, all of them qualities to assist in business administration. It is not unexpected, therefore, to find that lawyers were readily accepted as Board members in many companies. Several lawyers interviewed acted as Company Secretaries, a post taken up with promotion in larger companies or together with an 'in-house lawyer' label in the smaller company. Membership on the company's behalf in trade or industry associations was also frequent. The Managing Director in a company operating without an in-house lawyer pointed out the increasing importance of lawyers for his industry by way of the example of the trade association to which his company belonged — the recently-retired Chairman of the Association had been a lawyer and he had been replaced by another lawyer — testimony to a recognition of the lawyer's general skills as well as to the increasing legal regulation of business.

In this respect, the in-house lawyer could be said to be emulating the traditional 'wise counsellor' role of the legal profession. 'Businessmen in particular look to their lawyer for objective advice on a wide variety of areas, apparently because they feel the lawyer is the last generalist' (Bartlett, 1982:15). Many of my interviewees commented that managers found they valued lawyers' analytical training.

Similarly, the qualities of legal training lead one to find a high number of lawyer-executives, a phenomenon noted particularly in the US, but also in West Germany (Rueschemeyer, 1973) and in Australia (Sexton and Maher, 1982). Max Gloor, a former managing director of the Nestle Group, and former corporate lawyer, has suggested the following advantages of jurist-managers, whether as lawyers or in a management role:

— He states facts objectively. He has learned to differentiate between important and less important facts.

— Closely connected with the ability to describe the facts is the gift not to get lost in details. He has learned to subordinate the individual case to the overall strategy.

— He has been trained to look ahead into the future and thus to recognise the various possibilities which the realisation of a commercial transaction might necessitate.

— The jurist has been trained to think logically and methodically, to concentrate upon a problem and to bring it to a conclusion.

— He knows that often for one problem not only one opinion or one solution exists. Therefore, he is used to consider also other opinions and discuss problems with others and only, thereafter, draw his own conclusions. This furthers teamwork which is most important in business.

— The jurist knows the technique of negotiation and, therefore, also the technique to conclude agreements.

— He is open for innovations because the legal world is changing rapidly and he has to deal with new regulations and facts all the time.

— The jurist does not avoid to make decisions because he has been trained to make decisions every day. (Quoted in Kolvenbach, 1979: 16–17)

Of course these qualities could be ascribed to outside lawyers as well, but the other advantages of the in-house lawyer described above contribute to this aspect being even more clearly to the fore where an individual lawyer can demonstrate such qualities effectively.

Managing outside lawyers

Finally, it is important to bear in mind that the employment of an in-house lawyer is not an 'either-or' choice for companies. There is nothing to prevent a company employing its own lawyer and at the same time continuing to use outside lawyers for certain services or certain sections or areas of the company. Indeed, it is common practice. The occasions when outside lawyers are used are spelt out in more detail in chapter 7. What is pertinent here is the advantage for the company in using an in-house lawyer to buy in legal services. It is, of course, equally possible for management to retain the practice of direct access to outside lawyers rather than go through the legal department, but this was not often adopted as practice, except where local managers had autonomy on smaller claims issues (such as debt collection, unfair dismissals, insurance claims). It was more often found in companies with relatively new legal departments where older practices had been retained, or in companies which practised a large degree of decentralisation.

The first clear advantage is the *quality of communication* where outside lawyers relate to in-house lawyers rather than to management. The in-house lawyer is already versed in the jargon, attitudes, and legal requirements of the profession and can, therefore, ensure better instructions on salient points than the lay manager. Linked to this is the ability of the in-house lawyer more readily to find the right people and places in putting a case together for litigation, relieving other managers of a potentially difficult role. The in-house lawyer will therefore often make a better 'surrogate client' for his outside colleagues than other corporate employees unversed in the law and with other matters demanding their attention.

The best way to reduce outside legal costs is to give the best possible instructions. That's a major role for the in-house lawyer — to ask the right questions and give the right information (Australian lawyer in media business)

I think it's delightful dealing with in-house lawyers, because they can translate. You can have sensible conversations. There's less chance of misunderstanding. (Employment law specialist in a City firm)

Most lawyers would probably say it's good to get instructions from in-house lawyers rather than other people in the organisation. They can crystallise issues and present things to you in a way that makes them easier to assimilate. In turn they have more understanding of the problems we face. (Partner in City firm)

A second advantage is in the *appraisal of the service provided*. A lawyer is in a far better position to judge the quality of the work of another lawyer than a layman. Inefficient or incompetent fellow professionals can therefore be avoided or replaced or further opinions sought, while conversely the more able can be identified. Important, too, is the ability of the in-house lawyer to *monitor costs* and take early action to settle a claim or to replace the lawyers as necessary. One in-house lawyer had adopted the regular practice of requesting fee estimates before work was allocated, and in a complex conveyancing project, requested 'presentations' from several firms as to how they would approach the project (a tendering system becoming known among lawyers as 'beauty contests'). In becoming effectively the company's purchaser of legal services, in-house lawyers are therefore in a position where they may have a powerful influence over the conduct of outside lawyers' business. These and other more direct advantages for the in-house lawyer in being able to use outside lawyers are discussed in chapter 7.

DISADVANTAGES OF THE IN-HOUSE LAWYER

The disadvantages of employing an in-house lawyer are less clear-cut or predictable than the advantages but I have set out some possible leads to consider, in order to present a more rounded appreciation of in-house legal work. They derive more from hypothesis than from evidence arising from the research work. Whereas an outside lawyer might have difficulty emulating the advantages to a company of an in-house lawyer, it seems fair to conclude that outside lawyers would not necessarily avoid the disadvantages of in-house lawyers except in a passive sense, while in most instances these disadvantages could be easily overcome by an effective in-house legal department.

Costs

The complexities of some of the issues of cost-benefits in employing an in-house lawyer were discussed earlier. Clearly some companies, particularly small or medium-sized (or larger if legal work generated is small), could not justify the cost of employing a lawyer for purely legal purposes, although they might gain an improved service for the work they do generate. However, where the lawyer employed combined legal services with other company functions such as Company Secretary or executive, then the equation might appear rather differently.

Problem-creation

Linked to the above category and to general business views of lawyers is another possible difficulty, that lawyers may create problems that would otherwise not have existed. Thus, not every infringement of law is noticed or enforced, so the extent to which a lawyer takes on a preventive role is not coterminous with problems avoided by the company. Also, if a lawyer tends to err on the side of caution (an occupational trait recognised in some popular stereotypes), then more obstacles will be laid in the way of management, for example, by way of unnecessary arguments over contract terms or caution over possible tribunal findings and so on. As outlined earlier in this section, in-house lawyers showed awareness of this dilemma by emphasising the importance of a *positive* approach — identifying solutions and not problems. Several, in fact, reported finding management over-cautious where legal action was a possibility, and others referred to this trait being found more commonly amongst outside lawyers who were less used to preventive law or who felt more impelled to raise unnecessary issues in order to justify their fees.

Objectivity

A number of lawyers recognised that possible problems of objectivity could arise where an in-house lawyer was concerned, less
in any ethical sense than in their advisory capacity. Anyone
working for a large organisation might become more identified
with its style and objectives or identified with a particular
project if the lawyer had been part of the management 'team'.
Their advice to the company on interpreting a contract might,
therefore, reflect that orientation, for example, failing to give
enough emphasis to the fact that a judge might be more inclined
to side with a small supplier against the large organisation in
interpreting the document or circumstances. The problem could
also arise in another guise if legal advice and commercial advice
began to overlap, as was not uncommon. The corrective to this
possibility was seen in the lawyer's ability to maintain his or her
professional status and independence, assisted by the lawyer's
training and socialisation, as well as the important point that a
second opinion could always be sought from outside lawyers.

Another aspect of the question of independence relates to
the in-house lawyers' position in the organisational structure.
Criticism of in-house lawyers from an ethical point of view,
namely that their professional standards may be compromised
in pursuit of their employer's objectives, has come from some
voices inside the legal profession rather than from industry (see
chapter 13). This did not strike lawyers I interviewed as likely
to be a problem for them although it was mentioned by three
of the outside lawyers interviewed. More commonly stated
(although again felt to be more of a theoretical possibility than
one occurring in practice), was the possibility that some
particular department or level of management might fail to
follow definitive legal advice (as against a mere outline of risk
probabilities, that is, what was lawful or unlawful, compared to
what was merely desirable in risk terms). In-house lawyers
valued in this instance the fact that they had, in most organisations, direct access (or access through the Head of Department)
to the Chairman or Board of the company. In this respect they
felt in a more independent position than other departments of
the company. The implication of this, of course, was that these
upper tiers of management would follow legal advice as to what

was lawful if it was put to them. This was the normal expectation.

Narrowness

A few in-house lawyers felt that they valued the fact that outside lawyers advised a range of diverse companies, so they were therefore more likely to know what developments were taking place in different settings. Outside lawyers could therefore be more advanced or creative in their analysis of legal problems. In other words, outside lawyers provided 'breadth' compared to the in-house lawyer's 'depth' of knowledge of his own company. Outside lawyers also stressed this factor. However, more frequently they talked of narrowness in cultural terms, namely that British society placed lawyers into a narrower role in commercial decision-making. They felt that American companies used lawyers more centrally in the business, that the US General Counsel had a higher status in the corporation than British in-house lawyers. This cultural factor would inhibit the employment or full utilisation of in-house lawyers.

> Managers see lawyers as a necessary evil at best and in bad moments as an unnecessary evil. This may be part of the reason why companies haven't been as ready as they might have been to build up their own law departments. I have a number of clients who think any money spent on lawyers is a waste of time. They may see that as an economy but it probably works to our advancement in the long run. They are sometimes caught on things it's not sensible to be caught on. (Partner in City firm)

THE MANAGERS' VIEW

While the research for this book did not extend to a detailed survey of managers, previous research supports the view that managers would place a high value on the advantages listed earlier. What the businessman looks for in a good lawyer and what in-house lawyers think he looks for are not appreciably different. Donnell (1970) in his research on this found 'remarkable agreement' on the criteria for effective communication between clients and counsel, although some differences of detail existed within the groups (56, 91). The eleven factors clients mentioned in order of frequency were:

(1) Professional competence (not mentioned but assumed, Donnell suggests).
(2) Understanding of the business.
(3) Positive attitude, imagination.
(4) Prompt service.
(5) Clear-cut advice.
(6) Accessibility.
(7) No attempt to dominate client.
(8) Easy to talk with, good listener.
(9) Comprehensible language.
(10) Not a 'nit-picker'.
(11) Takes initiative.

My own discussions with managers tended to confirm this list, managers' negative comments on lawyers revolving around questions of difficulties of communication (understanding points made by lawyers), failure to get clear-cut advice, delays and cost (the latter two mentioned often in relation to outside lawyers).

A NEW PROFESSIONAL IDENTITY?

Returning to the theme stressed in the Introduction — that there are many worlds within a survey of one occupation, the in-house lawyer role, like most occupational roles, has a degree of 'role ambiguity' in its objectives and performance. There are many ways for individuals to 'play' the role, according to the advantages and disadvantages they identify for themselves and their clients, as well as in the way the work environment (including client demands) shapes their behaviour. Equally, this ambiguity provides scope for individuals or 'opinion leaders' in the profession to articulate a vision of the 'good in-house lawyer', thereby perhaps extending and developing current practice and attitudes. The advantages outlined above have been used to set some of the parameters by which the in-house lawyer can be judged.

Perhaps the most significant aspect of the in-house lawyers' identification of their advantages over their colleagues in private practice, at least within the wider debate about the legal profession in society, is the refinement of the 'service' aspect of the legal profession to make explicit what 'good service' may signify in a particular professional context. The experiences of, and demands on, lawyers in business, are leading to the articulation of new professional demands, and to a new professional identity, which can perhaps best be described by the expression *'the integrated lawyer'* — a lawyer only distant from the client in terms of problem-solving objectivity, *but a lawyer who is otherwise intimately familiar with and responsive to wider client goals than the solution of a legal problem per se.* Implicit in this emerging occupational identity is a critique of some aspects of the image of the traditional lawyer — allegedly aloof from the client and his wider objectives. How this position relates to developments in the legal profession in general is taken up later, where we shall see that this role-image also has relevance to emerging trends in private practice. The concept of 'the integrated lawyer' and its implications for legal work inside the modern corporation are also discussed later, but first a word should be said about the day-to-day work of the in-house lawyer.

NOTES

1 Taken up in greater detail in the chapters to follow on the 'integrated lawyer'.
2 Because this study was limited to an analysis of the in-house lawyer role, it did not extend to a survey of management decision-making where companies were appointing an in-house lawyer as a new post in the company. Further research on this particular stage of in-house growth would be very helpful in pinpointing management 'weighting' of the advantages of in-house lawyers and the degree of variation in this process.
3 As would be true of all 'staff' roles in a business.
4 For example, the CBI ran a conference in 1983 on 'Managing Legal Costs', reflecting company concern on rising legal costs. See 'Managing Legal Costs' (1985).
5 Johnstone and Hopson (1967) in the 1960s noted a reluctance amongst in-house lawyers to refer to cost advantages, and a few of my own respondents echoed this, but in the more cost-conscious climate of the 1980s, it is more frequently mentioned as a distinct advantage.

6 The salary figure I have used is drawn from the median base salary of in-house lawyers in 1985, in a survey conducted for the Commerce and Industry Group of the Law Society by Hay/MSL (1986). It does not include the cost of additional non-salary benefits.

7 See the CBI publication, n4.

8 Kolvenbach (1979: 71) has suggested another route to assessing when to think of employing an in-house lawyer, based on the number of employees in a company. He suggests a reasonable estimate for a manufacturing company (and highly regulated industry) in Europe would be one lawyer per 1000 employees.

4 The Work of the In-House Lawyer

THE NATURE AND ORGANISATION OF IN-HOUSE WORK

In-house lawyers work in a range of diverse company settings, thus not only covering different types of legal specialisation but also of company structures and 'cultures'. In addition legal departments vary in size from the one-man/woman legal department to legal departments with over 50 lawyers, and larger numbers still, sometimes into the hundreds, in companies in the United States, although the largest department in my own research employed a mere 37 lawyers in a department of around a hundred staff (including para-legal staff such as legal executives,[1] and secretarial). The range of work of in-house lawyers is also influenced by the extent and manner in which outside lawyers are used as a resource to service company needs, either generally or for specific functions or particular parts of the company. This is dictated by company traditions and in-house lawyer preferences, and is more appropriately discussed separately (see chapter 7), but also therefore plays an important part in the work of the in-house lawyer.

Thus, any general discussion of the nature and organisation of in-house legal work must bear in mind this diversity and its effect on the experience of in-house legal work. However, there were clear patterns which emerged within this diversity and this chapter attempts to outline them, both with regard to the structure of legal departments and to the nature of the in-house lawyer's work. As a starting point it is worth stressing that, despite the wide range in the size of legal departments, the majority of in-house lawyers work in departments of between one and five lawyers, with perhaps a quarter of in-house lawyers working in companies with six to ten lawyers and under a fifth in companies with more than ten.[2] The most common situation for an in-house lawyer is therefore that of being one of a small departmental team of lawyers.

Most of the lawyers interviewed reacted with amusement to the request to describe a 'typical week's work'. 'No such thing' was the repeated response. This reaction did not refer so much to a repeated need to learn new legal specialisms as to the diversity of fact-law situations and detailed questions that came across their desks. (For an example of this, see the diary outline at the end of this chapter.) The majority of the lawyers, in fact, covered a range of legal specialisms, at the same time expecting to perform a 'general practitioner' role within these broad guidelines, an understandable position given the diversity of legal issues raised by the activities of a large company and the small number of lawyers typically involved. Most referred to this variety, and the uncertainty over what they would next be asked to advise on, as a plus factor in terms of job satisfaction and felt that work in private practice lacked the diversity of in-house work. Several also referred to the possibility that they could switch the emphasis of their work in the future if they wished (by transfer of work to colleagues or to outside lawyers). Thus it is difficult to classify in-house lawyers neatly as generalist or specialist, as much will depend on the size of the department, its role in the organisation and the special fields of law which affect the company's operations. They are likely to be both generalists in the sense of knowing a range of company and commercial law, and specialists in particular areas relevant to their industry.

You never know what's coming over your desk next. The one danger, of course, is that you can't become specialist. You're expected to have a working knowledge of every area. You're eventually a Jack of all trades and master of none. You also become more of a businessman than a lawyer — well, let's say there are commercial considerations in everything you do. (A one-man department in a consumer goods subsidiary of a multinational corporation. His reference to not being a specialist, however, ignored his own expertise in consumer law affecting his company's products.)

There are not many outside lawyers who would know thoroughly all the aspects of North Sea legislation — licensing, international treaties, pipelines legislation, legislation relating to facilities, the construction and design of platforms, health and safety on them, etc. I'm not suggesting it's very difficult to acquire that knowledge, but if you went outside, you're not likely to have the people with it, because they just don't get the exposure to it. Though one reason for that is the fact that all the big companies have their own in-house lawyers working on it! (A lawyer working in an eight-man department of an oil company.)

The potential areas of work for a 'general practitioner' in a major company are, of course, substantial, whether by way of advising on, or monitoring or documentation of, company transactions, involvement in relevant meetings and negotiations, or dealings with courts and other regulatory agencies. Areas covered might include, for example, agreements on raw materials and other goods and services supplied by and to the company; distribution and carriage arrangements; product descriptions, warranties and advertising claims; packaging, trademark and copyright regulations; sales on credit or leasing, and the protection of the seller's rights; infringement of competition laws or restrictive trade practices; property transactions, charges and planning regulations; product liability claims; insurance agreements on product and employer liability; employment contracts, confidentiality and competition restrictions; tax and financing arrangements; devising new corporate structures or overseeing acquisitions, disposals and joint ventures.

General advisory work on the details of legislation affecting company practices, and work on commercial contracts, are probably the two most common activities of the in-house lawyers I interviewed. Two recent surveys support this, while also indicating as I found that 'generalist' can cover areas which many lawyers in private practice might have little contact with. A questionnaire survey conducted for the Law Society Commerce and Industry Group[3] indicated that almost half of the solicitors surveyed described their work as primarily generalist, only 15 per cent as specialist, but almost 30 per cent saw themselves as primarily engaged in commercial work. The principal areas of work in which respondents indicated some involvement were — contracts and negotiations (73 per cent), general advice (62 per cent), company law (48 per cent), conveyancing and property matters (46 per cent), employment law (43 per cent). Acquisitions and takeovers, intellectual property and litigation were mentioned in over a third of cases. More senior lawyers were likely to be more heavily involved with commercial, company and tax matters. This survey can be compared with another questionnaire survey conducted by the Association of Graduate Careers Advisory Services (AGCAS, 1984) which found the most frequently mentioned areas of work to be financial (tax, investments, trusts, banking, claims, acquisitions, and so on), employment, property/conveyancing, contracts, litigation, intellectual property, the first three being clearly predominant.[4]

The somewhat different findings of the surveys (for example, the lower emphasis on contracts in the AGCAS case) may partly reflect the different forms of questionnaire or samples drawn. However, it also again confirms the point I made earlier that it is difficult to classify easily in-house legal work, since in some respects it is almost inevitably specialist (in terms of coverage of one industry only) in relation to many outside lawyers, but at the same time is more generalist because of the wide client community covered within the organisation on any areas of law relevant to business operations. This contention is more readily appreciated if one examines the profile of a company legal department's work coverage, and examples of an in-house lawyer's case-file and of a weekly diary are set out at the end of this chapter.

The variety of work involved was also reflected in comments made on the problem of the rhythm of work. Workload over the year did not follow a consistent pattern. Rather, there would be periods of dealing with many smaller items, interspersed with sudden major problems or chunks of work, for instance, a major product liability claim against a pharmaceutical company, or an important company acquisition or a major batch of staff transfers, and therefore conveyancing and contract questions, or redundancies (therefore questions of employee consultation, dismissal notices, severance terms, tax implications).

Much of the advisory work was done over the telephone, in face-to-face meetings, visits to company sites, or by memoranda. There were few examples of regular briefing meetings with management (although Heads of Department were more likely to attend Board meetings or other regular meetings of senior management). By and large that is, in-house lawyers worked on the basis of acting as 'professionals', responding to their 'clients'[5] as and when required on an individual basis. (Apart from sitting on Boards of Directors, either a main board or the Board of a subsidiary company, the most frequent committee presence mentioned was Health and Safety Committe membership. Membership of *ad hoc* 'policy' groups, drawing up company practice on specific issues, was also common.)

This 'professional' orientation was also reflected in the fact that few departments had any systematic job descriptions for lawyers which detailed job responsibilities and authority.[6] Given the uncertain nature of the law-business environment, and the personal nature of lawyer-client service, a strong case can be made out that such an 'open system' approach is functional in organisational terms, allowing for adaptability, swift response to problems, good relations with clients, and — crucial for the lawyer's work — independence and objectivity (Donnell, 1970). Of course, as in other areas of company practice, support from senior management is an additional vital factor in ensuring that the work of a legal department is effective and respected by fellow staff. In this respect in-house legal departments are normally greatly advantaged, since the activities they cover are often central to major company initiatives, thus bringing them close to senior executives in any case. However, there were also clear signs that in the more 'professional management' climate of the 1980s legal departments were being required to justify this 'natural' model, a number of companies undertaking 'effectiveness and efficiency' studies, which included the legal department's work. I have more to say on these later in this chapter.

Legal specialisation and law department organisation

Not surprisingly there was most evidence of specialisation of legal skills in those companies with larger numbers of legal staff. However, even in these larger departments, specialisation was not rigorously followed. This arose from the acceptance again of a 'professional' ethos as against a 'division of labour' ethos. Thus, where there were a number of lawyers working together, work often divided on the lines of individual preference for types of work rather than a strict allocation of duties. At the same time, it was accepted that clients arose for members of the department through personal contacts as much as through any other means. That is, if a manager of a particular factory came to know one of the lawyers over, say, an unfair dismissal claim, that manager was likely to approach the same lawyer again over other legal questions. Those questions were likely to be taken on board personally for the client rather than the lawyer referring him to another member of the department (although the lawyer might in turn approach a colleague in the department for advice). Frequently, therefore, a 'matrix' work system developed involving specialisation both in clients and in law.

> Our work is almost like a private practice; we all have our own individual clients. It works on the basis of some people get on with you, you get on with them, and perhaps you particularly like the work they give you. That's how we allocate work. Our clients are the individuals inside the company. (Pharmaceutical company)

However, this looseness of role was not as dramatic as it might appear to be because of the common split in legal department activities and staff into two broad areas. The most frequent division of functions in legal departments was that of a section dealing with 'commercial' matters (contracts, licensing, and so on) and a section dealing with all other operating matters of the company. This latter came under various headings, most frequently 'litigation'.[7] It covered what one interviewee described as 'lawyers' law', that is new legislation, conveyancing, leases, acquisitions, Road Traffic Acts, health and safety, employment legislation,[8] trading standards, food labelling regulations, and so on. Thus, the specialist character of the former probably led to contacts wtih management levels with more specialist legal interests (in sales and marketing) and who were less likely to return with issues arising in another field of law. Thus the lawyer who referred to work as allocated on the basis of individual choice went on to elaborate on this:

> The assistant solicitors all have their own particular interests. We are quite lucky in this company in that respect. One of the assistant solicitors deals with mainly commercial work and conveyancing. Another also deals with commercial work, but for different divisions. For myself, my main area is litigation, particularly product liability litigation, and employment and personnel work, plus some conveyancing and

commercial work. The clients would come to me generally because that is my speciality. For example, with product liability claims, I have a lot of contact with scientific staff. Their legal problems would be likely to fall into my area of expertise. But don't get the impression that we specialise completely. We are all expected to do all the work of the legal department if necessary.

A few interviewees, as this one did, referred interestingly to this broad division of function within legal departments as being more than a question of division along the lines of *company* legal function. They regarded the division as a sensible *professional* division, that is that the type of legal work required a different type of mind and personality, and a person who would be suited to one branch would not be so readily suited to the other. This was partly due to the nature of the thinking process required for commercial contracts, a 'commercial flair', and partly attributed to other connected facets of the work, for example, a greater amount of extensive travel required by the work and the ability to enjoy 'mixing' (in both senses) with others in negotiating situations.

There is no formal allocation of work. It doesn't happen that way. We tend to allocate among ourselves on the basis of our preferences and known abilities. B in the next office has a commercial flair. He is good at negotiating and dealing with people so he tends to assist in commercial sales of distributorships and agency questions and so on. I tend to handle lawyers' law . . . also all the work on regulations — health and safety, cylinders explosives, Road Traffic Acts — which B finds boring. (Manufacturing company lawyer)

On the other hand, once this personal specialisation was established into a more set pattern, it could lead to differences of view on the best method of organisation:

The department probably just grew according to the capabilities of particular people. The organisation is an *ex post facto* rationalisation. To some extent we are stuck with history but we have made a conscious decision to stick with it. Some individuals would have liked the change, mostly 'young men on the make'. There's no harm in that. I expect it happens in universities too. They see that there are plum jobs they may not be getting and think there may be opportunities if they change the organisation. It's not being cynical. It happens and organisations do have to accommodate. (Oil company lawyer)

The clearest two cases of specialisation in the research study were those of a lawyer who worked entirely on conveyancing matters, and one who worked in the newspaper industry where the legal role was principally concerned with monitoring press articles for possible libel, contempt of court, and so forth. The former occurred in the largest legal department encountered in the study (already mentioned) where conveyancing was a central part of the business operation because of the frequency of property investment transactions (an insurance company). In the newspaper case, lawyers had traditionally carried out this more specialist role, although there were indications that this was changing because of the dual effects of increasing employment law concerns and company diversification into other businesses.

These two types of specialisation also recall another relevant distinction in linking lawyer specialisation to industry type — the division of the profession into barristers and solicitors. While there are more solicitors than barristers in industry, some sectors employ more or less barristers than other sectors,[9] partly out of tradition, partly out of the separate professional skills of the two groups. The newspaper industry has relied more often on barristers, for example, whereas industries with greater conveyancing issues, such as construction and insurance companies, are more likely to have high proportions of solicitors. Similarly, more barristers are likely to be found in advisory roles in trade and professional associations. Some aspects of this division of the profession in the in-house context may be in a process of change, a point we return to in chapter 12.

In conclusion, the organisation of legal departments reflected the high degree of independence of professional employees, a fact which is not necessarily detrimental to the client organisation given the need for professional employees to be both motivated and flexible in their ability to respond to client demands. The clearest structure evident in the larger legal departments was a 'matrix' of clients/competences. That is, most lawyers specialised (although not in a narrow way) both in certain areas of law and in certain client units of the organisation, whether individual managers, plants or divisions of the company. Most felt this had emerged fairly naturally in their work development and that they could equally opt later to change their emphases if they so desired. However, there were obviously certain limits to this, and degrees of structure imposed both by the nature of the company's organisation and work and the interests and contacts of existing members of the department.

There were also signs that this perceived fluidity of work organisation was likely to face more rationalisation in the future. First, the issue is sharpened once departments reach limits on size, since questions of career structures will emerge, particularly for younger lawyers. Second, some in-house lawyers had begun to recognise the need to be as 'professional' in their managerial, as much as their legal, functions. In any case, in the harsher climate of the 1980s, with companies more cost-conscious, all company departments are likely to face appraisal or are asked for self-appraisal of their activities. A few I encountered had been through such exercises. For example, one had been required to record and categorise all its activities, assessing which services were being given to which departments. Both the lawyers and the departments were then asked to rate the importance of the activity, its costs, and areas of possible cost savings. In this way, various categories of activity received ratings of how essential[10] they were and costings. The next stage was to decide which of those areas could be the target for cost saving, and to take action, followed by an evaluation of the results. As a result of this activity, the legal department adopted the practice of time-recording all activities as a routine practice. While the exercise did achieve some savings, and the department felt it had been useful, much of the savings were made in work which had formerly gone to outside lawyers, a fact reflecting the points made in chapter 3 on the relative costs of in-house and outside lawyers.

As an example of the approach involved in these exercises, the general headings (the 'purposes' of the legal service[11] within which the particular activities in this company were analysed — (rated and costed) are set out below, including functions which were linked to the law department's activities, functions which in some companies might be quite discrete. Under each head,

there were a series of sub-headings in which particular activities
were timed according to their allocation to specific departments
of the company.

LAW
(1) Draft contracts.
(2) Advise on existence, content and application of laws.
(3) Convey and receive other useful information.[12]
(4) Represent the company.
(5) Administer and conduct litigation.
TAX
(6) Generate profit improvement through tax planning.
(7) Advise personnel on tax laws.
(8) Ensure compliance work is completed to the Group's best
advantage.
REAL ESTATE
(9) Advise on and negotiate purchase of real estate.
(10) Manage real estate.
(11) Control real estate expenditure.
(12) Achieve, negotiate, manage real estate sales.
(13) Provide specialist valuations.
PATENT
(14) Coordinate European patent matters.
ALL
(15) Maintain professional knowledge and skills.
(16) Administration.

Another example of such an exercise is recorded by Fischer
(1984) in the Alcoa legal department in the United States. As
a result of the analysis, the department recognised that it had
five 'missions' in the company:

(1) to assist in *compliance* with all applicable laws, regulations
and mandated company policies;
(2) to *advocate* the company's position in legal proceedings an in
other matters where it is customary to have legal representation;
(3) to establish the company's position in *transactions* and ensure
it is legally effective;
(4) to *counsel and advise* the company regarding the legal aspects
of business decisions and the formulation of company policy;
(5) to provide *competent lawyers* to serve the needs of the

company, including in such matters as training, recuiting and administration.

Fischer reports that, as a result of the exercise, they decided to organise their work by a client/competence matrix system, indicating that the 'natural' division of labour reached by many of the departments I studied was also a 'rational' one.

The area of greatest cost identified in the Alcoa study was also in work going out to litigation and outside lawyers — approximately 60 per cent of Alcoa's legal budget (and 76 per cent of this in litigation matters in 1983), was going in fees to outside lawyers whose hourly costs were double those of in-house lawyers. As a result, one of the targets set following this exercise was to reduce these cost areas by bringing additional litigation specialists in-house and planning a litigation-avoidance campaign.

Allocation of costs in legal departments

Two basic methods were used. The simplest method was to charge the legal budget to the central or general administration budget. Other companies allocated costs on a notional basis to different divisions according to the extent to which they used legal services. The former was said to have the advantage that no one was discouraged from seeking legal advice on financial grounds, and also it spread the cost evenly instead of a division bearing it which might have more legal problems not through managerial ineptitude so much as the nature of that business compared to others of a different kind. On the other hand, allocation of costs meant greater cost control consciousness, and also had tax implications in certain cases.[13]

The effect of company type on legal work

The nature of the company's operations affected the content of the work of the legal department in a number of ways. The obvious effects were to be seen in the types of problems encountered, and hence their legal content. Thus, those lawyers working in the retail industry were likely to spend more of their time on food labelling regulations and trading standards questions than the generalist lawyers in other industries; in the oil business, with oil licensing regulations and petrol station distributorship arrangements; in the pharmaceutical industry, with product liability and drug licensing; in banking, with loans and credit agreements; in newspaper publishing, with libel and related matters.

Less obvious, but nevertheless important, factors were to be found arising from the issues which concern organisation theorists, ranging from the 'hard' dimension of company structure to the 'soft' one of company 'climate' (or 'corporate culture' in the more fashionable terminology). These influences were evident frequently in comments made by interviewees. Those lawyers who had worked for more than one company almost invariably referred to the difference of 'style'. For example, one referred to the contrast between working for an old-fashioned English manufacturing concern where senior management insisted on doing business as 'gentlemen' (which in turn 'played down' bargaining and contract enforcement strategies, and also made for a highly autocratic management style) compared to his current position in a US-owned subsidiary where it was regarded as scandalous to 'leave a dollar on the table' in negotiations and where open, consultative management was the norm. Another referred, somewhat wistfully, to his last company's ability to make every section of the operation 'profit-conscious', which ensured greater emphasis on product quality at every level.

The structure of the organisation in some cases modified the 'product' specialisation referred to above. The research brought home to the author the impact of trends in industrial concentration of ownership. Most of the companies studied not only had many separate premises or 'plants' with which the legal department was concerned, but also many subsidiaries which had been developed or acquired for expansion, diversification for tax purposes both in the UK and overseas. The legal department, usually based in the Head Office of the parent company (or the European Head Office or a branch of it if a US-owned company), also dealt with these arms of the business (sometimes through overseeing the work of a lawyer/legal department based in the subsidiary). Diversification of company interests ensured consequent diversification of legal interests, whether into different products, legislative and regulatory requirements, foreign systems of law, or being able to adapt to different styles of management or company policy in a subsidiary. One might say, therefore, that the typical 'in-house' lawyer has many 'second homes'!

Product specialisation had an obvious impact not only on the content of the legal work but on the amount and type of legal servicing which was necessary for the company. For example, where the large retailer could normally work according to its own standard form contracts since suppliers were more dependent on it rather than it on them, a group of small cosmetics manufacturers/retailers were dependent on frequent transactions of varying character according to market and sales circumstances.

> Our agreements are so many and so varied in size and in the nature of the supplier relationship, that they virtually all have to be negotiated separately. It's not like British Aerospace who can insist on standard conditions which suppliers must fulfil. Therefore all I can do is to emphasise the general points and deal specifically with some of the major deals. We may be stronger or weaker in particular circumstances and you have to adjust to that. . . . One has to compromise a lot in business. It's a case of what's possible more than what's legally ideal. That's one difference from private practice.

The retailer, on the other hand, had large numbers of shoplifting prosecutions to process, frequent industrial tribunal claims to defend, and trading standards concerns.

This last example is also relevant to the question of the role of the legal department. Although the frequency of legal transactions was clearly a factor in the growth of legal departments (for example, in the case of the long-established department in the insurance company), it was not a conclusive factor. The tradition in each of the retailers was to farm out to private practice the legal work in shoplifting prosecutions, because it was so extensive as to prove too burdensome for an internal department (and possibly for political reasons, to distance the company to a degree from enforcement processes). Participation in litigation was normally regarded as excessively time-consuming for in-house lawyers, not easily fitted in alongside the many other more pressing in-house demands on their expertise, although some did become involved relatively frequently where they tried to keep work in-house.

The nature of the communications system in the company was also seen by some interviewees as important. One, for example, referred to the centralisation of decision-making required by the nature of the business (with daily decisions necessary on ordering stocks for the company's shops). This fostered an equally swift ability to respond in the legal department, made easier by the location of the legal offices in the same corridor as the directors. Office location was also seen as relevant in many of the departments to other questions, for example, the clients one came to know best or the requests one received for help with personal advice.

Finally, the history and traditions of the company and its legal department were important in determining how widely the legal function was defined. That is, there are many areas where there is a link between law and other fields such as tax, insurance, patents. The extent to which these were separate or worked closely with the legal department clearly varied from company to company. Some in-house lawyers saw this as a challenge to the legal department to prove its worth by absorbing or at least decisively influencing these other functions.[14]

In-house and outside lawyers

The ability to 'sub-contract' legal services to outside lawyers gave in-house lawyers additional room for flexibility in terms of the areas of work they chose as the most effective for them to pursue, or as a means of coping with workload or in-house political pressures. A fuller discussion of the occasions when outside lawyers were used is contained in chapter 7. Chapter 9 on the career of an in-house lawyer also contains further observations on the distinctiveness of in-house legal work. For example, in the context of this chapter's emphasis on structures it is possible to reinterpret many of the comments made on the difference between working in-house as against working in private practice, as itself reflecting different 'corporate cultures'. Thus, one was working, in the company environment, with a more highly educated and sophisticated range of clients (engineers, geologists, pharmacists, senior managers) than could be met in private practice. This kept the lawyer more on his or her toes as advice was more often challenged at an intellectual level.

At the same time it was a more smooth process. 'One is aware of working as part of a smooth, well-oiled machine'; 'One's instructions are — how shall I put it — more "well ordered" '. These and other comparisons with work in private practice in fact typify the distinction between working for a large concern and working for a small business. The work in private practice for many had been dissatisfying because of the excessive time spent chasing clients for fees (debts) or avoiding clients who demanded more (in time and answers) than solicitors could give within the constraints of a small business.[15]

THE WORK OF THE IN-HOUSE LAWYER — CASE STUDIES

Reference was made earlier to the generalist character of the in-house lawyer's work. Three examples of this follow. The first section contains an example of a legal department's description of its structure and activities, set down as part of a company-wide exercise (a pharmaceutical company) to evaluate its structure and organisation.[16] The second example sets out the subject headings within one lawyer's employment law case file (another pharmaceutical company). The third was the answer given by one interviewee who, when asked to describe a typical week's work, read out the contents of the previous week from his desk diary. (In each case, details which might identify the companies have been omitted.)

X plc Legal Department

Commercial Section

To provide legal services in respect of all commercial contracts including distribution, manufacturing, supply, research and patent licence contracts, confidentiality agreements, company acquisitions and formations, copyright, company law, EEC law, restrictive trade practices, weights and measures, product labelling, pricing, advertising, trade competitions, consumer credit schemes and statutory company secretarial matters.

Litigation Section

To provide legal services in respect of all employment matters and litigation including unfair dismissal claims, customer complaints, claims for personal injuries, complaints and prosecutions by inspectors under Trade Descriptions, Weights and

Measures and Food and drug laws, criminal and security matters.

Conveyancing Section

To provide legal services in respect of the Company's land and buildings, including conveyancing of retail, office and industrial premises and advice on planning law. The section provides advice to the Company's Pension Fund in respect of its investments in land.

Trade Mark Section

To act as trade agents and advisers to the Company in registering, maintaining and defending its trade marks throughout the world. This involves advising on the choice of trade marks, handling infringement proceedings and registering licences. (Trade mark agent and no lawyers in this section.)

Board and Company Secretaryships

Staff in the Legal Department act as secretary to the Divisional Boards and certain subsidiary companies. (There was also a house purchase and debt collection section without any lawyers which reported to the litigation section.) In this company the legal department was within the Company Secretary's Department with a Deputy Company Secretary who acted as Principal Legal Adviser.

An employment law file

(1) Advice on the position over company accomodation for an employee who was leaving the company — can we get him out?

(2) Some problems with pay on transfer grievances.

(3) A secondment of staff problem.

(4) A possibly difficult redundancy.

(5) Issues in a transfer to a lower grade of someone who was disabled.

(6) Bridging loans to employees being moved.

(7) Sickness absence 'fibs' case.

(8) Relocation expenses.

(9) A difficult sickness termination.

(10) A mental illness problem.

(11) Drafting a consultancy agreement.

(12) Some fixed-term contracts.

(13) A work permit problem.

(14) Maternity absence problems.

(15) Whether we can recover sick payments from a third party for an employee who was injured by that party.
(16) Sports and social club issues.
(17) Possible sex and racial discrimination claims.
(18) Disclosure of information to trade union claim.

A week in the life of an in-house lawyer

Monday   Sports and Social Club (I went through the problems with them on insurance quotations etc. such as problems of borrowing yachts from the Club and so on.)

Contract with Water Authority.

Personnel — I advised them on a consultancy matter, an employee in the department was leaving and was retained as a consultant.

Charity matters.

Reviewed advertising material.

Drew up consultancy agreement.

Made arrangements for the Board meeting.

Long US telephone call from our South African Company — it used to be our subsidiary but has been transferred to the US company but they are always ringing us up because South African law is similar to ours rather than the law in the US.

Tuesday   Purchasing terms and conditions.

Engineering contracts with South Africa.

Dutch legal matter concerning EEC regulations on new substances. It's a core inventory that the EEC is aiming at where they must be notified of any new substances and approve them etc. if they are not on current list. So we had to go through all our 168 products to make sure they were on the list.

Property discussion with surveyor on sale of some of our property.

Pension plan — change of custodian trustees.

One hour on various County Court actions with my Debt Collection clerk.

One hour on an easement in Cheshire — water pipe line.

Development land tax.

Reviewed a guarantee.

Minutes of AGM of our Credit Union — yes we have a credit union of our own. I was Secretary of it when it began.

Wednesday   Two or three contracts.

County Court work.

Road traffic accident.

Thursday   Barclays Bank Motor Club arrangements. They were using our car park for their annual rally.

Tax matters.

Formation of an Irish company.

Saw our outside solicitor on some current litigation.

Three people on different weights and measures problems.

Insurance department about employee disqualified from driving. (That was an interesting problem. He was disqualified and asked if his unemployed father could act as a driver for him going round his engineering operations. I told him it was OK as long as they didn't use the vehicle for any private use because the insurance does not cover private use. Anyone can drive our vehicles on business.)

Friday   Charity matter.

Advice to our transport department.

Dealt with Personnel Department on a new staff handout — I talked to them about it and reviewed the draft the following week.

Dealt with computer department — they are entering into a contract to try out some software.

Plant sale to Saudia Arabia.

Computer Department on a computer maintenance contract.

These summary 'case-studies' of legal practice inside business organisations, confirm the point made earlier as to the combination of generalist and specialist aspects in in-house legal work. The in-house lawyer is a member of a specific business 'community' and is likely to be required to deal with the range of issues arising within that community from core business matters to more peripheral concerns. The diversity of material this may bring to what is normally a small-sized department reveals the factor underlying comments on the 'openness' of the in-house lawyer role — the importance of which contacts one made inside the company, of the scope to vary the emphasis of one's work, of the diversity compared to many private practice contexts. The three examples given only refer to headings, of course, rather than providing case-studies in detail of the actions taken. Exploring the latter would, however, further confirm that the individual lawyer can 'play' the role in a number of ways. Nevertheless, the current business climate is providing impetus for lawyers to seek to approach this range of work with more 'businesslike' judgements on cost-effectiveness. This emphasis is merging with a more longstanding debate amongst in-house lawyers, an attempt to articulate a distinctive professional-managerial approach for the in-house lawyer. It is to this issue that we now turn.

NOTES

1   In this study I did not survey the role of para-legal staff in companies,
    although comments made by interviewers did not disclose any difference
    to their use in private practice for more of the routine functions of lawyers.
    For a more detailed description of the use of these para-legal support
    staff, see Kolvenbach (1979: 98–103).
2   The figures are taken from a recent survey of in-house legal departments
    conducted by Hay-MSL for the Law Society Commerce and Industry
    Group (1986). They confirm the sort of distribution I found in my own
    smaller sample. A survey of legal departments by AGCAS (1984) obtained
    slightly higher figures of staff — just under 50 per cent with more than
    five, nearly 30 per cent with more than ten.
3   By Hay-MSL management consultants.
4   The AGCAS survey also suggests that international law advice is a
    growing area (16).
5   The nature of the in-house lawyer's client provides some intriguing issues
    for the nature of professional practice. See the discussion on the integrated
    lawyer in the following chapters and chapter 12.
6   For a more detailed 'job description' of a legal department, see Kolven-
    bach (1979: Annex).
7   In the larger departments, a 'litigation' section was more specifically
    involved in the direct aspects of litigation; in smaller departments, outside
    lawyers were more likely to be used.
8   Employment contracts were treated in all companies with this division
    as a distinct category of contract, that is, they were dealt with by special-
    ists in the 'other law' branch rather than by those in the commercial
    contracts function. Most interviewees attributed this to the recent
    historical development of employment law. It provides in that sense
    additional support for those academic lawyers who have argued that the
    principles behind employment contracts are, or should be, distinctive
    from other areas of contract law.
9   AGCAS (op. cit.) noting the almost complete dominance of solicitors in
    the building/civil engineering sector. AGCAS found, not surprisingly,
    that more solicitors than barristers are employed in business, the highest
    proportion of barristers to solicitors being in professional/advisory bodies
    (36 per cent of lawyers in that category).
10 Another intriguing aspect reported by this interviewee but not developed
    was the fact that some of the areas which the lawyers had rated as not
    essential for legal department involvement, the managers had rated as
    indispensable — reflecting presumably the misconceptions about law
    which many laymen hold.
11 The trend for management consultants and businesses to seek some defi-
    nition of purposes, 'corporate objectives' or 'mission' is linked to the need
    to assess effectiveness, which is difficult unless one sets goals as criteria.
    Choka (1969) argued strongly in favour of such an exercise since a legal
    department has no quotas, efficiency indices or even common grounds of
    comparison with other departments to guide its effectiveness. My own

interviewees were often surprised when I asked 'How would the company know you were doing a good job?', nor were there clear answers to this question.

12　This category referred to checking sales authorisations and other company documentation, to attending meetings (Board, safety policy, management committees, other subsidiaries), providing information on request, commenting on reports from others in the company, and so on.

13　For a more detailed description of the methods used in cost allocation, see Kolvenbach (1979: 93–8).

14　There are arguments for such specialisms as patents and tax to be within the jurisdiction of a legal department (Kolvenbach, 1979: 79), but whatever their merits, clearly there is a strong case for effective liaison between such areas and the legal department. Similarly, effective coordination within the department is as essential as effective coordination with management. Combination of specialist legal knowledge with specialist organisation clients is probably the ideal (Kolvenbach: 82), but organisational structure primarily depends on the structure of the company which determines the best mode of response.

15　It is an interesting reflection on how much lawyers retain their professional outlook that those interviewed often attributed the differences between inside and outside lawyers as a difference of approach to practice rather than an outcome of the different organisational settings of the two groups.

16　For an example of a standard manual of work practices for a company legal department, see Kolvenbach: 109–26.

5 The Integrated Lawyer (1): Preventive Law

We have gained some sense of the legal content of the in-house lawyer's role in the last chapter. Clearly most in-house lawyers carry out functions which are similar to those of lawyers in the profession generally, particularly those concerned with the technical matters of legal work — drafting contracts, servicing property transactions, drawing up appropriate documentation when initiating or responding to legal actions. Equally, the need to advise clients of whether a course of action is legally feasible or advisable is common to both groups of lawyers. However, the organisational setting of the in-house lawyer creates distinctive opportunities and choices in the area of the *delivery* or *management* or *style* of legal services. Indeed, such choices may move beyond questions merely concerned with the organisation of legal work, to shade into differences of substance between in-house and outside professional practice.

The primary source of these possibilities derives from the incorporation of the lawyer into a client's business, thus creating the opportunity to build on the advantages of in-house lawyering referred to in chapter 3, in order to *integrate* legal practice with organisational practice and objectives, creating 'the integrated lawyer'.[1] The relationship of in-house lawyer and client can therefore become one with both a past and a future, and one targeted on the organisation's primary purposes and situation, rather than one concerned with an isolated legal 'problem' of the moment which necessitates calling in a legal specialist.[2] Thus, the in-house lawyer can re-create the 'family lawyer' tradition, in organisational 'role' terms as well as in personal terms (good personal relationships figured highly in most in-house lawyers' descriptions of their role). This option separates in-house legal work from the large sectors of private practice which deal with separate, occasional and often 'one-shot' clients.[3] It is a working situation which leads to an emphasis on professional 'imperatives' that are not necessarily given a similar emphasis in private practice lawyering (although part of a later

74

argument of this book is that they are qualities which ought to be intrinsic to private practice). These professional imperatives are particularly evident in the written culture of in-house lawyers, but this reflects and is reflected in their working methods and aspirations. Espousal of these occupational beliefs, of course does not, guarantee that individual in-house lawyers actually practice them successfully, but they do indicate what they aspire to, and distinguish the typical 'practice management' concerns of in-house lawyers from those of their fellow lawyers in private practice.

The distinction is particularly evident in the stress laid, both in the literature and in interviewees' comments, on the 'preventive' or 'proactive' role of the in-house lawyer. Defined broadly, 'prevention' of legal difficulties might be said to apply at any stage up to and beyond a court judgement. The good lawyer may not only prevent a breach of law but thereafter advise on effective defences or claims in mitigation, or on limiting legal costs and damages or reducing the impact of the legal enforcement mechanisms. However, we shall distinguish for our purposes between legal skills in responding to causes of action once begun, and legal skills involved in forestalling litigation by ensuring that client behaviour takes a course with least potential legal hazard. 'Proactive' or 'preventive' lawyering is generally taken to refer to the latter. The crucial ability referred to is the capacity to *anticipate* that problems might arise in order to forestall or limit them, a less defined skill amongst lawyers (and others) than the skills of *responding* to problems (Stichnoth and Dolan, 1982).[4] One might also extend the scope for preventive lawyering even further to include *attempts to influence law creation or reform*. Only a minority of in-house lawyers referred to this activity as preventive lawyering,[5] but since a number of them engaged in it, it is also dealt with in this chapter.

A second area where one can sense the special character of in-house legal work is in terms of the in-house lawyer's role in the *translation of law into practice*, that is, the capacity to guide and influence practical business behaviour in the light of an interpretation of the likely applied meaning of abstract legal rules. This aspect was evident in the frequent references by in-house lawyers to the need to be 'positive' in their approach to legal advice — being helpful rather than stating the obstacles to action. This ability is also integral to the lawyer's capacity to be proactive. The lawyer's role as translator is considered in more detail in the next chapter.

Out of these two symbolic functions, of proactive law founded on translation skills, one can argue that a new occupational identity is being forged for the in-house lawyer with characteristics which, as we shall see, represent an equally important but less easily attainable target for the outside lawyer. There were frequent comments made to me of the importance for in-house lawyers to be seen by their clients to develop the necessary skills to sustain this professional aspiration of what I have termed the 'integrated lawyer' — 'professionally sound and practically helpful'. Such comments also carried with them explicit or implied criticisms of aspects of the more traditional private practice lawyer model.

It's a problem in Australia. . . . I don't think many companies really have come to grips with how to *use* lawyers. Instead they feel the need for someone there who 'understands these things'. Lawyers are partly at fault too. Lawyers are mainly reactive — it's the outcome of their training. Throw them a problem and you get an answer. But how many lawyers think creatively? (Lawyer in a consultancy firm)

I blame UK lawyers for the situation we're in. They ought to be more *professional*. If a lawyer is as thick as two short planks and wet behind the ears, he's treated only as a walking law book in the company. Sometimes when we're negotiating contracts, we ask the other side 'Why didn't you bring in your law department?' They say 'Oh no. We don't want to bring in bloody solicitors on the subject.' And I think — Oh no. They've got the wrong sorts of lawyers working for them. . . . To my way of thinking, the role of the law department depends on the personality of the individual solicitor. If he's a 'dopey conveyancer', as some from private practice are going to be, no one is going to value his advice or talk over problems with him. He would just be the office boy doing the few jobs he's given to do. (Manufacturing company lawyer)

We see ourselves as part of a team, not an outside adviser who happens to be employed by the bank. When the law department was first formed, they treated lawyers *as* lawyers, i.e., essentially a high-powered clerk who sits there with a stamp in other words. We're now moving into the commercial deals. (Banking lawyer addressing conference of in-house lawyers)

What elements of their work allow lawyers to become 'proactive' or 'positive' or to engage in 'preventive' lawyering? The legal practice-management skills[6] which underlie these abilities, and the facets of in-house work which particularly encourage their development are considered below and in the next chapter. It is important at the outset to stress again that they need not be unique to the in-house lawyer although we shall see why they can be more readily available than to the outside lawyer. At the same time the qualities they require in terms of managing legal services are certainly not fixed but admit of a range of decision-making options in terms of how an individual or legal department can choose to exercise them. Thus while few in-house lawyers disagreed with the aspirations underlying the concept of the integrated lawyer, there was considerable scope for debate about which working practices best ensured the exercise of such skills in legal practice.

PROACTIVE LAWYERING

In order to anticipate potential legal difficulties (or, less frequently, opportunities — to develop market share, and so forth) for a business it is necessary as a first stage to scan the environment in order to identify existing or emerging legal issues.[7] Environmental scanning is a recognised management skill, although one that has received limited attention in management training and in organisational theory relating to general management.[8] It is useful for our purpose to distinguish between the organisation's *external* environment and its *internal* environment.[9] Legal difficulties may arise from the former principally by way of new or impending legislation (including case-law developments) having implications for current or likely future organisational practices. From the internal environment they may arise from new business developments (or existing practice brought for the first time to the lawyer's attention), taking forms which might be questioned under existing or emerging laws.

The external environment

Monitoring legal developments was a consistent occupational concern of the lawyers interviewed, a natural approach arising from their training and interests as lawyers. The areas of law they tried to keep track of related closely, of course, to the service they provided for the organisation, whether commercial or consumer law, employment law, property law, banking law, or legislative developments in overseas markets. However, it was common practice also to scan the literature for more general legal developments, in part from the fact that most had generalist roles, in part from professional interest. The prospect of an important development going unnoticed by them was a recognised 'occupational nightmare'. At the same time maintaining an up-to-date knowledge of business law and of their specialist fields was regarded as intrinsically satisfying. Many expressed to me their appreciation of the fact that they found this easier to do, and something more expected of them, in a company legal environment, with all its back-up resources, than in the more chaotic, fee-chasing world of private practice as they had experienced it.

Keeping up-to-date was overwhelmingly seen as an individual professional duty rather than an additional specialism within the Legal Department. In only three of the companies was an individual allocated specialist responsibility for the Legal Department as a whole in keeping abreast of legislation, in order to take relevant action for the company (as against keeping track of developments relevant to one's own legal work in the company). In two of these cases this was a part-time responsibility. Only one company had created a formal one-man post, the 'Legislation Secretariat', to monitor all forms of legislative developments. In this respect, therefore, in-house lawyers had carried over the style of private practice rather than created a new approach, but were aware that the requirement to keep up-to-date was facilitated by their work situation.

Most of the lawyers interviewed used a 'net' system of scanning for legal developments, that is, scanning a variety of sources for legal changes — journals, law reports, specialist 'encyclopaedias' and a range of non-legal sources. The principal journals read in common were the *Law Society's Gazette, New Law Journal* ('generalist' journals with professional news as well as information on current legal developments), and *Current Law* (a journal devoted entirely to summaries of case-law and statutory developments). A range of other journals or reports were scanned for information relevant to general interests (principally the All England Law Reports) or to specialist interests in food or consumer law, employment law, commercial law, and so on. They were normally circulated around the Department and articles highlighted or photocopied if someone spotted a relevant development.

A second type of source used for broad updating were the various encyclopaedias on employment or consumer law or other pertinent fields, regularly updated in loose-leaf form and structured and indexed according to the structure of the subject area.

Non-legal sources were also frequently mentioned, perhaps because many of the interviewees still did not find as much time as they would have liked to read journals in detail. The Parliamentary column of *The Times* was several times referred to, as well as general press and television news for major developments. Equally helpful were the journals and publications of trade and employer associations. Many lawyers were first given notice of developments through contacts in trade associations. Major legislation was generally preceded by government consultation with trade or industry associations. Legal departments were frequently involved in such consultation processes or active in the trade association, so had prior notice of legislation, another advantage of being part of a large business organisation.

In addition, other specialists in management played an important role in bringing lawyers' attention to new regulations. Such specialists in Personnel, Health and Safety, Transport Departments or Regulatory Control (the latter a technical-legal specialism within one pharmaceutical company) were able to highlight new areas because of their own updating process through technical journals or trade/professional associations. The fact that these were major companies meant that their technical experts were in touch with most of the leading developments and were consulted on government thinking regarding regulatory policies.

The breadth of sources available to most company lawyers

means that few lawyers were 'caught napping' over a legal development they might have missed. Only two examples were quoted to me of lawyers missing an important development, although in both cases their attention was then directed to the change by a Personnel specialist. One lawyer had missed the arrival of an important set of employment law regulations, the Transfer of Undertakings (Protection of Employment) Regulations 1981; another had been surprised to find that the qualifying period of employment for making unfair dismissal claims had recently been doubled by the government.

Only in two cases, both of them concerning Departmental 'specialists' in scanning, did lawyers rely on checking Parliamentary legislative lists, that is, look to original sources. The most highly developed specialist mentioned earlier, the Legislation Secretariat, referred to all lists of new Parliamentary statutes and statutory instruments as well as European one,[10] the person concerned ordering all original material that might bear on company practices (from new offences in relation to sales of solvents to new Road Traffic regulations), then summarising or photocopying it and distributing it to any relevant staff in the Legal Department or other areas of management. The same individual was responsible for collecting and synthesising company (and a professional/industry association) comments on proposals for legislation emanating from government departments or the EEC. (For a fuller discussion of this aspect of preventive law, see the final section of this chapter.)

Such a sophisticated system was, however, exceptional. The system used in most company legal departments for scanning the business legal environment was relatively informal and relied largely on individual professional skills and motivation. However, the resources of the large business environment, in terms of time, materials and technical specialists, meant that the updating capacity of the in-house lawyer was of a sufficiently broad character as to be a reasonably successful system for maintaining awareness of legal developments.

Finally, an important aspect of monitoring the external environment relates not only to developments in *substantive* law, but also to *applied* legal developments, such as changing interpretations of the law which become apparent in practices of business competitors or in new legal mechanisms for achieving business objectives (for example, in product and advertising claims, new financial instruments, restructuring of loan agreements, and so on). Lawyer attention to these matters was not a recognised function in the way that keeping up-to-date on legislative changes was, but could be an important element in effective in-house lawyering. However, it was at least implicit in comments made reflecting in-house lawyers' close, personal interest in the business, interest in market and industry developments, and again in contacts with other sections of management and with industry associations. However, its significance is that it would require different scanning skills from those discussed earlier, the more traditional areas of legal practice.

To the extent that such a role is unclear to lawyers practising in-house, it is obviously an area where there could be benefits in developments in specialist training.[11] While the situation of the in-house lawyer is again conducive to maintaining such knowledge, this is an area where outside lawyers could in some respects offer a particular advantage, given their experience advising a range of firms in the marketplace, and the requirements placed increasingly on leading commercial firms to provide highly specialist and 'creative' advice to their business clients.[12]

Monitoring the internal environment

Most legal issues for in-house lawyers arise from the day-to-day operations or developments inside the company rather than from the need to consider company operations in the light of new legislation (although there will be periods when major new legislation will dominate the work of an in-house lawyer). Thus, problems requiring legal solutions or advice will regularly be brought before the in-house lawyer for action, problems covering the whole spectrum of legal and quasi-legal issues raised for in-house lawyers — from advertising slogans and consumer competitions to questions of employee ill-health retirement.

The significance of the distinction between the external and internal organisational environment lies in the differing content of the two areas, and the different scanning systems used. Monitoring the external environment was largely seen as a question of the lawyer keeping professionally up-to-date with legal developments. In-house issues tend to be much more mixed 'law and fact' questions. As already mentioned, few of the lawyers interviewed referred to any need to keep up-to-date with *external* business or law-in-business practices in their industry or in relation to competitors. Such 'business strategy' questions were seen primarily as the concern of senior management, the in-house lawyer being ready to advise on the legal validity of new practices if he or she was referred to, although the significance of the area was at least implicit in comments made. In-house lawyers are more likely to attend explicitly to competitor business practices where their company is in a keenly competitive situation over its products and this 'culture' is imparted into the lawyer's thinking (as, for example, in current developments following the deregulation of the financial services sector, or where there are a few major competitors making claims as to the superiority of their products[13]).

The external-internal environment distinction is also relevant to the scanning process. Interviewees were primarily proactive in their approach to legislation (actively sought out information on current legal developments), but predominantly reactive in relation to in-house legal issues (responded to requests for advice or legal drafting). This is not to suggest a value judgement of the contrast — to some extent it is inherent in the nature of the two areas; however, it is worth alluding to the distinction as it is an issue *which many in-house lawyers saw as an important challenge for the development of effective in-house legal practice*. The reactive mode of dealing with legal problems was seen as the typical form of client relationship necessarily adopted by private practice — to wait for the client to come through the door (although the in-house lawyer still had greater advantages of familiarity, ready accessibility and none of the 'fees fear' attaching to the outside lawyer).

Some in-house lawyers argued that their position inside the client organisation gave them an opportunity to be even more proactive in both encouraging client attention to legal questions and being practically helpful, thereby making for a more effec-tive preventive role for the in-house lawyer.[14] In particular, early involvement of the lawyer meant not only that fewer legal problems would arise, but also that the lawyer could intervene at a stage when it was still possible to structure a transaction so that it was both commercially *and* legally effective. Later involvement gave the lawyer a limited role which more often would be an obstructive one. Instead, it was important to be involved in the 'architecture' of a deal. Various routes to such an end were suggested or adopted. For most lawyers it was sufficient to emphasise the quality of 'accessibility', that is, becoming known as a helpful and valued adviser.

If the company lawyer's advice makes it possible for the manager to achieve good results, he will be considered not only as a competent lawyer but as a good friend as well. The good relationship with individuals will make it possible to study the problems thoroughly at their earliest stages and at a time when a constructive solution is possible. This will establish a sense of confidence in the lawyer's judgement and integrity. And it often results in a sound leadership position in non-legal cases. (Kolvenbach, 1979, 24)

Other, more active, ideas suggested were in the form of legal department newsletters or 'updates' circulated to managers drawing attention to regular or current legal questions; legal 'surgeries' held at regular intervals/locations, a meeting or telephone call where management in an area could raise whatever issues might be arising (thus allowing lawyers to come in at an early stage on a problem a manager might not otherwise have thought to raise); or merely down to the lawyers making sure that whenever they called on or telephoned a manager, they remembered to ask 'is there anything else coming up in your work at the moment that might be relevant?' Finally, there were areas where, as a matter of routine, the legal department was required to 'vet' company material such as advertising slogans, consumer competitions or nutritional claims for food products. These options for a more active role are considered in more detail in the next chapter.

The most frequent style adopted, however, was perhaps the least 'proactive', namely a belief in the importance of 'being accessible', relying on the informal development of contacts. This, of course, is in keeping with the traditional custom in the outside profession of relying on reputation in the community rather than acceding to the demeaning practice of advertising.[15] However, in this respect, too, the in-house lawyer can have considerable advantages over the outside lawyer, because his organisational position allows contact to be made with most levels of the organisation to create a network of 'clients', a very different position from the outside lawyer who is limited to contact with whoever has formal authority to consult an outside lawyer. In some cases, perhaps with the 'right sort of lawyer' in the right environment, accessibility in itself is no great problem.

I had this big fear when I came that people here would resist contact with a lawyer. So I was friendly, tried to be helpful, approachable and fast. The response was quite the opposite. I almost had the door knocked down in the first week. You see people used to need Departmental Head and Company Secretary approval before they could go to a lawyer outside. They feel a lot easier now there's someone to talk to and it doesn't cost them anything. And they know I'll do it if needed and take it up the corporate ladder if it's necessary. (Australian lawyer in media business. He went on to give an example of a junior employee bringing to his notice an article in a magazine about to be published which defamed his own company. He then successfully sought an injunction to prevent publication.)

Regular meetings with management on any formal basis were not common, except where lawyers attended the Board of the company or one of its subsidiaries, or sat on a health and safety or other policy committee or where the Head of the legal department was a member of a senior management committee (by virtue of being a senior manager rather than a specific legal adviser). Most of the lawyers interviewed did not think formal meetings would, in fact, be helpful, judging (probably correctly) that personal relationship and access were more important. Also a few regarded an emphasis on a proactive role as likely to lead to treading on managers' toes or raising the status of the legal function beyond what was desirable, and all recognised the dangers of taking the concept of proactivity too far — 'a business has to run as a business, is isn't there for lawyers'.

Tempting as it may be to dismiss a proactive perspective in this fashion, such a judgement may perhaps be too attractive in its simplicity (and its appeal to the professional 'style' of the lawyer). The more fundamental question remains of what is the most effective and efficient form of providing a legal service inside a company, and there are likely to be varying degrees of preventive lawyering within that ideal (which explains why the subject was a prominent theme in in-house lawyer professional debates). A reliance solely on a belief in 'being accessible' hardly sounds like a professional *managerial* viewpoint, nor one which would be sufficient or advisable for all situations. In particular, the newcomer to the in-house lawyer role is faced with a considerable task in becoming accessible and known on an informal basis to company personnel. Few companies, for example, had any form of induction procedure for new lawyers. At the other extreme, well established lawyers who relied on their informal network of contacts might find themselves abundantly busy with telephone calls and requests for assistance from all sections of their company. However, this method might lead to severe time-management problems and to the exclusion of more considered 'legal-managerial' systems by way of, for instance, developing standard operating procedures (with regard, for example, to disciplinary practice or Trading Standards investigations) or conducting a 'legal audit'[16] to establish the more important areas of legal need inside the company, statistical trends in cases against the company or particular departments, and so forth.

As in most questions of effective management systems, one cannot lay down absolute rules for a variety of organisational environments as to which policies and practices will be effective or efficient for the organisation or sub-unit or the individual manager. However, it is important that the options and skills relevant to different practices are at least known so that they can be tried out or applied to appropriate situations — an approach known in current management theory as 'contingency management'. This must be equally true of the 'legal management' role and has therefore an important bearing on the training of in-house lawyers.

For example, differing legal specialisations and tasks have differing implications for the nature and extent of scanning activities required. This is also influenced, of course, by the nature of the company environment. Thus, certain business transactions require an established legal service which may be or may develop into a routine for the company and lawyer where clear legal tasks are involved, triggered by regular company practice. Such routine legal form may be found in such areas as Annual Reports, conveyancing, patents and trade marks, insurance and tax documentation, contracts and conditions of purchase documentation or certain food labelling practices. In these areas, the business practice is often directly tied into a particular legal form, and it is a simple matter for management to be aware that the appropriate documentation must be drawn up or vetted by the legal department. An effectively-managed legal department is also likely to have available to it an 'information bank' of past contracts, policy documents and company case-law so that its lawyers can readily identify important areas of precedent or policy in company transactions.

More difficulties may occur for the lawyer in scanning areas where business developments which might contravene legal requirements take place on an irregular or localised basis — the effect of new technology or new operating practices on health and safety, for example, or decisions to run price-cutting marketing campaigns in a local department store, or to change temporarily the raw materials used on a particular production batch, or staff dismissal decisions — all of these may have legal implications not anticipated by the operational management involved. In these areas the in-house lawyer is more likely to be brought in in a classic reactive role where the issue leads to trouble with outside authorities. Because of this, an effective preventive legal service not only has to educate managers with regard to potential legal hazards to alert them to the occasions when it is worth first consulting the company lawyer, or to guide them into legally effective ways of operating, but also has to be run in a manner which ensures that the lawyer stays in touch with developments in the business. Choka (1970) has described this as the 'detective' role[17] and graphically outlines the 'organisational politics' inherent in proactive lawyering:

There are few things more pleasant to watch than a good, sneaky legal department at work. Every legal department should acquire the talents of a legal footpad, creeping quietly about the company, disturbing no one and, without anyone knowing, effortlessly filching the legal problems off desks all over the building. (1015)

Corporate counsel is engaged in a continuing battle for information. It is a continuing battle because what your client, the company, is doing changes every day. . . .
    How do you find out? . . . educating the client . . . is

certainly an important method of keeping track of affairs. But equally important are the unofficial techniques. Techniques like the setting up of your own Baker Street Irregulars, a network of agents scattered throughout the company. This isn't hard to establish because a number of psychological drives can be appealed to. First are those people who genuinely want matters in their department to be shipshape, the little-old-ladies-in-tennis-shoes types. Second are those to whom anything about the law strikes fear to their hearts. They can scent a legal problem in a trip to the bathroom. Third are those with a natural love for intrigue and gossip. Unfortunately, those outnumber all the others. Fourth are those who are flattered by the attention paid to them by a lawyer. And so forth. . . .

And there are less devious techniques such as insisting that the members of the legal departments have lunch regularly with members of other departments. Such as having lawyers sit in most meetings. Such as having lawyers regularly tour the departments and ask people what they're doing. Such as, in general, wooing clients. (1019–20)

INFLUENCING THE LEGAL ENVIRONMENT

In-house lawyers were primarily concerned with the interpretation and application of existing law rather than with influencing the processes of law-creation and law reform. Thus, although their day-to-day work involved them in preventive law, it was preventive primarily in the sense of preventing the company's operations clashing with legal restrictions rather than in the sense of preventing the creation of legal restrictions on the company's operations or of repealing existing legal impediments to, or costs on, business operations (although this effect was directly achieved in respect of legal department involvement in case-law developments, that is, either fighting or defending legal actions on points of law or building up an informal case-law through negotiations with regulatory officials of various kinds).

However, preventive law in the broader, more political, sense was nonetheless an important, if occasional, element in the activities of most of the company legal departments. Just under half of the lawyers interviewed[18] took an active part in the work of one or more[19] trade, industry or employer associations, and some also participated in the government lobbying activities of the legal professional associations. There was also knowledge of, and occasional liaison with, other technical specialists in the company who participated in trade or industry associations. Finally, lobbying also took place directly from the company if it was sufficiently affected, although it was usually seen as more effective to work through a trade or industry association.

The approach to lobbying activity was predominantly 'rational' in manner rather than seen as derived from mere self-interest, summed up well by one interviewee — 'We lobby in the usual way — we try to bring the facts to the people involved.'[20] The methods of lobbying depended on the stage legislation had reached. Often, it would be simply a question of writing a paper in response to a government consultative document issued to the affected industry. The usual manner of preparing this was for a small sub-committee (usually those with relevant specialist knowledge) of the trade association executive committee (or its legal section) to meet and draft the necessary document. At a later stage in the progress of legislation, lobbying would be centred on Members of Parliament or Ministers rather than the civil servants. This would be done by means of letters, and meetings if time allowed (it usually did not). On an important issue, there would naturally be more intensive lobbying through Parliamentary agents or by providing opposition MPs with speaking notes on the issues.

Once legislation which was seen as adverse or ineffective was on the statute book it met with 'grumbling non-resistance' as one interviewee remarked. 'After all, what can you do about it?' However, industries were not always passive at this stage. If a provision was seen as badly drafted or to be working badly, the association or company would draw it to the attention of relevant government departments or Ministers either in the course of the regular contacts with them or as a separate initiative. Similar activities took place in relation to EEC legislation, although it was felt to be more difficult to penetrate or influence the European dimension partly because of the values guiding the EEC civil servants and partly because of its complex structure. It would seem likely, however, that this area of activity will increase as EEC legislation grows more extensive and

British lawyers and companies more sophisticated about its workings.

The values behind these lobbying efforts could broadly be classified, in the words of one interviewee, as 'for [in favour of] industry and commerce'. The same interviewee felt EEC staff tended to be influenced by an 'anti-industry' viewpoint and this made it more difficult to affect them. Being 'for' industry meant opposition to regulations on grounds, for example, that they unjustifiably imposed extra costs, or that the regulations were merely an ineffective irritant or that they were imposed for a political rather than a practical purpose, (for example, in requiring Annual Reports to include an item on employee involvement, s. 1 Employment Act 1982). They identified with the client in supporting the rights of industry interests to be allowed to pursue their operations without 'excessive' or unwarranted interference from legislators.

In this latter respect most interviewees (insofar as the issue emerged) thought there was a somewhat moderately more favourable environment under the current Conservative administration than under the previous Labour administration, a recognition that business should be allowed to get on with the job of creating wealth and providing good or services, rather than be shaped for social purposes. A couple of interviewees, however, dissented from this view on the grounds that law-creation was fuelled by other sources — the EEC was a major source of the legislation affecting industry; the civil servants were the real source of law-creation by the nature of their role; and governments had to be seen to be doing something if a scandal occurred, for example, a major accident. This issue of the growth of regulation is discussed in chapter 10.

It should be added as a caution to this section, lest it give too much emphasis to the activity, that political lobbying was not seen as a major function or interest of in-house lawyers. However, it clearly did occur occasionally and some interviewees were quite active when it did take place. More apparent was the fact that they were aware that the process of lobbying could achieve results, and that the trade, industry or employer associations were there partly to provide this service. Also, the large companies for which these in-house lawyers worked were seen as having a significant voice both within the associations and in respect of government and civil service contacts.[21] Given the prominence of legislation and regulation within the political arena, the in-house lawyer has potentially an important part to play within these developments and one likely to increase rather than decrease in significance with the emergence of the new breed of 'integrated lawyer'.

CONCLUSION

In summary, the research findings underlying this work indicate that the delivery of in-house legal services does not of itself necessitate legal services of a noticeably different character from what one might expect of any professional lawyer in private practice. However, the organisational setting of this area of legal services clearly *facilitates* the creation of a role of a different kind and provides the means by which such a role can be exercised. First, by way of back-up resources and contacts (in terms of time, specialist colleagues in technical areas, trade and industry association contacts, and prior notice of legal reform) to allow the in-house lawyer more scope to keep abreast of, and at times influence, significant legal developments; second, by giving the in-house lawyer a stable presence[22] in management's working environment with ensuing access to information and clients such as to allow for greater contact, understanding and influence between the lawyer and his multitude of 'clients' in the organis-ation — not only with those with major political influence in the organisation,[23] but also with others who would not normally have a line of contact to an outside lawyer.

To some extent one can detect parallel developments within private practice towards 'client responsiveness' — both in the City firms by way of their adopting a more proactive role in terms of their marketing, client seminars, law-guide publications and legal audits; and in the provincial commercial firms which are seeking to acquire more resources and compete in a national market through mergers and specialisation. However, these would seem to be parallel or complementary, rather than ident-ical developments to those which I have described as influencing in-house lawyers.

The organisational features of in-house work, together with the activities of opinion leaders within the occupational group in creating a new professional 'culture' for this branch of the legal profession, are encouraging the growth of a professional image which I have described as the integrated lawyer. He will have a far keener eye towards the complex goals of the client than the traditional outside lawyer can normally hope to achieve, and be more able to engage in preventive lawyering and to assess the value of legal advice in terms of its utility to the client. While in-house lawyers tended to emphasise the preventive law element of their role as the primary aspect of their work distinguishing them from outside lawyers, the value of the integrated lawyer did not end there. Some further aspects of the role are considered in the next two chapters.

NOTES

1 This closeness is also said to have its own drawbacks, expressed by some critics in terms of the danger that the in-house lawyer may lose some of the outside lawyer's objectivity (in professional judgement) or independence (of professional ethics). These points are dealt with elsewhere in the text, particularly chapter 12.

2 Restricting a lawyer to a legal opinion without a depth of awareness of the client's situation, of course, does not make it inevitable that such an opinion will lead to a *narrow* legal solution. Some opinions may overestimate the client's capacity to respond in practice, while others may underestimate it. Knowledge of the client provides a more realistic assessment of the practical options.

3 See, for example, Rosenthal (1974), Carlin (1962).

4 Stichnoth and Dolan (1982) suggest a preventive style is not common partly because corporation resources are limited, but mainly because it is not part of legal training, it involves foresight and innovation which are difficult mental achievements for anyone to accomplish, and finally because a proper allocation of resources between preventive and reactive functions requires management skills which few lawyers have had training in. The most successful legal departments in anticipatory work, they suggest, are those which most effectively practice management techniques of planning, budgeting and resource allocation.

5 For discussions of legislative reform as part of the preventive role, see Ruder (1968) and Maddock (1968).

6 The preventive role has been described in terms of 'management' (Stichnoth and Dolan, *supra*), or 'leadership' (Maddock, *supra*) skills. I prefer to refer to it as a management skill, separate from a leadership role a lawyer may play in developing corporate morality. (See chapter 10.)

7 I have restricted the discussion in this chapter to law which is emerging

in a definite form. Some writers have made great play of the in-house lawyer's role in sensing 'inchoate law', that is, law being formed within social developments, although not yet crystallised in reform campaigns. This is also discussed in chapter 10.

8   For a discussion of this skill and of the failure of management theorists to acknowledge the importance of environmental influences on a business, see Pfeffer and Salancik (1978).

9   For an early discussion of the in-house lawyer's information needs, see Laughton (1968). He recommends that the lawyer's supply of information should cover both general information (foreign and domestic law, general business and political affairs, professional affairs) and company-specific information (legal department experience, contract obligations and history, and information about the company — its situation, product, policy and structure, and its industry policy and structure).

10 For example, the *Weekly Information Bulletin* from each House of Parliament, *Hansard Official Reports*, the *Official Journal of the European Community*, and so on.

11 See chapter 8 on training.

12 See chapters 7 and 12 on the role of outside lawyers.

13 As in the example given by a lawyer at a conference, where his company were seeking to produce a 'low-calorie' shandy. Food regulations prevented such a name because of the requirement for a product described as shandy to contain a minimum quantity of alcohol, and hence more calories than the term 'low-calorie' could justify by another part of the regulations. A competitor had come up with a 'slimline shandy with low-calorie lemonade' claim which apparently satisfied the regulations.

14 Another aspect of preventive lawyering sometimes referred to is the in-house lawyer's role as 'corporate conscience' or the 'policing' function of the in-house specialist. See, for example, Stone (1975: 42, 240). This is inevitably a part of a lawyer's role insofar as he is successful in altering company practice which is out of line with the law. However, in-house lawyers tended to reject the description otherwise — see chapter 10.

15 See chapter 13 on the shifting attitude to advertising. Despite the apparent faith in community reputation, lawyers have always had more subtle ways of attracting business. See Podmore (1980) (participation in community organisations), and Mungham and Thomas (1983) (duty solicitor scheme membership).

16 See Brown (1965) for an account of the process, and Patterson (1971) for an example of an audit applied to the legal position of an acquired company.

17 Other roles Choka identifies are: Craftsman, Administrator, Educator, Translator, Soothsayer and Perfectionist.

18 The sample of in-house lawyers interviewed, however, possibly overestimates in-house lawyer involvement in lobbying activities because of drawing on contacts made through the legal professional associations.

19 It was common for these major companies to be affiliated to more than one trade or industry association.

20 Compare Kolvenbach's (1979) comment:

Especially in countries where legal departments have either themselves or through business associations close contacts with governmental agencies which draft new proposed legislation, it is very important to use such contacts. Often the officials charged with drafting legislation are grateful for information from practitioners because frequently legislative projects are very theoretical due to lack of information. (33)

21 In this sense, the study bears out the contention of Michael Useem (1984) that we are witnessing the formation of a new political elite within big business in response to the business crises of the 1970s, built around an increasing concentration of ownership of capital. However, if this is the case, it is an elite serviced by a wide range of technical specialists including lawyers.

22 The lawyer has a 'stable presence' not only in contrast to outside lawyers but also in some companies in relation to management. The lawyer's role of record-keeper, combined with high degrees of management turnover contrasted to the lawyer's less mobile career, ensures that lawyers often have more information about the organisation and the reasons in history for company policies than many managers. This is obviously an important source of influence and control.

23 The status of the legal department in a company may be critical to its ability to succeed in proactive law. (See the section on legal department management at the end of the next chapter.) At a basic level, if a company does not have sufficient belief in its legal department or in the value of lawyers, to provide sufficient resources (or staff), its in-house lawyers are likely to be forced into a role of crisis management rather than the 'strategic planning' role envisaged in the integrated lawyer model.

6 The Integrated Lawyer (2): Translating Law into Practice

In my last company there was a very good in-house lawyer. He was a translator — he put things in a way managers could understand. I find the trouble with most lawyers is that they don't seem able to move out of their own language system, and all the provisos and qualifications that go with it. It can be very difficult for a manager to understand what's being said. He really needs to know in relation to his problem what his options are in terms he understands.

Managing director of a textile company

Previous chapters have given some indication of the legal areas and issues that confront company lawyers, and the prevailing emphasis amongst in-house lawyers on 'proactive law', which I have preferred to refer to in broader terms as 'integrated' lawyering. The last chapter dwelt on the preventive aspects of in-house legal work, ranging from the lobbying activities of in-house lawyers to their more immediate and central work of preventive law through environmental scanning, both internal and external. The skilled lawyer, however, is more than an information-gatherer scanning the internal and external legal environment. How do in-house lawyers translate legal infor-mation into client behaviour and decision-making? How do they influence the day-to-day actions of the business? We have already touched on aspects of this in the previous chapter, but this chapter focuses more directly on the *applied* skills of lawyering, on the lawyer's role in guiding client actions, on the lawyer's *effectiveness*.

To achieve effectiveness in this translation process inside an organisation the in-house lawyer can be said to face three basic challenges: (1) how to integrate legal judgement with practical judgement (relating the language and logic of law to everyday decision-making); (2) how to integrate legal judgement with commercial decisions (relating legal analysis to business goals); and (3) how to achieve influence inside the organisation (integrating the lawyer function with organisational processes and politics). The resolution of these tasks does not admit of single solutions, but it is important to be aware of the range of issues and options raised. Nor is it inevitable that in-house lawyers and outside lawyers will differ in their response to these challenges.[1] As in relation to preventive law, however, the in-house lawyer is placed in a position which facilitates a distinctive style of legal services, particularly in relation to (2) and (3). Indeed, in respect of the last issue, one can argue that in-house lawyers *must* adopt a different approach to that of the outside lawyer in order to fulfil the potential their position makes available to them.

THE NATURE OF LEGAL JUDGEMENT

A first issue that merits some consideration is the content of a lawyer's skill — what service is a lawyer providing? This is a harder question to answer well than might appear at first sight. A 'hard' answer would simply require a statement that a lawyer will convey his or her knowledge of the law so that a company either does not run into legal difficulties or, if it does, will know how to mitigate the adverse effects of these difficulties. Thus, in practical terms, the lawyer will provide appropriate forms of documentation, of wording, or of guidance as to conduct such as to achieve these ends (or at least will advise against inappropriate communications or action).

In many cases the lawyer will have little difficulty in achieving just this effect — the client can be given clear guidance on what actions are necessary or available in his case, or provided with the supporting documentation required for his actions. However, in many other cases, possibly a majority, such a simple analysis is misleading in that it fails to acknowledge the often problematic nature of law, of the behavioural alternatives available within the terms of the law, and the problems of proof, evidence and enforcement in the application of legal rules to behaviour. Legal rules are generally abstract 'essence' statements which are designed to apply to a range of diverse fact-situations usually by way of prohibition or of mandatory guidance. The problematic nature of legal rules is particularly clear in modern regulatory controls over detailed business practices, although it is also at the heart of the common law. Thus, unfair dismissals are in most instances assessed in terms of whether the company acted 'reasonably' 'in all the circumstances'; what does this standard on its own really tell anyone about guiding behaviour in practice? Similarly ambiguous criteria can be found in many other areas of law from negligence to health and safety legislation or rules regarding certain exclusion clauses in consumer contracts. Added to this core element of obscurity in many legal provisions is the uncertain nature of factual evidence and the interpretation of that evidence in court — what facts are available to support the evidence for one's interpretation of the legal rule? Can they be used in court? Will a witness tell the same story in court? What evidence will be put forward by the other party? Will particular aspects of the situation carry special weight with the judicial forum? Will an issue be presented adequately by counsel? And so on. Finally, the enforcement of a law may also be erratic, uncertain or unlikely. What is the lawyer's particular function in giving management guidance on practice where the law, its processes and its judgements[2] are frequently (and perhaps inherently) ambiguous?

Lawyers faced with these decisions of applying often problematic rules to complex fact-situations are likely to resort to a range of techniques of statutory interpretation (assisted by commentaries on the legislation), to case-law precedents, to any guidance notes or Codes of Practice which might accompany the legislation, to their skilled 'intuition' and experience of judicial attitudes, litigation and pre-litigation processes. At the end of the day, like the judges, they are likely to have regard to 'all the circumstances' in passing a legal judgement. Thus the importance to lawyers of knowing the facts of a case[3] as well as knowledge of the personalities involved, of the history of the particular area of dispute, of similar or related fact-situations, of considerations of 'public policy' — all these and more, are likely to enter a skilled legal appraisal. Equally, they will have considerable regard to 'expert' advice on technical matters, namely current industrial practice on safety or technical standards or in disciplinary procedures, and last, but not least, on client policies, objectives and attitudes measured against wider social norms. One can argue that the most competent lawyers, as in other professions, are those who can best handle such 'grey' areas of judgement, can best identify the appropriate legal rule-patterns in the 'legal and operational mosaic' (Rast, 1978: 813) of business practices.

> Certainly I use the broad brush approach in the way I write to people here. I become jaundiced being a lawyer when you can never give a certain answer, only pros and cons. But it's difficult to be categoric often in questions of commercial risk. (Lawyer in food products company)

> All lawyers know that you are very lucky indeed if you can give a black-and-white answer to a question of whether you will win or lose a particular case. The compromises you make follow the legal assessment of the situation. And our advice follows from that. (Lawyer in food retailer)

In making a legal judgement lawyers therefore are often only in a position to assess 'risk' rather than offer any absolute guidance. This characteristic of law is one that generally puzzles non-lawyers[4] who expect law, almost by definition, to admit of clear rules regarding their particular affairs rather than be a 'puzzle' even to the lawyers. It partly goes to explain the image of cautious nit-picking sometimes associated with the legal profession since there are numerous cases where one must say 'it depends'. If one adds to the uncertainty involved in predicting the application of legal rules, the propensity of lawyers to resort to the archaic language of legal tradition, it is little wonder that, like the manager quoted on p. 94, laymen may find themselves exasperated by law and lawyers.

While, therefore, the lawyer can often assist the practical position of clients by engaging in legal transactions or advice or guidance which is reasonably certain, there will also be numerous occasions where the language and logic of law is difficult to translate. The challenge to the lawyer is to learn how to handle this ambiguity and uncertainty in professional understanding without 'losing' the client in an exposition of the intracacies of law and legal process. In this, one may say, lawyers are immediately handicapped by aspects of their training which, because of the nature of lawyering (particularly the common law system), emphasise attention to detail and the

importance of legal technicalities in relation to detailed fact
considerations. The client's need in approaching the lawyer is
not usually to test these intricacies but to achieve certain basic
outcomes — to avoid a fine, to obtain compensation, to prevent
copying of a trademark. The lawyer's ability to assist these
outcomes is dependent on mastery of the intricacies of the client
situation in relation to the intricacies of legal rules and practice.
The stress amongst in-house lawyers on preventive law reflects
the importance of the opportunity to *create* the facts of the client
situation rather than react to the situation imposed by the client.
Re-adjusting particular elements of the mosaic may alter the
total picture. Where the lawyer guides the transaction as it
happens, he can ensure he will 'feel comfortable with the facts'
should the actions come to be tested in law.

   The first basic challenge to the lawyer in practice is therefore
to learn how to 'translate' — from the client's initial situation
into the rule-system of law (its principles and practice), and
back again into recommendations for action which will marry
the two to further client objectives (or perhaps to convey bad
news regarding these objectives, given the client's situation).
Such translation activities occur at a number of levels in legal
practice. At a minimal level, the lawyer may engage in a form
of translation even where there is no assistance one can provide
for the client. The process of 'labelling' the problem, of giving
the issue its legal name, may as in medicine ('you have incurable
disease X'; 'you have no remedy because of exclusion clause Y
in the contract'), be an elementary form of service to the client.
Where there is no satisfactory translation possible (law is of no
relevance to the client's situation), the lawyer may fall back on
other systems of assistance to the client, on the practical guidance any intelligent lay adviser might give. At the other extreme,
'creative lawyering' may involve restructuring client actions or
lawyer documentation in order to make a novel re-adjustment
of the legal position.

   Learning to be an effective translator therefore contains a
number of skills basic to professional practice, though not all of
these are explicitly dealt with in legal education and training,
partly because of a lack of research into this process in legal
practice.[5] In the interviews with in-house lawyers three related
themes relevant to translation can be discerned. These were: (1)
being clear; (2) being decisive; and (3) being positive.

(1) *Clear.* One of the commonest complaints about lawyers is the obscurity of their language. This partly reflects the influence of ritual and tradition on lawyers (for instance, the use of archaic forms of expression in standard precedent forms for wills, contracts, deeds), partly the nature of legal judgement described earlier — provisos and qualifications are inevitable. It has also derived, however, from the failure of some of the profession to respond to the needs of clients — lawyers have often been happy to emphasise the mystique of law via its language system. Working in the client organisation does not inevitably ensure a lawyer will drop this style. However, it provides both an incentive and a pressure to speak in 'plain English'. In-house lawyers are dealing regularly with clients who are *colleagues*, compared to the outside lawyer whose colleagues are lawyers. The distance that can be maintained between the outside lawyer and client is not readily available to the in-house lawyer. If he does maintain a degree of distance from the client, he risks losing some of the opportunities available to in-house lawyers of, for example, practising preventive law.

Conversely, the in-house lawyer is better placed over time to educate the client in the language of law, thus achieving a more sophisticated client who is in turn more able to understand the problems of matching legal rules with everyday practice. Clients who have a grasp of the legal issues will be better able to know how early to consult a lawyer, and the type of help they will get, and vice-versa. 'When both parties are keen and sophisticated in the other's area and have the personal relationship advocated earlier, the payoff comes in the frequently occurring situation in which legal inventiveness is required to accomplish the company's objective within the law' (Donnell: 1970, 185).

(2) *Decisive.* Learning how to cope with the problematic nature of legal judgement is a task all lawyers face — how to express to the client the degree of risk and probability in a legal analysis and recommendation. In-house lawyers were very conscious that they worked in an environment where there was an emphasis on decision-making. Advice which failed to take account of this was likely to be of little practical value. This did not mean avoiding an explanation of risks but it did require avoiding opinions which were so littered with provisos as to be of little value, and it meant taking a realistic view of the risks involved.

We break young lawyers in, and into leaving their old habits. They've got to be bright but above all have to have good personalities so they can relate to commercial people and give good, short, practical advice. One-and-a-half or one-page advice saying this is what you do. The number of times we see advice from barristers and solicitors who just indulge themselves. It's just not on. (Australian oil company lawyer)

'As from next week, what do I have to do?' 'You have to do this.' That's what managers want to know. 'You have to do this.' I know what they must do so I can tell them that sort of thing. Though I may have to check if I'm not sure of company practice, for example driving schedules or where tankers are left by drivers. They have to be left in a safe parking position. I may have to check with the transport manager what is the current practice. (Manufacturing company lawyer)

After reading the law, studying its history, understanding its purpose, analyzing the trends bearing on it, filling in the gaps, swapping judgments on the matter with other knowledgeable lawyers, and then pulling forth from his own experience the ultimate feel for the matter, corporate counsel must say, 'We shall operate in my company as if the law governing this matter were as follows . . .' My own fellow lawyers are a little tired of one of my pet phrases, 'We're going to pretend the law is as follows . . .' (Choka, 1970: 1022)

The need to be decisive was another reason to practise preventive law; early participation in decision-making meant one could offer suggestions of routes to an objective which lessened the legal risks to the point where one could 'feel comfortable' with them.

The Bargain Offers Order is so complex, even lawyers don't understand it. And our managers want answers instantly often. Or used to. Just on the point of going to the printers they would come to us and say — is this alright? We do tend to get 24 hours' notice now instead of 5 minutes' notice. They're getting to know us. (Lawyer in food retailer)

Some lawyers pointed out also that there is no feasible way to indicate adequately to a non-lawyer the degree of risk in an action without in any case biasing the decision by the way one presents the risk equation, so that there is an onus on the lawyer to *participate in the decision*, to make the decision for management in areas of risk. (See Choka, op.cit., and see further below.)

(3) *Positive.* The emphasis on action in business organisations and the in-house lawyer's need to be seen as a helpful adviser, combined to lead to a stress on 'being positive'. It was unhelpful for lawyers merely to advise that planned actions were unlawful. Where possible the lawyer should suggest alternative routes to achieving the commercial objective. Otherwise the law department would be seen merely as an obstacle to decisions rather than a source of assistance in enacting them. From the comments made to this effect it was clear that this is an inherent problem for lawyers, at least in terms of the perceptions of law and lawyers held by many laymen. This experience was particularly predominant in dealing with sales and marketing managers, for whom contractual clauses could be seen as an obstacle to their achieving sales.

A lot of one's time is spent dealing with questions where management want an answer and if you won't give them the answer they want, they'll go to someone else. So it's a case of finding out how to tell them what they want or how to stop them continuing to try to achieve something that's not legally possible. (Construction industry lawyer)

Of course, in many cases, laws may be less restrictive than non-lawyers imagine — in the law department efficiency exercise mentioned in chapter 4 clients of the legal department rated a far higher proportion of their current activities as 'too great a risk to drop' in assessing cost-saving ideas than did the lawyers in assessing the same activities. In such cases being positive was relatively easy. However, the stress on being positive also implied a need for in-house lawyers to be familiar with commercial objectives, thereby assisting them in matching legal and business options. But how far should this go? Should the lawyer become involved in the business transaction itself to the extent of taking business decisions?[6]

LEGAL JUDGEMENT AND COMMERCIAL JUDGEMENT

Commercial judgement, in the sense of advising on the most sensible commercial decision to take, was something of a two-edged sword in interviewee comments. On the one hand it was an asset for a lawyer to develop this ability in order to better grasp client affairs, but on the other hand most felt it was important to separate legal from commercial judgements in advising management, at least in the sense of stating clearly which type of judgement was being used. A few felt managers were likely to resent lawyers gratuitously offering commercial advice.

Competence in business language and logic is one of the assets an in-house lawyer is in a position to acquire through familiarity with business if nothing else. In this sense, the ability is again merely the extension of a quality that would be desirable for most legal practitioners, namely what are the relevant circumstances of the client's case and what are his objectives in seeking legal advice? The in-house lawyer was far better placed than the outside lawyer to know company practices, policies and procedures, company personnel, products and markets, and company objectives. All of these could be relevant to assessment of legal risk equations, and to situations which called for legal creativity. Being 'positive' meant being able to respond with suggestions of alternative methods that would be legally effective where management sought to implement business decisions in legally ineffective ways, as against merely returning a note to say 'it can't be done'. A typical example was in the provision of car wash facilities in petrol stations. The in-house lawyer advised against the garage licensee being allowed to build the structure (as there were possible Landlord And Tenant Act problems) proposing instead that the company take ownership of the structure, then license back to the garage licensee. Of course, a lawyer in private practice might have given a similar alternative, but it was obvious that in-house lawyers felt both that they were better placed to make such suggestions, and also that they were under more pressure to do so to retain their credibility as an integral part of the company's operations.

The question of the exercise of commercial as well as legal judgement arose not only in the context of the need to be positive, but also in relation to the expectation found in certain companies to the effect that the in-house lawyer had to acquire certain commercial skills because of his presence in a business where he or she was expected to contribute, along with other members of management, to business decisions, that is, *as a member of the management team*. The lawyer could not (or should not), many said, draw a ring around the legal department and pretend it was independent advice merely stating probabilities for management to decide on.

Essentially I see us as part of the management team helping them to make a decision on something. It's your job to help them solve a problem, not to generate difficulties. For example, if there was a legal risk, I might still say 'go ahead' and, depending on who I was writing to, might or might not tell them about the risk element. (Lawyer in manufacturing company)

It should apply to any lawyer worth his salt in industry. He shouldn't feel constrained by his instructions but should try to achieve a contract that's commercially sound. The difference in being in industry compared with private practice is that you are closer to your client — because he's your colleague. Also you have a more personal interest in the company's success and should think commercially as well as legally. Of course, the commercial people set up the deal and bring in the lawyers for the points of detail, but that's no reason why one, particularly one with a lot of experience, shouldn't comment on how the contract can be improved commercially. . . . You are more at liberty to question the client's judgement and, of course, you know the business so much better so you are better placed to do so. (Pharmaceutical company lawyer)

Quite a lot of our work is concerned with setting up systems for handling things, 'routinisation' we call it. For example, in our service stations. It's a cooperative effort. It would be artificial to analyse it as 'lawyer-client' since the law department has taken on, in effect, property management functions. . . . What it is is that there is a legal content in the system and the lawyers are taking on the initiating role in changing things. For example, at the moment we are reviewing the credit-related aspects of the business. (Oil company lawyer)

Any solicitor who says that the commercial matters are not his responsibility will very soon get a kick up the pants. I can give you an example of this. I was on a visit with other managers to the USSR. We were negotiating in Moscow. We had a difficult problem with the agreement and it was a time when the telephone lines to the UK were down. So we met in our room and the Sales Manager said: 'Let's make a joint decision on this and at least come to a decision.' When it came to me, I said: 'It's not a legal problem, it's not for me to say.' Well, he blew his top. 'We're all part of one team,' he said, 'and when we get home I want us to be able to stand together and justify the decision together. We don't want anyone going back and then standing to one side and pretending to be separate from the decision.' He was absolutely right. I felt two inches small after he had spoken. After all, I was there on behalf of the company as a manager of the company and had to act as part of the team. The same would happen if I failed to report a mistake I'd noticed in the accounts to the Chairman, for example. I'd be out of the company in two weeks if I'd failed to report an obvious mistake and then said that's not my business, I'm a lawyer. His answer would be: 'Anything that goes on in this company is your business.' (Manufacturing company lawyer)

Whereas the lawyer in private practice, by reason of his separation from the organisation, could quite easily perceive the legal problem brought to him as *the* problem, the in-house lawyer's working experience was likely to lead him to a humbler view of the role of law. In the day-to-day process of commercial decision-making lawyers were merely one of the many sources of information essential to senior management decision-making in mixed law-and-fact situations.[7] For example, whether to proceed with an important contract to obtain a particular construction company for planned oil pipeline work before planning permission was obtained; what were the chances of planning permission being refused (and the cost of terminating the contract) and how did this weigh against the possibility of the development being unable to proceed if the builder was not retained? Senior managers received advice from a variety of professional advisers — geologists, tax advisers, pharmacists, engineers. Thus, law was an important element, but only an element, of commercial decision-making and risk-analysis. Further, the experience of senior executives not only meant they were often already fairly sophisticated in their understanding of legal issues, but, in receiving and dealing with advice from various specialists, were well-qualified to assess its quality or challenge its judgement (although some lawyers mentioned also that many managers were frightened of the law and lawyers.)

While on the one hand this business setting therefore led to a more modest view of the importance of law, on the other hand many in-house lawyers were of the view that they received a great deal of valuable learning by 'rubbing shoulders' so frequently with other experts. This applied not only to the other professional specialists in the business, engineers or accountants, but also to senior management. Over time, therefore, this experience contributed a great deal of informal learning to the in-house lawyer's understanding and approach. In turn, this led to an ability to comment on the commercial aspects of a legal situation just as the commercial managers often questioned the legal judgement of their 'colleagues'.

You do pick up commercial skills. You're involved even at a young age with difficult problems of the corporation compared to routine ones. It's the difficult problems that are brought to this department so you develop a damned good business sense. In fact I believe, and I wouldn't say it too loudly, but people here are amongst the most advanced commercially. I'm surprised sometimes at the naivety and lack of common sense out there. (Australian oil company lawyer)

From a different perspective many in-house lawyers had also experienced situations where managers, in seeking advice, wanted to give the responsibility of making a decision to the lawyer, thereby passing the buck if it was a difficult area of decision, and shedding any blame if it turned out to be wrong. Whether in-house lawyers took this on or not was seen as a matter of personal judgement linked to the experience of the lawyer, the nature of the issue and the level of management. In

general it was unlikely that such situations arose with senior
managers, but it was a common experience in respect of middle-
and lower-level management. However, given the variety of
situations and managers that in-house lawyers were likely to
have encountered, it was likely that they could in such circumstances offer a view of the best course of action, a view likely to
reflect practical business judgement or company policy on the
matter in question as much as of legal skill. In any case, some
argued, the way one presents risk equations in law to clients
inevitably suggests the decision that need to be taken. In-house
lawyers may also become involved in commercial decision-
making in many cases almost by inadvertance — because the
business people may be hazy about the details of an agreement
and the lawyers end up filling in the details; because businessmen may have a biased view of how lawyers approach a
problem[8] and expect complex advice, failing to recognise that
the law is often essentially merely common sense on good practice (and sometimes not[9]); because many matters that seem of
a policy nature are in fact matters of inchoate law or matters of
prophetic legal judgement. (Murphy, 1968, and see chapter
10 on the question of the lawyer's involvement in commercial
judgements and 'inchoate law'.)

The mixed responses to the question of legal and commercial
judgement perhaps can be summed up by stating that it reflects
the typical interaction of law and fact judgements, set against
appraisal of the client, that any lawyer is called on to make in
ordinary legal practice, but given added emphasis by the fact
that the in-house lawyer has a deep familiarity with one client
setting in a hierarchical organisation, knowledge of which
consistently influences and guides the legal decision-making
process. Although the boundary between legal and commercial
decision-making seems readily to prompt debates of principle
amongst lawyers and managers,[10] it is perhaps more helpful to
see the issues as merely offering a classic example of 'contingency
management' of the crucial points of balance in the lawyer-client
relationship (given even greater significance by the problems of
dealing with and for an organisation[11]); both types of judgement
will play a role but the appropriate emphasis will vary from
situation to situation with the knowledge of the lawyer, the
sophistication of the client, the area of law covered, and so on.
'Part of any negotiations relates to commercial factors, part to

legal, and you're debating them separately, or together, or seeking trade-offs' (Pharmaceutical company lawyer).

A lawyer who, in such circumstances, is guided by principles of 'participative' client counselling (Rosenthal, 1974) — involving the client in the analysis and assessment of options; or who acts in an open, helping role (Donnell, 1970); or who sees himself as a 'consultant to the corporate decision-making process' (Rosen, 1984) rather than a technical expert in risk-analysis[12] — is likely to achieve the best translation of legal principles into client practice. As Donnel notes (180), once one adopts the idea of an open role definition for the in-house lawyer based on the nation of a helping relationship, the question of what is a business issue, and what a legal issue will become irrelevant. In the initial development of a relationship, however, the lawyer may want to state when he is commenting on a commercial aspect of the situation outside his territory, in order to foster good relations with the client. Equally, the question of how early the lawyer should be consulted becomes less significant, as indicated in Donnell (1970):

> Given the kind of client-counsel relationship that has been described, the attention of both parties will be on the problem and the contribution that each can make to finding the best solution to the problem, rather than on jurisdictional boundaries. . . . [L]egal and business aspects of a problem cannot completely be separated, and the final decision is an amalgam of both and *is best arrived at by a mutual weighing of the imponderables of both.* [author's emphasis]

INFLUENCING THE ORGANISATION

Whether one is concerned with outside or in-house lawyers, recognition should still be granted to the unique status of organisations as clients. Legal fiction ensures that lawyers can deal with the company as a 'person', since that is how the company will be treated in law. However, behind this fiction, the reality is that lawyers are dealing in a fragmented way with at most spokesmen for a 'community'. The company is a collection of individual departments, divisions, subsidiaries, managers, directors, shareholders, employees. Advice to one sector/individual (or instructions from one sector/individual) does not *necessarily* represent the collective interest of the company as identified at law. This gap between the company as legal fiction and as sociological reality has led to a number of situations where the law has had difficulty in reconciling the two aspects, for example, in determining the respective rights of shareholders and directors, in deciding the ethical requirements on lawyers acting for companies, or in determining the appropriate sanctions and locus of responsibility to punish or deter 'company' wrongdoing.[13] In practice, lawyers rely a great deal on the common sense position[14] that companies are fairly unitary in nature and that the fiduciary/employee nature of the role of director or manager ensures that most actions or requests are therefore in the best interests of the company. However, the organisational problem remains of how in practice a lawyer ensures that legal advice is communicated throughout the organisation, of how the lawyer's voice is able to influence actions and behaviour of the relevant sections of the organisation. The in-house lawyer's position in this respect is distinct from that of the outside lawyer. He is part of the organisation and able therefore to apply different techniques and understanding to legal practice than those an outside lawyer can apply.

What were the specific techniques adopted by in-house lawyers to achieve a proactive lawyering outcome; what means did they use to establish an effective presence in the organisation whereby they could not only stay in touch with relevant internal developments, but also contribute positively to business practice within the organisation? I have identified eight methods of 'communication and control' adopted by the in-house lawyers interviewed: (1) accessibility; (2) policy/practice guides; (3) 'checking-off' systems; (4) formal accessibility; (5) written communications; (6) education and training; (7) organisational status; and (8) reactive law. They are outlined briefly below. All of these were used by in-house lawyers, although the mix of techniques and emphases differed across different legal departments and lawyers.

(1) Accessibility

Mention has already been made of how in-house legal departments cultivate preventive law by fostering individual lawyer contact with a range of individual manager 'clients' and emphasising their accessibility and helpfulness. Much of their work then comes from these clients by way of telephone inquiries, memos or personal visits. In terms of organisational communication this approach thereby ensures an advisory service can be available at all levels of management, an 'open system' approach that avoids hierarchical or mechanistic lines of communication from the top down. Its corresponding disadvantage is that it is dependent for effectiveness on the accessibility principle — if the manager does not know the legal service is available or does not wish to use it, then there will be less preventive law, except to the extent that the manager can bring legally sophisticated judgement to the issue (by his own efforts or through advice from other managers or staff specialists).

The overall aim is to become sufficiently embedded in the company's 'culture' to ensure that the legal service is seen as readily available and helpful on all occasions. A law department which succeeds in this respect is likely to build up a reservoir of deep knowledge about company affairs and hence to be able to advise individual managers not only on law but on practice and policy elsewhere in the company, thus assisting with its communication needs. The in-house lawyer can become a communicator of, and contributor to, the 'internal law' of the company, not merely an adviser on external law.[15]

(2) Policy/practice guides

A hierarchical approach to organisational communication was adopted in cases where the issue was sufficiently serious in its implications to require an 'organisational effort' by way of statements of company policy and practice. The information from the interviewees indicated that this normally occurred where a sweeping legal reform affecting company practice was introduced, or where a policy decision was taken at a senior level which had legal implications. It seems likely that British companies will increasingly follow American ones in their emphasis on company policy documents to cover important areas of company practice (including, for example, the status of the company legal department and its rights for direct access to the Board in certain cases of disagreement with senior management).

In the former category, interviewees quoted examples such as the period following the Industrial Relations Act 1971 or the Employment Protection Act 1975 when employment practices were extensively reviewed.[16] The typical form taken by such a review was a review committee of specialist managers, for instance, personnel, in employment law matters, senior line management and legal department representatives. The committee would go through the statute, consider its meaning and its implications for current practice, and draft a statement of policy and/or practice for the organisation or its parts. The lawyer's role in such situations was as one of a team, able to advise particularly on the technical interpretation of the legislation. The predominant emphasis was on company practices and the managers involved in these exercises were usually seen to be fairly sophisticated in their knowledge of, and approach to, law and practice questions.

In the second category come decisions taken at senior level to have an extensive review of current policy or practice, for example, in regard to payment systems or contracts. In such cases again in-house lawyers were often incorporated into the review process so that any legal implications could be attended to. The outcome of both processes would be a statement of company policy or directives issued to the relevant levels of management with regard to changes in practice. Beyond that stage the in-house lawyer's role usually reverted to that of accessibility, requests for further clarification, or in response to legal actions.

Some companies also used briefing documents for sales personnel:

> We have standard contracts with almost 10 000 customers. If the customer says to the sales engineer I don't like that clause, we like the engineer to be able to reply. So every engineer has a briefing document to explain what the clause means and why it is there. For example, why we cannot warrant gas as being fit for the purpose, because half the time we don't know what the customer's purpose will be. (Manufacturing company lawyer)

(3) 'Checking-off' systems

In certain instances the in-house lawyer was charged with the duty to 'vet' practices/products of the company so that legal approval or disapproval could be given before the practice was finally accepted. Such an approach was more prevalent in certain types of company activities but was also at times practised in an informal manner. The areas where legal department 'control' was most often found in the study were contracts (other than employment contracts), food labelling (ingredients listing or nutritional claims) advertising campaigns and employee relations manuals.[17] It was fairly common in these areas for new labels, and such like to go to the legal department for checking before being given approval. In some companies, it was required practice, while in others it took a more informal course, with management using the legal department only in cases of doubt.

Such practice could develop out of the 'accessibility' route rather than through a more formal company policy. For example, several lawyers referred to management 'getting their fingers burnt' when they had proceeded without legal department assistance, for instance, on commercial contracts. Where such experience made managers more cautious, they would be readier next time to use the legal assistance available. This was notable, too, in the area of employment law, where legal departments not previously involved with personnel matters were increasingly approached because of the greater legal complexity surrounding a traditionally informal human relations area. The degree to which this occurred depended on other organisational factors, for example, how 'cautious' the management culture was, the degree of sophistication of other specialist management (such as Personnel), the lines of communication to the legal department and so on. But the overall pattern was clear — the more regulated the area, the greater the likelihood of the legal department being involved in work control systems.

> Generally speaking in [this company], they do tend to say 'Have you cleared this with the legal people?' so I get things from them I wouldn't get from other sectors [of the parent company]. . . . they are very cautious people, very jealous of the company's image, therefore there are very few non-routine

letters that would go out without being cleared by the
immediate supervisor. And one of the questions a supervisor
will ask, if he can't think of anything else, is 'Have you cleared
it with legal?'. So it's a self-perpetuating thing and after a
while, having seen a lot of these, I can be quite helpful I
think. (Oil company lawyer)

(4) Formal accessibility

It was not common for the lawyers to have regular, formal
meetings with managers, other than in the case of Heads of
Department attending senior management meetings or as
advisers to the Board of the company or one of its subsidiaries.
The other area most frequently mentioned for lawyer involvement was health and safety committees. This method of preventive law was not therefore commonly used nor popular (nor is
it with managers), other than Boardroom meetings. Some
lawyers, for example, found they resented the time they spent
in health and safety committees when only a small proportion
of the business was relevant to them. They preferred to be called
on if legal advice was required.

(5) Written communications

Lawyers also used the written communication of information to
influence and inform company practice, using a range of media.
The internal memorandum was the most commonly used,
pointing out to a Department Head or other relevant manager
some new regulatory requirement. Of course, as with techniques
of influence in organisations, the decision of what and how to
communicate in writing is too easily taken for granted. Lawyers,
like other managers, have to learn how to communicate.[18] Most
lawyers also contributed to company manuals issued to
managers as a reference system on company policies and practice. This was common, for example, in the case of employee
relations handbooks issued to departmental or plant managers.
These covered topics such as disciplinary procedures, recruitment practices, holiday and overtime arrangements, and so on.
Most of the in-house lawyers were at least consulted on these,
and one or two drafted substantial sections themselves. Work
on these, of course, overlaps with the earlier heading of 'control

systems' as they contribute to determining management responses to various situations.

Other media used were newsletters. One or two of the interviewees had contributed an occasional article to the company newsletter (for instance, on sex discrimination). Also a couple of departments produced their own legal newsletter for management circulation, highlighting new legislation or company case-law to draw attention to the legal issues that managers had to keep in mind.

(6) Education and training

Nearly all the lawyers had contributed to in-house courses for various levels of company personnel. Some examples were employment law lectures; health and safety legislation; criminal law (for security staff); contracts (contract negotiators); race and sex discrimination; defamation (journalists). Usually their contribution formed part of a more general training course for those groups established by training departments rather than being a self-contained legal department course. The lawyers interviewed felt these activities were again useful, firstly for drawing attention to the occasions when legal problems can arise, secondly for making managers more aware of the legal department in the company (thus establishing better contacts for 'accessibility' purposes). Only a few, however, emphasised this area as an integral part of their work. Compare Choka (1970):

> Each department (sometimes each man) needs a custom-tailored course in layman's law. And when they have learned their law throughly, a new course must be started because the people forget and new people come in. In addition, the procedures set up to double check all legal matters start deteriorating. The job of education is a continuous process. (1021)

Again, the skill in using the technique is at least as important as the content — for example, using a requested lecture session not merely to impart information about, contract law, for instance, but doing advance preparation so that one knows the real problems of the audience, thus establishing oneself as a

constructive adviser (Maddock 1968); or using the experience
of the legal department to identify where company practice
was ineffective — explaining to managers the need for annual
appraisal sheets to be written up honestly if the company was
later to protect itself from unfair dismissal claims.

(7) Status in the organisation

Like other staff specialisms, it was not surprising to find in the
literature written by in-house lawyers a stress on the importance
of being given due recognition by senior management for the
law department to be fully respected and influential in the
organisation.

> The chief executive officer who places his chief company
> lawyer in a hierarchical position of equality with the top
> managers responsible for the other decision components will
> look upon him as a true adviser and not only as an assistant
> for the execution of legalities. . . . If the work of the company
> lawyer is considered to be of only marginal importance, a
> kind of insurance against accidents, or if he is regarded as a
> kind of company fire brigade for the removal of break-downs,
> then the words of Martin Luther can rightly be applied:
> 'Der Jurist, der nichts ist als ein Jurist, ist ein arm Ding'
> (Translation: "The Jurist who is nothing but a Jurist is a
> poor fellow").' (Kolvenbach, 1979: 18)

Or, in the evidence of the Law Society Commerce and Industry
Group to the Royal Commission on the Provision of Legal
Services:

> [S]tatus is not merely a matter of personal or professional
> pride, but an essential element enabling the lawyer to carry
> out his duties properly and effectively . . . the name of the job
> is not necessarily everything, it is how the job relates to other
> senior management that matters. It is desirable that there
> should always be (and in fact there almost always is) a right
> for the in-house lawyer to have direct access to the Board or
> at least to its Chairman or Managing Director. (Law Society,
> 1977: para 2.8)

Nearly all the law departments in this study had achieved this access to either the Chief Executive or the Board of Directors,[19] not surprisingly in view of the significance of law in company practice, either commercial or in terms of operational risks. Most stressed, however, that this gave them a place in councils on company policy rather than being used as a means of going over other managers' heads in a 'policing' function (see chapter 10). If, as described in the earlier section on commercial judgement, the lawyer had succeeded in creating a position where legal and commercial distinctions were less relevant than problem-solving, then the in-house lawyer at this level is likely to be involved in senior management discussions on corporate social responsibility committees or corporate strategy planning[20] and in all stages of important negotiations in the company.

The aim of becoming a valued adviser to managers was also part of the process of achieving status in the organisation. The lawyer's task 'is to build on the ongoing machinery and commitments of the organisation to make law compliance mesh with organisational routines and channels. The influential lawyer must educate, organise and respond. The influential lawyer must be a master of organisational analysis' (Rosen: 317–18).

(8) Reactive law

Inevitably, in-house lawyers also were referred to by management where the company or manager was faced with a legal 'problem' by way of litigation or regulatory controls. These situations were more typical of the role of lawyers in private practice, but also gave the in-house lawyers an opportunity to advise on future practice by using one of the other methods listed above. It was also in this area where there was likely to be most frequent contact with outside lawyers. The handling of reactive law, and the areas where outside lawyers were used, are discussed more fully in the next chapter.

MANAGING THE IN-HOUSE LEGAL PRACTICE

In-house lawyers, therefore, have a range of tools available by which they can affect company behaviour and can practise preventive law. Typically, they approached their role on a case-by-case, client demand basis, as befitted their professional training and approach. Only a few adopted a structured, systematic or department-wide analysis of how best to perform that role (sometimes prompted by company efficiency exercises) but rather allowed it to develop in an organic, individual fashion. (One should, of course, bear in mind that the evidence suggests that equally few managers determine their work on any analytical, planned basis.[21]) The advantages of such an approach by way of flexibility are evident, and can be justified in organisational theory — the role ambiguity in an 'organic' style of management (openly defined roles as against more rigid job definitions in the 'mechanistic' style) has been noted to be more functional for companies and personnel operating in a rapidly changing environment compared to a stable one.[22] Donnell, for example, concludes from his role analysis of corporate counsel that:

> a fairly high degree of ambiguity concerning the functions, duties, authority, and mode of operation of the law department and corporate counsel is functional. It is submitted that the nature and quality of the relationship between counsel and client is a very important determinant of the effectiveness of the corporate counsel and that detailed specification inhibits the development of the desired relationship. . . .
> It is a personal, helping relationship that goes beyond providing specialised knowledge and offering legal opinions on fact situations defined by the client. . . .
> The ideal environment for such a relationship appears to contain certain features that appear salutory for the constructive use of ambiguity by counsel. . . . Minimum organisational structure, close colleague relations, and support of a general counsel who is perceived to have influence with the executives. These factors are also the preconditions for the independence and objectivity that are essential for having counsel's advice reflect the legal environment accurately. (173–4)

It follows that attempts to define too narrowly the in-house legal role by way of job definitions, allotted tasks, control procedures, reporting requirements, legal issues, authority of the legal department, and so on, may be counterproductive, both in misunderstanding the nature of the role and in undermining the importance of the professional identification and motivation of the in-house lawyer. Nevertheless, taking account of the professional status of the lawyer to this extent may lead to an underestimation of the capacity to improve legal *management* techniques. There is no inbuilt professional understanding which provides lawyers with immediate skills in organisational communication or in organisational politics. To be influential in the organisation may require additional training and capacities. Equally, in large departments, problems of allocation of work, budgeting, staff management and motivation, choices of whether to 'divisionalise' or centralise legal services must already be tackled in some manner.[23] At the least, lawyers would benefit from learning relevant techniques so that they are aware of them and able to practise them. This is not to circumscribe the professional role of the lawyer but to enlarge his potential for working effectively inside the organisation, his capacity to translate law into effective business practice.

NOTES

1 Rosen (1984) argues that both in-house and outside lawyers have the responsibility to become 'influential lawyers' in the sense discussed in this chapter, giving less weight to the distinctiveness of the in-house lawyer's position than my own analysis. His work is a critique of corporate lawyers who restrict their role to technical risk-analysis and fail to engage in a consultancy role with the political complexity of organisational actions. He suggests the process has gone further in England, thus not only impoverishing service but resulting in loss of work to other professions. (31–3)

2 Not the least of the ambiguity of legal practice and advice is that many areas of the lawyer's craft are not tested because they are never the subject of litigation, or only tested many years later.

3 The importance of the facts to lawyers was emphasised in Donnell's (1970) finding that corporate counsel mentioned more than anything else 'disclosure of all pertinent information' as one of the criteria for a good client.(67) The others mentioned in order of importance were: 'consults corporate counsel early', 'is intelligent and generally aware of the legal environment', and 'demands high quality legal service'.

4 For a similar discovery in the field of criminal law by a sociologist trying to understand the legal processes involved, see McBarnet (1981) (who identifies this ambiguity of law as a means by which the rhetoric of

individual rights can be sustained in judicial reasoning while denied to defendants in practice).

This elusiveness also plays its part in the mystique of law. What can be more mystical than a statement of what the law is which is not only veiled by the need to know where and how to look for it, but which turns out when you find it to be provisional, particular, and only really ascertainable for your specific question if you take it to court? . . . People may not be bamboozled by the wigs and ceremony and jargon of law, but they are quite likely to be bamboozled by the law itself. It is not just that they are in their ignorance puzzled by the law. It is also quite simply that the law is a puzzle. Its particularistic *post hoc* form inevitably makes it so. (165)

5 But see Cain (1983) for a study of translation processes in legal practice. She sees translation as the core activity of lawyers' work.

6 Tomasic and Bullard (1978), in a questionnaire survey, found that just under half of the corporation lawyers they surveyed felt they spent more than five hours a week making business decisions.

7 Cf. de Butts (1978):

> The questions that come to top management to decide are characteristically shrouded in complexity, ambiguity and uncertainty. And, more often than not, the exigencies of time demand that such questions be decided in the absence of sufficient information to assure without question that what is decided is decided right. In any event, the essence of the corporate manager's job is a never-ending and never-satisfied quest for some reasonable balance among the overlapping and often directly competing interests of the various constituencies to which his business is in greater or lesser measure accountable. . . . all the manager can be certain of is that what best serves everybody will meet the perfect satisfaction of nobody. (de Butts, 1978)

8 Not the least of the roles inherent in this educational process is that of eliminating the myriad misconceptions which exist about the law. . . . Oddly enough, the 90 per cent errata are generally restrictive or prohibitive in nature. Most misconceptions tend toward indicating that something *cannot* be done, not that something *can* be done. A review by the lawyers generally opens vistas the operating people thought were not accessible. (Choka, 1970: 1021–2)

9 . . . there are archaic laws on the books, not enforced for good reasons of public policy, and, also, there are laws so poorly drawn or which have been so interpreted by the courts that no black-or-white areas of legality or illegality can be drawn under them. It is in areas such as these that the corporate counsel's exercise of business judgement can be of value in helping the corporate executive to decide whether proposed action is, in fact, the kind of activity that the law really was intended to prohibit, or whether the results the company expects to

obtain are worth the risk involved because of the uncertainty of the law. (Binger, 1968)

10 See Donnell (1970) and Kolvenbach (1979) on the conflicting views of businessmen as to whether lawyers should participate in business decisions. Kolvenbach (op.cit.: 63) suggests that lawyers in England are more likely than elsewhere to maintain a distance from management by acting more like lawyers in private practice because of their close ties with the legal profession and the division of the profession. By contrast, the US General Counsel he claims has more of an accepted policy role within companies.

11 Rosen (1984) identifies two major influences narrowing the scope of the lawyer's 'problem' as set by the organisational client — the *fragmentation* of the case from its context (such as a department view versus company-wide view; lack of information on the full background or on responsibilities at stake; failure by managers to learn from experience of failures, and so on): and the problem of the *timing* of the consultation with the lawyer (the later the lawyer is called in, the less there is room for influencing the range of outcomes, and the more such influence will revolve around issues of 'power') (137ff.). Lawyers forced to work with such organisation 'pathologies' 'are likely to misserve their corporate clients. . . . To overcome these pathologies, the lawyer must be involved in the corporate decision-making process' by 'mending information nets and engaging in intra-corporate political processes' (154, 158) — influencing the chain of command and guiding the exercise of managerial discretion. The reality of organisational decision-making is such that the professional in the organisation has a responsibility to assist in *setting* goals, not merely processing them (155, f80). Otherwise, in sheltering behind technical expertise, the lawyer is ignoring the weight his opinion will give to particular sub-units or coalitions within the organisation in relation to differing views of its best interests.

12 Cf. Rosen (1984: 1) on corporate lawyers in the United States:

> . . . to effectively serve a corporate client, the lawyer must not merely supply technical information about the law. Such information is likely to be inadequately processed by the corporate organisation. To be of service, the lawyer must study his client's organisational structure and utilise corporate resources — policies, political coalitions, and cultures — in presenting his recommendations. In effective corporate legal service, the lawyer becomes an influential member of his client's decision-making team and therefore cannot readily evade responsibility for the consequences of the decisions he recommends.

13 See chapter 10 and Stone (1975).

14 Organisational theory, however, tends to emphasise the 'disunity' of organisational life. See Rosen *supra*, n 11.

15 Cf. Rosen's useful discussion of how lawyers can draw on corporate culture and on company policies to assist their influence in their consultant role to management. (239ff)

When a lawyer mixes legal and business advice and draws upon the corporation's conception of itself embedded in its cultures and policies, he becomes an influential member of the corporation, an exponent of not only the external law of the state, but also the internal law of the organisation. (Rosen, 1984: 257)

16 The period of employment law reform following the election of the Conservative government in 1979 had not led to the same overall review, probably because its effects were largely aimed at trade union, rather than employer, practices.

17 Also newspaper industry departments which vet copy for possible libel difficulties and so forth, and of course some areas which invariably require a legal input — conveyancing, litigation.

18 See, for example, Choka's (1970) description of how two legal departments handled the introduction of major new regulations on finance, one by a lengthy memo, followed by an ineffective major meeting of nearly all the department managers, compared to another which sent round a brief memo on the broad outline of the change and a note that more specific information would follow. The specific information came in individual operational messages to departmental heads, composed in a meeting between the lawyer and the senior finance manager.

19 For examples of formal company policy statements safeguarding in-house lawyer access to a Board, see Kolvenbach (op. cit.: 26–7). For a discussion of the problems of lawyers as *members* of Boards of directors, see same, 47–9.

20 A survey in the United States found that all the companies surveyed reported involving in-house lawyers in strategic planning of the company (cited in *Business Week*, 1984: 93). This may relate to Kolvenbach's (1979) suggestion that US corporate lawyers are more often placed in a policy adviser role in their companies than lawyers in Europe. Without further comparative research it is difficult to test the accuracy of this claim.

21 Cf. the work of Henry Mintzberg (1973).

22 See, for example, the classic studies of Burns and Stalker (1966) and Lawrence and Lorsch (1967).

23 On the question of law department organisation, see Kolvenbach, chapter 5.

7 The Integrated Lawyer (3): Reacting to Legal Difficulties

Despite the emphasis by in-house lawyers on proactive lawyering, inevitably a significant aspect of in-house legal work consists of assisting the company to deal with litigation and other direct legal processes. All the lawyers interviewed spent at least some of their time (and a few specialists spent most of their time) in this area of 'curative' rather than preventive legal work. It should not be assumed that this necessarily signified the failure of proactive lawyering. Apart from the inevitable degree of human error and intentional lawbreaking (usually attributed to lower levels of management) in management processes, companies sometimes faced situations where preventive law did not prevent other parties pursuing litigation to the point of failure. Equally there were occasions where the company sought to enforce its own legal rights against other parties for actions which could not have been anticipated or avoided by the legal department.

Nor does the concept of the 'integrated lawyer' break down at this point. Intimate knowledge of company objectives, personnel and practices can assist at this stage too in a variety of ways: risk-analysis of the likely success of litigation; gathering appropriate evidence and expert witnesses from inside the company; remedial measures which can be taken by way of mitigating the damages or cost to the company; measures to prevent a formal legal action (by way of settlements or a negotiated withdrawal of the action); and in the effective use of outside lawyers.

This chapter outlines the typical areas where such legal problems arose, the way the legal service in the company was organised to cope with them, and the attitudes and approach of in-house lawyers engaged in this work. It also focuses on relations with outside lawyers since this was the area where they were most frequently used. Outside lawyers were also widely used for

specialist advice but this usually arose in the context of existing
or planned company practices raising legal 'problems' for the
company or in-house lawyer, and so was in that sense also
'reactive lawyering'.

LEGAL PROBLEMS

The large company's involvement in litigation is potentially
quite vast, given the significance and size of the companies
studied — in their economic and commercial dealings, their
property transactions, their production or service operations,
their consumer and employee transactions. This breadth of
activity explains why in-house lawyers felt themselves to be
involved in a more diverse range of legal issues than they would
have confronted in private practice and their day-to-day work
to be correspondingly less predictable.

Nevertheless, within this diversity it was apparent that
companies had distinctive patterns, with core problem areas
depending on the nature of the business. These patterns were
fairly predictable: manufacturing companies dealt more
frequently with industrial accident and product liability claims;
bank and finance companies with debtor actions; retail
companies with theft cases, trading standards actions and unfair
dismissal claims; consumer goods producers with 'passing off'
actions and trademark litigation. Where the company's operations were diverse, it would experience each of these core
problem areas within the relevant subsidiary part of the
company.[1]

The in-house lawyer's role

The bigger legal departments usually had a specialist or
specialist unit dealing with litigation. (The smaller departments
also coped with this work but were likely to use outside lawyers
more heavily.) All, or most, matters which had reached a point
of litigation, such as product liability claims, applications for
injunctions and so on, were then passed on to this function which
became responsible for processing the relevant court procedures,
liaising with outside lawyers, collecting the evidence and documentation inside the company. The advantage of litigation

specialisation was said to be in the degree of specialist knowledge necessary to conduct court business although there was the corresponding problem of a degree of loss of knowledge where the specialist took over a case previously handled by another member of the department, in having to learn the background to the case all over again.

All in-house lawyers, however, were involved with litigation some of the time but most avoided too detailed an attachment to it. The general view was that it was very time-consuming to spend time in court acting for the company or instructing counsel, so in many cases lawyers restricted their role to liaising with outside solicitors and helping them by way of collecting together the relevant evidence and documentation inside the company. Also, there was a widely-held view that court procedures demanded specialist technical knowledge and familiarity only available to those who practised regularly in them. (A fuller account of the allocation of work between in-house and outside lawyers is given later.)

In a number of cases, company legal problems of a particular type were allocated entirely to outside lawyers, in-house lawyers concentrating on policy matters, commercial or preventive law. The type of problem dealt with on a substantial scale by outside lawyers were those of a routine or local nature, such as supermarket theft cases (by non-employees) or debtor actions from bank branches. This was partly a division of labour on efficiency grounds but also could arise from tradition, if the in-house lawyers had been introduced into the company to be responsible for more recent or diverse business law matters.

Many companies coped with routine legal work by the employment of law graduates or para-legal staff such as legal executives or clerical-administrative staff in fields such as conveyancing, industrial accidents (for collection of evidence), debt collection or customer claims. In a few companies, too, personnel departments handled most of the individual employment law claims and resorted to legal departments only in what were regarded as difficult cases for non-lawyers to handle. (Although several other interviewees noted that their personnel departments had initially tried to take on industrial tribunal case work only to find that it was a more appropriate forum for the skills of a lawyer.)

Courtwork is, of course, only the most visible area of legal

problem situations for companies. All companies also dealt with
regulatory agencies or government departments of various
kinds — health and safety inspectors, trading standards officers,
tax inspectors. Legal department involvement with these was
more limited. In most cases, other specialist or general managers
had first contact with these agencies, any issues raised only
coming to the legal department if there was a legal rather than
'technical' problem, that is; a possible prosecution or an enforcement notice of some kind. More often the legal department had
been involved at a preventive stage, helping other specialists
in the company to interpret the meaning and application of
regulations, or drawing up guidance notes for staff. The lawyers
in one of the retail companies studied were the most active
example found in the study in terms of contacts with Trading
Standards Officers. They had regular contacts with them at
local branches when queries were raised with regard to breach of
trading standards, and had issued to branch managers standard
report forms as an aid to evidence for the legal department of
what took place on an investigation or caution, in case a
summons might be issued.

> My job is to get the Retail Branch manager selling and get
> people like the Trading Standards Officer off his back. So I
> inform him of his legal rights [when there has been a caution]
> and what to do about it. They have my telephone number
> and standard forms so that I will have consistent and proper
> information for my investigation. . . . Have law will travel I
> suppose is my motto. We don't even need to tell District
> Managers that we are on a visit. We're welcomed with open
> arms because usually we are getting them out of a hole. We're
> fire-fighting and we arrive and all we have to say is — where
> do we point the hose? (Retail company lawyer)

In-house lawyers saw themselves clearly as there to act in the
best interests of their client — to defend or promote the interests
of their client, subject to not conspiring to commit an unlawful
act or to conceal evidence from a court. There was no evidence
from the interviews that this professional role posed any
particular ethical dilemmas for them within the context of
working for a single company as client. (See chapter 10.) They
did feel better placed, however, to assess the reliability of

company witnesses in determining the chances of success in a legal action. A businessman commenting on business-lawyer relations summed up this issue neatly:

> Too many executives do not function well in situations where they exercise little control. They make poor witnesses. They provide confusing statements and really can lose the total thrust of your position. You must in your risk-reward equation look at what is going to happen when you put that executive . . . in what is essentially a hostile environment. (Kelly, 1978)

Also, in-house lawyers felt they were in a position to help determine future company practices, should a legal problem disclose existing practices that were inadequate to protect the company from future action. Thus, in one case the company introduced a formal disciplinary procedure for its employees because of the advice of the legal department following some experience of unfair dismissal claims. In this way, reactive law was intimately linked with preventive law, insofar as lawyers passed on relevant insights from experience of company litigation or attempted to create effective strategies and structures to deal with the problem. In these cases, the reactive role could be more clearly seen as a law enforcement role than in cases of preventive work. Where someone 'had their fingers burnt' in this way, it was also often an opening for the law department to achieve more future influence in that section of the organisation.

> We didn't get involved in the original agreement and would have said 'it's not on.' It grew out of managers sitting around a room — in the old Australian style. It's only sinking in now that you don't reach agreements and contract afterwards. It takes 20 years as it did in the United States to get the message home. You have to get it into business schools and out from there. We find out about them. Things start to bubble up — agreements don't sound right, people make snide comments or 'ho-ho-ho', and we fix them to the wall with a knife in their throat to tell them off. . . . It's a termination case if it happens — the company is fined and its reputation at stake. (Australian transportation company lawyer, talking about a price-fixing case)

I had kittens every time I appeared before an industrial tribunal anticipating the inevitable request from the chairman to see our company's disciplinary procedure. So I repeatedly advised we must have a formal, written disciplinary procedure. Eventually one was produced. (Insurance company lawyer)

We had a struggle to get a legal input into the shipping market side of the business, even though there are vast sums involved in demurrage claims or in cargo shortage claims. Why? Because the managers involved had never used lawyers and were reluctant to get in the extra legal expertise. It was partly the inertia of the large organisation again; they are used to doing without legal interference. But I think we have succeeded now because of the fact that (a) we've been pushing to be involved and (b) I think some of the consequences of insufficient legal advice have been coming home to roost on the managers. (Oil company lawyer)

Determining the best interests of the client is not in itself unproblematic. The client's best interests may not relate, in the client's mind, solely to winning or losing a case, or losing at least cost.[2] Company attitudes, policies and public relations practices also influenced the role of the in-house lawyer. A more flexible approach was evident in cases involving individuals suffering hardship arising from company actions (for example, leasehold or mortgage eviction actions) or cases where the company's image or commercial reputation might be at stake or its relations with another party such as a local authority. Thus companies did not always enforce their legal rights under contracts nor contest nuisance actions by local residents, although their legal assessment was to the effect that their case might be upheld in court. In-house lawyers picked up these company policies over time or in negotiations and to some extent incorporated them into their advice. Sometimes, however, there was a feeling that the company was insufficiently rights-minded. Three interviewees commented that their company was too 'soft' in enforcing rights under contracts or in its fear of possible legal action, suggesting that lawyers normally take a more robust view of litigation. However, where companies felt an important business principle was involved they were more likely to press a case, for example; cases of theft of company property by employees in the case of a retailer.

There was little evidence from the interviews that any refined distinctions were made (by the lawyers or by their colleagues in the company) between different types of legal action, whether on grounds of cost or morality.[3] Legal action against the company was a cause for concern, whether it involved health and safety, trading standards, discrimination claims or breach of contract actions. Some types of action, however, were of a regular nature and seemed to elicit less concern than action which infringed important business activities or which involved claims affecting company reputation (such as discrimination, compared to the less controversial area of health and safety, where claim frequency and a tradition of insurance-based protection have perhaps lowered the level of concern, although this statement would need support from direct research). The legal department was responsible for tackling all of these issues and it was left to it (within its budget) to decide how much time and resources to devote to cases. The cost to the company in any particular case was, however, often an important factor in determining whether to fight a case or not, as in the case of another retailer who had been cautioned by a Trading Standards Officer over some stock to the value of £1.3 million of ladies' nightdresses which, in line with fashion changes, had moved to a mini-style. The Trading Standards Officer had suggested the length might bring the clothing into child night-dress safety regulations. The company argued they were unsuitable for young children and that they were prepared to fight the case to the House of Lords if necessary. 'The Trading Standards Department looked at its budget and decided to drop the case.'[4]

Client culture also determined rights enforcement responses, whether it was a case of taking a 'soft' line (associated in traditional English companies with a tradition of 'behaving like gentlemen') or a harsher, legalistic standard:

We do have some morons working for us, driving our trucks, so we have situations of products getting smashed up in crashes. People didn't see the exclusion clause, and our rates are based on not insuring. So we don't pay. And we use our commercial muscle to last out any action. I don't like saying that. It's not really a very warm, loving statement. But that's the truth. (Australian transportation company lawyer)

Finally, other client attitudes perhaps rubbed off on in-house lawyers. Over half of those interviewed criticised the delays and costs involved in litigation and felt there was room for improvement by the legal profession, a question dealt with in a later chapter.

RELATIONS WITH OUTSIDE LAWYERS

In-house lawyers dealt fairly frequently with outside lawyers, perhaps most often in the context of litigation. One of the early arguments about the in-house lawyer branch of the legal profession was whether in-house lawyers might supplant the work of outside lawyers. In this study, only two of the legal departments said they tried in principle to do *all* legal work in-house (that is apart from litigation in the higher courts where counsel had to be used). In both cases, they had not been entirely successful because of work pressures necessitating some work going outside. As to whether in-house legal departments have *reduced* rather than replaced the work of outside lawyers, this is harder to say. In-house lawyers undoubtedly have some cost-saving effects but it is difficult to assess the strength of the converse argument that the presence of an in-house lawyer encourages more attention to legal issues and hence more work in turn going to outside lawyers.[5]

It is more self-evident that the in-house lawyer may alter the *character* of the client-lawyer relationship for a company. The in-house lawyer mediates between managers with limited knowledge of the law and lawyers with limited knowledge of the company. It can be expected therefore that there will be improved communication and a more sophisticated presentation of the client's case. On the one hand the in-house lawyer is better placed to locate the relevant evidence inside the company — documentation, witnesses, technical experts or recommended expert witnesses, and to educate the outside lawyer on business details such as trade association standards, competitor share of the market, competitor trademarks, and so on. On the other hand there is also improved *control* of the case for the client company. The in-house lawyer has a better understanding than a manager liaising with outside lawyers not only of law but of the procedures, delays and cost factors in the work of the legal profession and is therefore better placed than any layman to make suggestions or criticisms or otherwise assess the quality of the service. He may also be able to 'translate' to management (in the sense of the translation goals outlined in the last chapter) the advice received, and in particular compensate for what was said frequently to be a common failing of outside lawyers — a reluctance to take any definite stand on the course of action the client should take or to assess the respective risks involved. (See Chan and Wilson, 1983.) Over time, therefore, outside lawyers who provide a poorer service will be more likely to be dropped in favour of others who are better, or the in-house lawyer may steer the outside lawyers more forcefully (and can do so not only because of his expertise but also because the outside lawyer is likely to recognise that the in-house lawyer is the effective buyer of future legal services), thus producing an overall improvement in the legal services to the client. 'You don't really want outside lawyers running riot with your management. You need someone who can shackle them and say whether what they're doing is sensible or not' (Manufacturing company lawyer).

At least one writer (*Business Week*, 1984) has suggested that this trend will lead to a situation where in-house lawyers come to be the dominant partner in the relationship (compared to the traditional view within the legal profession that it was a second-best role). The trend in modern business to greater consciousness of costs (litigation and use of outside lawyers are often large elements of the in-house legal budget[6]) and to greater integration of specialists into business thinking, will accelerate such a process. For example, several of the in-house lawyers interviewed regularly asked law firms for fee quotations for anticipated work and one described how he had, in a recent major conveyancing project, asked several firms to put on a presentation of *how* the work would be handled. It is clear that as in-house lawyers become more integrated with their companies and more 'businesslike' in their approach to proactive lawyering, such practices will become more common. Most in-house lawyers spoke of the gradual breakdown of the traditional 'family' firm approach by companies to their outside legal services. Outside lawyers were being selected for their competence as specialists as much as for the fact that they were regular suppliers of law service.

Some of the outside lawyers I spoke to were also becoming more sensitive to the need to work as partners with the in-house lawyer, recognising him to be the effective judge of their services. There could at times, however, be some tensions in the relationship.

The effect from my point of view is that it saves time, effort and money. But, on the other hand, it produces a much more demanding client, in terms of wanting a precise and low-cost — and the emphasis is on low-cost — solution. Corporation lawyers obtain a reasonable stipend. When they go to an outside firm like this with its quite huge overheads, I think they feel the hourly charge is excessive. And because executives get essentially 'kerbside stuff' from in-house lawyers, they expect a considered view will be given as cheaply and quickly as the kerbside stuff. (Australian commercial lawyer in private practice)

However, both groups tend to emphasise that the relation is now more clearly a case of partnership, or teamwork, rather than the traditional lawyer-client model. The trend was towards identifying more clearly the *strengths of each branch* for their role in tackling an issue — the in-house lawyer's intimate knowledge of the company and business practice as against the outside lawyers's strength in litigation experience, legal specialisation, or breadth of experience across a range of companies.[7] Also, there were signs of recognition of the need to work more system-atically together as a team, that is, to 'manage' the in-house/outside lawyer liaison by way of agreeing in advance a checklist of stages and activities, allocation of responsibilities, agreement on costs monitoring and discretion. The broader issues raised by these developments in the relations between the two branches of the profession are discussed further in chapter 13.

When are outside lawyers used?

The occasions when outside[8] lawyers are used most often by in-house lawyers can be categorised under the following headings:

Local knowledge
Firms of solicitors will be used for cases where a local dimension is important, either in terms of collection of evidence, knowledge of local courts and judiciary, or knowledge of local legislation (either local bye-laws or other legal jurisdictions in the United Kingdon or abroad), or merely because it is much cheaper for the lawyers on the spot to handle a case.

Specialist knowledge
Particularly in the case of the smaller in-house legal department, there will be a need to obtain advice on specialist points of law, either through outside solicitors or directly from counsel. Larger departments will more often have the experience, expertise and resources to carry out legal research.

Second opinions
In-house lawyers valued at times the opportunity to check their judgement on new, complex, uncertain or crucial areas of decision by getting an outside legal opinion (sometimes more than one if they felt unhappy with the first opinion!).

Litigation
Litigation is extremely time-consuming and requires knowledge of court procedures or regulatory agencies (and personnel), which are best picked up by those who regularly appear before the judicial forum. Many in-house lawyers felt they could not justify the time they would have to spend waiting in court when there were other legal tasks to be done in the company. Others referred to the fact that their contact was infrequent enough to make them too unfamiliar with the procedural aspects to be comfortable in doing it. So in many areas of litigation such work was delegated to outside solicitors and counsel after appropriate conferences. However, some legal departments carried their own specialists in litigation so that the in-house influence was present in court either in terms of advocacy (in the lower courts or other tribunals) or by way of assisting counsel.

Overflows
In-house lawyers valued the opportunity to pass out work when their own resources were limited. The work they did in-house was of a varied character and sometimes major projects (such

as litigation on product liability claims or a major acquisition of another company) would take up a great deal of their time. On these occasions they were thankful to be able to pass on some of the other items of work on their desks.

'Political' issues

Although infrequent, outside lawyers were sometimes used where there was a sensitive aspect to a case. This could arise where there was significant internal management conflict over a decision and the in-house lawyer could avoid 'taking sides'; where the decision was seen as one of high risk; where the in-house lawyer needed political support in advising against a venture which management favoured; or where it looked better to the outside world if the name of a prestigious outside firm of lawyers were to appear on documents (for example, a share prospectus, debt collection or acquisitions).

NOTES

1 Analysis of the statistics in a particular type of industry would indicate, however, that there are variations between individual companies in the frequency of legal actions of a particular kind, due to factors such as differing standards, a more effective legal preventive role, and so on.

2 One lawyer made the interesting observation that managers were more heated about unfair dismissal claims (which usually involved small amounts of money) because of their 'personal' nature than they were about decisions whether or not to settle contract claims which might run into many more thousands in costs.

3 This statement, however, needs to be qualified in that there was insufficient scope in the interviews really to explore this topic in depth.

4 This example was quoted at a conference of lawyers.

5 In the AGCAS (1984) survey, the majority of departments questioned about future trends in the department saw no likely change in the amount of work going outside; of the rest almost equal numbers expected an increase as a decrease in the work going out.

6 See Fischer (1984) for an example of a departmental review which identified litigation costs as the major item of the law department's budget. The remedy was to employ more in-house lawyer litigation specialists.

7 See Kolvenbach (1979), chapter 3, for an analysis of this relationship between outside and in-house lawyers in terms of it being a necessary partnership.

8 Note that many of these also cover situations when in-house lawyers should consult with *colleagues in the law department*. Cf. Donnell (1970: 181):

> A counsel should be quick to confer when it appears that no legally safe way can be found to reach his client's objective, when he needs additional specialised knowledge, when he has any doubt about his own objectivity, or when the matter has particular importance or a widespread effect on the company.

8 Training and Development of In-house Lawyers

The issue of education within the professions has become one of pressing importance within the last 20 years as the professions have become subject to increasing specialisation, faster rates of social, technological and knowledge-base changes, and a more sophisticated and critical public. Most professions have had to re-evaluate their basic professional training in terms of preparing entrants for working in a changing profession, and in particular have had to consider the option of more extensive continuing or advanced professional training.[1] Equally, the education providers or partners in professional training have been forced to re-evaluate their contribution in these areas.[2] For example, a significant development during the period of the study was the launch by the Law Society of a system of mandatory continuing education for newly-qualified solicitors, involving credits for courses taken from a range of specified courses within three years of qualification (Page, 1985). Other jurisdictions have also recently opted for mandatory continuing legal education. Although these developments were too recent to be covered specifically in the research interviews, the author's interest in continuing education was reflected in some of the issues covered in the research on in-house lawyers. What were their views of the suitability of basic training, of their need for, and experience of, continuing education, of their training needs compared with those of outside lawyers?

The first part of this chapter gives a brief account of the views on education and training of the in-house lawyers interviewed. The second part contains a training analysis of the work of the in-house lawyer, arising out of a request to the author by the Law Society Commerce and Industry Group to present a paper to their annual conference on the training needs of in-house lawyers. As a result of that paper, there was an agreement to devise a pilot two-day course for younger in-house lawyers.

The second part of this chapter also describes that course, and possible further developments in the education of in-house lawyers.

EDUCATION AND TRAINING: VIEWS OF THE IN-HOUSE LAWYERS

Nearly all the interviewees expressed themselves reasonably satisfied with their basic professional training. None of them felt that it took particular account of the in-house lawyer, being geared towards a career in private practice. However, all felt it did provide the basic *legal* knowledge which was a necessary basis for any lawyer's work. Some of the older lawyers felt that the courses had probably improved from their day, with at least some attention now given to more 'relevant' topics such as advocacy skills training, and less emphasis on courses such as, for example, Roman law. Most felt it unlikely that the courses could be altered to give special weight to the in-house lawyer's needs because of the number of those seeking to enter private practice, although company and commercial law courses provided some grounding. In addition, many felt that it would be inappropriate to cater for early specialisation when one was beginning a career with a range of career paths. There was less unanimity over experience of the period of articles, it being felt that much depended on the quality of the legal practice and the lawyers to whom one happened to be attached. It was possible for solicitors to take articles in a company and for barristers to take a part of their pupillage[3] in a company (a recent innovation won by the efforts of the Bar Association for Commerce, Finance and Industry — BACFI). However, there were mixed views amongst lawyers as to whether this was an appropriate route unless a young lawyer was sure his or her career aspirations lay in company work,[4] experience of private practice being seen as a more general introduction to the profession. In any case, many felt that it was difficult to offer adequate training support — unlike private practice, the department had no goal of expanding legal services and the work involved left little time for training support.

There was also some scepticism regarding existing continuing education provision or possible extensions to it by way of mandatory continuing legal education. Broadly, existing provision for continuing education fell into four types of voluntary provision. It was either provided by attendance at lectures on legal topics organised by the College of Law,[5] by lectures and the annual conference organised by the Commerce and Industry Group of the Law Society or the Bar Association for Commerce, Finance and Industry; by lectures or conferences organised by various other commercial or academic centres; or by personal reading and updating. There had been no experience yet of the operation of the new compulsory continuing education system for solicitors, although it was clear that the recognised courses being established for that system were largely content-based (rather than skills-based) and developed with the focus primarily on private practice.

As far as courses were concerned, most praise was reserved for the courses organised by the in-house lawyers' own professional association, as being most in tune with in-house legal work. College of Law lectures were also seen as occasionally useful for exposition of new directions in specific areas of legislation. Least praise was given to the commercial course agencies. Experience of these had been that they were of variable quality, often providing little knowledge that could not be gained from personal reading.

However, this last comment was frequently felt applicable to most lectures and conferences of any kind. 'You were lucky if you could come away from one of these with three new items of information.' The predominant method of continuing education adopted was, therefore, personal reading and study. Most of the lawyers felt that their basic training and professional standards had given them the ability to keep up to date in their own areas, and that there were sufficient journals and circulars of various kinds in those areas to allow them to do so. Time was the only problem in this respect. So one might summarise the diverse comments by saying that lectures (for that was the main teaching method of all the other provision) were most useful (1) when one had insufficient time to read up the information, (2) when there was a new area of law and the lecture provided a way of becoming familiar with its outline, and (3) to reinforce existing knowledge.

The mainly sceptical view of external provision of continuing education also carried over into views regarding possible compulsory continuing education. Most of those interviewed (more obviously the older interviewees) thought there was not likely to be much of value in such a scheme, given their existing personal commitment to knowledge updating. In any case, it was felt that such a scheme would suffer from the fact that there would be areas of law covered which were of no interest to a practising in-house lawyer who had already developed areas of specialisation. (The use of credit-type choice systems to some extent answers this criticism, of course.) However, it was apparent that the fundamental objection related to perceived professional competence — one already had sufficient skills to maintain up-to-date knowledge levels; sitting in another course was not going to add particularly to one's professional abilities.

A number of points arising from these attitudes are worthy of comment. First, it has to be recognised that basic legal training, *by virtue of its intrinsic character as a discipline*, focuses on updating requirements. The professional lawyer should not need to be told of the importance that new legislation or case-law has for his professional discipline and competence to provide legal advice. This is reinforced by a professional literature that lays great emphasis on updating — regular law reports, loose-leaf encyclopaedia formats, a wide range of journals almost exclusively devoted to new developments, and recently the introduction of information-retrieval computer systems geared to the legal profession's requirements. Adversarial practice also contributes, creating 'a systematised struggle that challenges lawyers to learn how to defeat one another.' (Houle, 1980: 304.) In this respect the legal profession is already attuned to continuing education in a way most other professions are not.

Against this background a fairly sophisticated analysis needs to be made to provide for lawyers a form of continuing education that can be justified on its merits. For example, an important question is to identify whether client perceptions of legal 'incompetence' relate to lack of updated *knowledge* as such or to other facets of legal skills, such as interpersonal skills in handling clients,[6] abilities in work organisation or case presentation, lack of motivation or opportunity to engage in continuing education, absence of specialisation. One suspects that lack of current knowledge is not a particularly salient factor. One of the lawyers interviewed who was in favour of a continuing education scheme, supported it as a stimulus to change structural professional relations in private practice rather than to enhance client assistance. His experience of private practice had suggested that when new areas of law emerged, senior members in the practice tended to pass the area over to young lawyers who then advised clients, rather than taking the trouble to learn it themselves. This 'traditional lawyer apathy toward self-improvement through education' (Johnstone and Hopson: 552) is an intriguing paradox in a profession so dependent on updating. If the comments on senior lawyers accurately describe the predominant pattern within legal practice, it seems unlikely that continuing education requirements for recently-qualified young lawyers will answer this problem so much as formalise it, unless one can assume that experience on such courses will induce habits of learning which will persist, an argument sometimes put forward in favour of such a youth-weighted scheme.

In this context it is relevant to suggest that in-house lawyers may be at an advantage over others in the profession in relation to their continuing education, arising from characteristics of in-house legal work which have already been noted. The fact that in-house lawyers appear to have greater resources of time, materials and staff back-up which the setting of a large organisation can provide; and the fact that they are seen as there to provide a comprehensive legal service to one client, a client who will not go away, may also act to produce a stronger motivational commitment to competence than affects lawyers faced with many one-shot clients (see Carlin, 1962).

Finally, it was noteworthy how much interviewees assumed that continuing education took the form (similar to basic training and the new Law Society continuing education scheme) of information-giving approaches rather than skills-based or action-learning approaches.[7] Lectures were the predominant method by which continuing education was delivered. Given what was said above about the professional orientation to updating inherent in acting as a lawyer, combined with self-perceptions of status and competence amongst the interviewees, it is hardly surprising that notions of continuing education did not receive much support. There was undoubtedly the sense, described by Houle (op. cit.) in relation to many professions' experiences of continuing education, of 'what seems to them to be a mindless proliferation of courses and conferences'.

Continuing education in the legal profession therefore requires greater refinement in knowledge of the variety of aims, methods and purposes of post-qualification educational provision, linked to the actual practice needs of lawyers. This would call for development along at least three dimensions — developing a coherent *conceptual structure* of the place of continuing professional learning within professional practice as portrayed in Houle's excellent text; wider appreciation of the principles of *adult learning* (Mackie, 1984) with their emphasis on making the adult *active* within the learning process, recognising and respecting existing competences and practical intelligence (Schon, 1983); *designing programmes* that build on such knowledge in order to link education to relevant areas of practice in an effective manner (Schon, 1987; Todd, 1987). It would seem obvious that this would also suggest the need for the profession to identify a *research prospectus* to underpin these endeavours. At this point it is appropriate to turn to a more detailed training analysis of in-house work.

The training and development of in-house lawyers

Most industrial training analyses start from an analysis of existing skills and operational procedures in the job or more precisely amongst those of whom it is commonly agreed that they are effective performers in that function. However, the more varied the work and the greater the discretion attached to its performance or to evaluating its performance, the more difficult this task becomes. Thus, it is difficult to analyse training requirements for managerial positions because of the complexity and variety of the work, the personal attributes individual managers bring to that work, the scope of discretion in managerial decision-making, and the difficulties in precisely evaluating the quality or competence of the outcomes of management decision-making.

In-house legal work carries exactly the same difficulties of appraisal for training and development purposes. Not only was there a variety of legal work between different companies, but interviewees spoke emphatically of the difficulty of describing a 'typical day's work' and indeed frequently cited that as a positive element of job satisfaction. Equally there is difficulty in arriving at measures for evaluating successful outcomes in legal work, much of the work being advisory and preventive in character.

A crude measure of 'legal actions against the company', for example, would be influenced by a range of factors not related to the performance of the in-house lawyer. (Incidentally, the author gained another impression of the 'professional' ethos of in-house lawyers in their response to the question of 'how would a company know the in-house lawyer was being effective?'. Most lawyers seemed a little surprised to be asked such a question as if it was an inappropriate question to put to them. Amongst the responses were such replies as 'I suppose a senior manager would know if a lawyer was making sense to him', or, 'I expect by the number of complaints to my Head of Department.').

Given these difficulties, therefore, I decided to approach the question of a training analysis in a similar way to management training profiles, namely to look at what the *objectives* of the work were and what this implied for necessary skills or knowledge base. Since the crucial issue here concerned the value of an in-house lawyer as compared to the service available from private practice, I chose to use as a starting point those areas where in-house lawyers were said to provide a more effective and efficient service than outside lawyers, as gleaned from the interviews and from the literature on in-house lawyers. From these headings, it was possible to suggest which skills and knowledge were implied, and the training requirements to achieve those skills. Finally, I made as assessment of where those skills were currently developed, according to whether they were met princi- pally from one of three sources, namely — basic professional training, formal continuing education, or informal continuing education (that is, personal sources). The analysis is set out in diagrammatic form in Table 2.

As one might expect, one finds a considerable degree to which successful in-house legal work is skills based or at least assumes a knowledge base which is only effective given the skill to *apply* that knowledge practically, in a business context. This same emphasis emerged from interviewee comments. However, both basic legal education and formal continuing education provision are predominantly information-based in the UK. Much of the skills training even in relation to legal understanding can there- fore be attributed to informal, personal learning efforts (or perhaps intuition is a more appropriate word here). However, one must bear in mind that much of the legal information-giving involves not solely an understanding of legal rules but of the implications and applications of these rules. To that extent, legal training does involve these *applied* knowledge skills. However, one's experience suggests there is not necessarily much effort in legal training to articulate the nature of such applied skills,[8] even less to a consideration of the skills of *preventive* law and its application to a business setting.

A second conclusion from the analysis is that it is clear that there would be great value for an in-house lawyer to have a knowledge base made up of both legal *and* business matters. This relates to the question of understanding the client's business and its problems. One could not expect a lawyer operating in a bank, for example, to provide a high-quality service if he knew little or nothing about banking practice, not to mention a general commercial understanding. In this area, it is quite clear that little legal education and training is directly relevant. Most in-house lawyers clearly have to 'pick it up as they go along' and were conscious that this was a process that was vital to their role.

Finally, there are personal skill areas which can be found in management training courses but for which lawyers mainly rely on extensive personal experience rather than on any formal courses, namely interviewing, negotiating, problem-solving, communicating, personal organisation and time management skills. (In addition, those lawyers who became heads of legal departments face typical management problems of staffing, staff relations, work control systems, budgets, and so forth.)

One is left with the issue, therefore, of whether or how the current training and development of in-house lawyers[9] could be improved. It is abundantly clear that legal education (as in other aspects of the legal system) is heavily dominated by traditions, and within that tradition the in-house lawyer is still given only marginal recognition. As a first step it would seem appropriate at least to consider whether the role merits greater attention in basic legal training. However, many in-house lawyers themselves doubted the value of this. They argued that there is more than enough material already to fit into a basic professional training, and in any case many valued their initial experience in private practice and felt that most young lawyers would be undecided on a career route at that stage (although they did think it would be useful to have more optional subjects that were directly relevant to commercial practice, such as EEC

Table 2 *In-house Lawyers — Training and Development Profile*

Advantages of the in-house lawyer	Objectives	Training/Development Requirements	Existing Training or Development P = from personal sources BT = basic education and training CE = formal continuing education and training
1 FAMILIARITY WITH 'CLIENT'	Enhanced capacity to solve in-house 'legal' problems. (that is, (a) commercially-oriented (b) constructive (c) practical (d) specialist)	Legal knowledge (1) relevant to company needs	→ P + BT + CE
		(2) knowledge of company — its products/practice/personnel/clients/regulatory agencies	→ P
		(3) skills to use legal/business knowledge effectively	→ P (BT)
2 ACCESSIBILITY	To ensure known in company as helpful adviser who can ease day-to-day problems	(1) advice and counselling skills	→ P (BT)
		(2) time management skills	→ P
		(3) familiarity with 'client'	(see 1 above)
3 PREVENTIVE ROLE	(a) anticipates legal problems in management developments (b) anticipates management problems in legal developments	(1) Fact-gathering skills and familiarity with 'client'	→ P (BT)
		(2) Communication and influence (persuasion and negotiation skills)	→ P (BT)
		(3) legal 'search' skills	→ BT/CE/P

4 COST BENEFITS → More efficient allocation of company resources by — → P

    (a) commercial assessment of decision-making options → P (BT)

    (1) knowledge of business and commerce and familiarity with 'client' skills to apply knowledge to legal problems

    (b) appraisal of value/cost of external legal advice

    (c) by carrying out regular legal work on salaried basis → BT + CE

    (3) relevant legal skills

    (d) preventive role

5 GOOD ADMINISTRATOR QUALITIES

    (a) organises and communicates information effectively → P

    (4) as above

    (1) communication and organisational skills → P (BT)

    (b) skill in handling meetings

    (2) knowledge and skills in meetings procedure → P (BT)

    (c) objective approach to situations

    (3) independent and broad-minded approach

law, which it had taken the legal education bodies some time to take on board). Assuming that viewpoint is justified, it leaves for consideration the question of advanced professional studies in relation to in-house work.

In the sphere of continuing education, occasional lectures on legal matters will clearly continue to have a place for the reasons mentioned earlier. Longer, formal courses concerned with knowledge updating would seem to have less justification, given that the basic professional training adequately prepares the lawyer for this process. There remain, therefore, issues of specialisation needs and of the 'skills' areas identified — legal and business — and also the need for basic commercial knowledge. Should greater attention be given to developing these at a more formal level?

One of the simplest means of acquainting someone with a business context is a company induction procedure of some kind. Only two of the in-house lawyers had been given an induction course by the company, indicating that companies also have something to learn about integrating the legal function with its business context. Of course, successful induction programmes are much more difficult to set up than might appear at first glance. The 'walk-round-the-factory' will only provide limited information to a new recruit. However, it is not beyond the wit of most large companies to ensure that a new in-house lawyer is provided with a short period whereby he or she can pick up a great deal of information, for example, by developing a project assignment such as a legal audit or a period working within a non-legal department on a project agreed between the head of that department and head of the legal department or in an alternative executive management role. Some of the major international companies had in fact recently begun to incorporate their in-house lawyers in their general management development programmes. In addition, some in-house lawyers, conscious of the need to make a career of in-house legal work, were tentatively considering expanding their qualifications by working for MBAs in business schools (although this aspect was stronger among Australian in-house lawyers and, from all accounts, US lawyers).

The fact that learning is informal and personal is in itself no bad thing. Most adult learning occurs like this. It combines the advantages of individual readiness to learn with motivation and commitment (see Tough, 1979). Nevertheless, it suffers from exactly the disadvantage that it is personal and therefore subject to considerable variations across individuals in ability and motivation, while losing the advantages of shared knowledge, experience and insights, as well as the reinforcement of group commitment. Further, the range and extent of the skills set out in the analysis suggest something of a major learning task for individual in-house lawyers, and suggest that at least an attempt should be made at constructing a viable continuing education programme which is seen as relevant and worthwhile by in-house lawyers. The Commerce and Industry Group of the Law Society in fact took up this issue and, with the author, organised the course described below.

The author ran a pilot, two-day course in association with the Commerce and Industry Group to assess the interest amongst in-house lawyers in a course covering some of the basic managerial skills identified in the training needs analysis. The course was entitled 'Negotiation, Communication and Administration: How to survive as an in-house lawyer'. Just over 60 in-house lawyers applied for 30 places. The sessions were deliberately made highly participative as well as providing a basic information input. Topics covered included an analysis of the work of the in-house lawyer; time management and office organisation (with small group discussion of a range of set topics in these areas); communication and interviewing skills (with a practical exercise on interviewing); and negotiation (with a role playing exercise in small groups). Further courses have since been held attracting similar interest (although the title has been changed to reflect the more self-confident attitude amongst in-house lawyers, from 'How to survive as an in-house lawyer' to 'How to succeed as an in-house lawyer'!).

The success of the course, launched despite initial doubts by some in the professional association, helped confirm the training analysis, but also indicated the extent to which in-house lawyers are conscious of their need to improve their abilities in areas other than legal skills or information. Beyond this area there is clearly scope for further developments in terms of business education. As in the case of induction courses, most companies seemed to pay only limited regard to management development of lawyers, only some sending lawyers on business-school or in-house management courses. Both companies and in-house lawyers could become more active in this regard. However, the strong professional identification of the lawyers and their sense of providing a highly specialist service to the company, is likely to limit the scope of such courses. It seems more likely that in-house lawyers will prefer to improve their applied legal/business skills by sharing the insights and experience of fellow lawyers in courses and contexts where the 'relevance' of the learning issues and skills is most obvious, yet conducted within the ambit of 'professional' development rather than general managerial development. To fulfill the ideals of the 'positive' corporate lawyer, clearly legal education generally has to recognise the need to rise above a narrowness and provincialism.[10]

Finally, it is important to note that in-house lawyers are not alone in recognising a need for education which broadens their skill and knowledge base into management practice, and which heightens their 'accessibility' to clients. There is also here a convergence with developments in the private practice end of the profession, although the reasons for the latter's interest seem more specifically related to office management and business practice needs arising out of the economic pressures on the legal profession at large. Thus, there are both commonalities and divergences between these, as other, branches of the legal profession. Legal educators must not only be able to recognise the 'core' skills of lawyering, but also to cater, with a range of 'boutique' courses, for the existing diversity of legal practice.

The demand for new kinds of interdisciplinary legal education was anticipated many years ago in Johnstone and Hopson's (1967) severe indictment of the English profession's apathetic approach to legal education.[11] Developments such as those outlined in this chapter, and current pressures on the profession, may indicate that the conditions are right for further major developments in English legal education.[12]

> law is concerned with the full gamut of human experience, and the education of lawyers should be one of the key points at which a society utilises the more astute and meaningful discoveries about human experience that other disciplines have made. (Johnstone and Hopson, op. cit.: 571)

NOTES

1 See Schein (1972), the Report on Continuing Education by the University Grants Committee (1983), and Houle (1980).

2 *Supra.*

3 A pupil barrister can claim an approved six-month period of a company pupillage for calculating the first six months of pupillage in chambers.

4 For one of the few articles on the subject, see Anderson (1968), who points to the division of professional training as one of the stumbling blocks in the way of company lawyer developments. She supports the expansion of training for articles and pupillage inside companies. The AGCAS survey (1984, 6–7) notes with surprise the low number of trainee lawyers in its survey of company departments. The Commerce and Industry Group, in its submission to the Royal Commission on Legal Services, noted that its members were evenly divided over the issue of in-house articles.

5 The independent 'training arm' of the Law Society.

6 According to the surveys by the Royal Commission on Legal Services (1979), client satisfaction and dissatisfaction with solicitors was related strongly to this factor. (See Sherr, 1986).

7 Compare Waterson's (1984) related finding amongst private practice solicitors, noting a preference for lecture style and factual topics.

8 See Twining (1986).

9 A similar skills analysis of lawyers in private practice would undoubtedly reveal equal gaps in formal education and training provision, many of them in similar areas. Given the current concern about the public image of the legal profession, such an analysis would be very relevant. (See Faulkner and Saunders, 1985).

10 Johnston (1982) suggests that lawyers have much to learn from other professions — from the medical profession in terms of its capacity to harmonise practical and theoretical education, to locate continuing education in the universities, and to develop the certification of specialists; from the accountancy profession in the way it has evolved business structures and services which relate directly to company needs and improved managerial performance.

11 Although it should be noted that these authors also advocated more practical changes in legal practice, in suggesting that the creation of highly-standardised, mass volume work provides ' . . . more promising prospects for improved client service than attempts at jacking-up individual lawyer competence by programs of continuing legal education' (Johnstone and Hopson 1967: 543).

12 Johnstone and Hopson suggested there was a need for more concentrated continuing education, that is, more than the token evening lecture, and probably certification with greater emphasis on specialist competence, which would be publicisable for client and client referral facilities. Also that there should be broader scope than traditional legal education offered in its segments of legal doctrine, for example, investment practices of large lenders, gas and oil company production and marketing policies,

organisation and management theory for government agencies, marriage
and counselling services, crime and delinquency causes.

Similar themes emerged in the Ormrod Committee Report on Legal
Education (1971), specifically in the call to establish an Institute of
Professional Legal Studies to innovate work of an interdisciplinary nature.
There has been no progress on this and limited progress in other areas
of the reform proposals. For a recent stimulating account of the crisis in
legal education, see Blake (1987).

9 The Career of the In-house Lawyer

The rise in the significance of the in-house lawyer, both in absolute and relative terms within the legal profession, and, in individual terms, the prospect for many of substantial lifetime employment in that capacity, raise questions of career and job satisfaction prospects. How does a career as an in-house lawyer compare with that of private practice? At what points are there or might there be movements between this role and other branches of the legal profession? Does working in a company or organisational environment create opportunities for other careers? These and other questions are considered in this chapter on the basis of comments made by those who participated in the research. However, it is important at the outset to recall the point made in the introduction that it can be misleading to treat comments made as a fixed and static summary of 'reality'. The in-house lawyer career is undergoing change not only as in-house lawyers and the profession at large, individually and collectively, become more aware of the in-house lawyer's significance, but as changes take place in company structures and in the wider 'business structure' of the legal profession itself. (For example, by the time this study came to be written up, growth in the economy, and the financial services sector in particular, had already created a severe shortage of commercial lawyers, which meant rapidly improving pay and career prospects in private practice.)

Individual attitudes to work are made up of a complex of factors including not only the daily experience of work, but individual life histories and expectations, cultural influences and group indentification. The case of the in-house lawyer has its own special features in that there is the issue, of long-standing fascination amongst sociologists, of the 'professional' working inside the 'bureaucratic' or 'hierarchical' organisation.[1] As a member of an ancient profession, the in-house lawyer has a clear point of comparison to make in assessing career possibilities and work satisfaction. The professional identification of in-house lawyers is again confirmed in the clear picture all had of what working in private practice would mean to them, and how it compared with their own work inside a business organisation. Most in-house lawyers not only dealt regularly with their colleagues in private practice and other companies, but had also spent at least a short period in private practice following qualification, although a couple had gone straight into industry (one because he had always intended to do so) and a few had worked in industry and qualified while doing so. The longest period in private practice was that of a conveyancing specialist who had been a senior partner in a London firm before deciding to join the company because there 'seemed nowhere to go' in private practice.

The most common reason given by the barristers[2] interviewed for not continuing in practice at the bar was lack of money in the first two or three years. The youngest barrister had left because he had not been able to find a place in chambers and had been agreeably surprised by what he found in-house work to be like. Most of the solicitors interviewed had opted for in-house work as preferable to the 'tedium' of private practice in terms of the prospect of being stuck with small conveyancing or probate matters. A few of them had found relationships with particular partners in private practice to be rather unpleasant, and this had contributed to a decision to leave.

The level of job satisfaction amongst the lawyers interviewed seemed very high. The impression given was that they found their work varied, demanding but not stressful (see Donnell, 1970, on this point) and satisfying both in terms of work content and or personal relationships at work. Several interviewees mentioned possible disadvantages of working as an in-house lawyer but these were usually not felt personally but were explained as possible disadvantages for some people or situations.

Obviously, there are dangers in relying on self-report in assessing work satisfaction (or comparison with private practice) because of the possibility of self-justifying statements. After all, most in-house lawyers had made a clear decision to leave private practice, the sector which legal education and training tends to convey as the 'natural' goal of the law student. However, some credence is given to the findings by their occurrence across different interviewees, by the interviewer's own impressions, and by the fact that most interviewees did offer suggestions on the *disadvantages* of working as an in-house lawyer. Finally, as mentioned earlier, most of the in-house lawyers had worked in private practice whereas the converse would not normally be the case, although two of the outside lawyers interviewed had worked as in-house lawyers.

Questions on work satisfaction in the interviews were directed particularly at this last aspect of the advantages to working as an in-house lawyer compared to working in private practice. An earlier chapter outlined the advantages and disadvantages to the *companies* of the in-house lawyer. In this chapter I set out the advantages and disadvantages to *the individual*[3] of working in-house, listing the various points mentioned by interviewees. The final section of this chapter discusses the career opportunities for in-house lawyers.

ADVANTAGES OF WORKING AS AN IN-HOUSE LAWYER

The advantages listed below can be summarised as the satisfaction of working for a large organisation with more resources, a more ordered and sophisticated environment and where there is a greater sense of being part of a team. This was the overriding impression from the interviews, but various headings are listed to give a proper sense of the variety of the comments. Of course, not all of the interviewees would have affirmed all the points on the list, nor, for that matter, the list of disadvantages, nor are the lists set out in any particular order of emphasis, but the overall character of in-house lawyer satisfactions is clear.

'Seeing the project as a whole'

There are several aspects to this. Many interviewees found satisfaction in knowing the background to the legal question by reason of familiarity with the company. Also, a sense of satisfaction was achieved because of involvement in projects from their initial stages through to completion, compared to being brought in from outside to act on a particular problem that arose in the course of others' actions. One outside lawyer spoke wistfully of this advantage — 'Rather than being the cipher of a client, there's always the chance to *be* a client rather than instructed, to be part of the decision-making process. That must be attractive.' Finally, there was also the pleasure of dealing directly with those involved in the company compared to getting instructions at third hand in the case of private practice (from whoever provided the link between company problems and private practice).

'Sophisticated clients/colleagues'

Many of those interviewed enjoyed their regular contacts with other levels of management. This partly arose in a *professional* sense, that is, instructions were 'better ordered', 'more sophisticated', 'very professional'; but also it was true in a *personal* sense, namely, being in regular contact with people who were intelligent and sophisticated in their own fields or work, whether engineering, geology, pharmaceuticals, banking or general management. In both respects private practice compared unfavourably, with a more disparate group of clients, many of whom were naive in their dealings with lawyers, and with whom one had limited or unsatisfactory personal contacts. (While some of these aspects might be less true of the clients of City firm lawyers, even they tended to have more limited contacts, moving from one major transaction and client to another. Perhaps reflecting their more technical, specialist interests, several outside lawyers also expressed their liking for dealing with clients through an in-house lawyer. 'You can have sensible conversations. There's less chance of misunderstanding.' 'They tend to smooth the way, in that we're working on the same track. They'll sort it out behind the scenes with the Chairman or MD. Some of the spadework you have to do with lay clients, they can do.') Clearly most in-house lawyers enjoy the intellectual stimulation of being regularly in touch with experts in different specialisms. 'It's like having an endless stream of experts on tap, which is nice' (Pharmaceutical company lawyer).

The people who ring up for advice, you know them. They know the basics. You don't have to start from scratch. They are competent in their fields and you can get advice from them. In fact in this company they would be major experts in their field, for example, metallurgy. It's almost a privilege

to get information from them. (Manufacturing company
lawyer)

'Friendly'

Related to the above, some interviewees mentioned the more
informal atmosphere inside a company compared to their experience of private practice. People were usually on first-name terms
and there was less abrasiveness in relationships compared to
private practice where relations within a small working group
were often highly strained. 'You are working for some decent
people compared to some of the s — — in private practice' (Oil
company lawyer). Also 'clients' would drop in or telephone on
an informal basis rather than being forced to rely on the formal
appointments system so necessary in private practice work.
While this could lead to some time-management problems for
the in-house lawyer, it confirmed the relaxed atmosphere of
being part of an organisation.

'Variety'

In-house work was felt to be more varied than that of private
practice. 'I had a worry that I might be getting more specialised
coming here, but in fact it's widened my area of work. I was
surprised and pleased' (Pharmaceutical company lawyer). This
was due to the range of potential 'clients' and the diversity of
client operations, with an ensuing diversity of approaches to the
in-house lawyer, especially given the ease of access to, and
preventive role of, in-house lawyers. For the same reasons, one
interviewee referred to in-house work as more 'exciting' because
of the range of activities a large company engaged in. Also, over
time one's areas of interests did not narrow as they tended to
do in private practice but one could, in fact, build up new areas
if one felt so inclined.

It's a lot more varied. They work you harder than practice I
find. And you have a far clearer picture of your prospects. It
was a difficult decision to leave the bar. I found the work
very stretching and demanding but at the same time limited
in a sense. It's demanding in the sense that you are always
living on your nerves appearing in court. The fact that

someone is relying on you — there is no one else you can look to. That's always a big worry. But it can be quite routine, too, once you've developed the techniques. Though the facts are different, you tend to always end up saying really much the same thing, for example in a bail application. You're also limited in that the sort of work you start off with tends to continue. I got into crime, for example, and not commercial work. Here it's equally stretching but in a different way. It's the variety that's stretching. And if you express an interest in something else, it tends to come your way eventually. (Bank lawyer)

'Travel'

Only a few lawyers actually mentioned travel, suggesting it was an advantage for the younger commercial lawyers working abroad regularly, but perhaps a disadvantage as you grew older or more settled (although in that size of company one could to some extent choose eventually to shift direction into more domestic legal matters). 'Commercial is more fraught and specialised — if you like dashing round the world drawing up contracts. But not everyone does after a few years' (Manufacturing company lawyer). Also, most of the in-house lawyers travelled around the UK to company sites fairly frequently, in other words went to the client rather than waiting for the client to call. This would be less available or desirable (in economic terms) to many lawyers in private practice.

'Avoiding client hassle'

Comments on client relationships in private practice were not particularly favourable. One's time could be wasted chasing clients for fees or avoiding other clients who regularly pestered you with questions about how their case was proceeding. 'You're not pestered by clients in the same way. You have a job to do and can get on with it without petty annoyances' (Pharmaceutical company lawyer). 'In private practice you spend a lot of time keeping out of trouble. You often spend more time avoiding clients shooting at you rather than dealing with the other side. And there was no time to look up the law so one felt one would grow to know less and less law . . . one couldn't help thinking one might become a bit of a conman muddling through' (Oil company lawyer).

'Back-up support'

Being part of a large organisation meant that one had access to the resources of that organisation, so in-house lawyers felt better served in terms of secretarial back-up, technology, library and research facilities and, to some extent, time, if they wished to concentrate on major projects or specialise (although the size of department and its range of activities were important factors in this respect).

'Money, security and working conditions'

Some lawyers had left private practice when it had been expected 'that you bought your way into a partnership' and they had been unable to afford this. Similarly, financial reasons had deterred some of the barristers interviewed from remaining at the bar. So there had been a prospect of greater security in company work, and the company car and other benefits. All of the lawyers interviewed who mentioned the subject were fairly satisfied with their salary level in the company. Most felt they were at least as well off as they would have been in private practice, often better between the early and middle years,[5] although some felt they might be worse off at more senior levels. However, by the end of the period of the research, a shortage of commercial lawyers was creating a boom period for salaries and partnership prospects in private practice which would influence the balance of advantage for a younger lawyer. Of course, this in turn was likely to affect in time the salaries companies would have to offer to attract in-house lawyers, so the situation was likely to balance out.

As regards working conditions, a lawyer in a City firm made an observation which echoed some in-house lawyers' observations of working conditions in private practice, although she stressed it as unique to the City firms.

If I was to move into in-house work, it would be for one important reason — so as to not work so hard. I did say, not *so* hard. I've no doubt in-house lawyers work hard, but not so hard. We have big transactions to deal with all the time. When we finish one, there's another one waiting the next morning. An in-house lawyer will have the occasional big transaction which will involve him and the company's senior managers working flat our for several weeks, but once it's past, he goes back to a more normal routine. We have them all the time. . . . Quite a lot of commercial lawyers are choosing to move out of the City into the big, merged firms in the provinces. They don't try to provide the 24-hour service we provide.

'Working for a large company'

It was apparent that most of those interviewed enjoyed being in business as part of a large company. There was a certain satisfaction and excitement in working for a business enterprise which was providing important goods or services and which, in many cases, was a household name. 'It is exciting just to watch the business and see how it develops.'

DISADVANTAGES OF WORKING IN-HOUSE

'If you're not organisationally shaped'

A few in-house lawyers thought that it required a certain personality to adapt to in-house work. There was an ordered, organisational approach to things and you were expected to fit in, to follow certain rules. 'There is an enormous big machine working around you so you have to keep your pace to the speed of the machine' (Retail company lawyer). If you were a more individualistic, 'abrasive' type, you might find it hard to adapt. This would be a disadvantage for the organisation as much as for the individual as you would then be less 'accessible' to the client. 'There are perhaps more "political" qualities required of the in-house lawyer' (Construction industry lawyer).

In the in-house environment, you've got to be more sensitive to people's feelings. There's an enormous difference dealing with problems by letter and telephone calls as most lawyers in large firms outside must do — you assess the case and give an answer or the implications. In here, you've got to be aware of internal sensitivities, departmental rivalries, ambitious people who feel they know everything. You still have to see them on a daily basis and have to work with them for years. For that reason it won't suit many lawyers. In fact the sort of guy who'd make a good barrister would not make a good corporation lawyer. Too isolationist. (Australian media company)

'The client doesn't go away'

In private practice you could, to some extent, avoid, deter or even repel clients you did not wish to deal with. In company work, as the above quote illustrates, you were stuck with them (namely, the managers inside the 'client'). However, it was not so much this aspect of client relations which some in-house lawyers saw as a problem as the fact that if you, the lawyer, made a mistake, then everyone else in the company knew about it. In private practice the dissatisfied client usually disappeared and you could forget the mess you might have made of the problem.

'Interruptions'

Being accessible or having an open-door policy had its problems. Managers would drop in to see you or telephone if they had a problem, sometimes often without notice. It was felt not to be good practice in a company setting to be seen to turn people away because it was inconvenient for you. You were there to provide a service and so should be available. Nevertheless, it could at times interfere with major projects you might wish to work on.

'Jack of all Trades'

The variety of the work also had its down side. You could end up needing to know a bit about everything compared to the pleasure of specialising in a few areas available in the larger outside firms. That work might be more intellectually satisfying. In-house work could at times be, as one Australian private practice lawyer remarked disparagingly, 'kerbside stuff'.

'Less freedom in the long run'

This partly relates back to the question of being 'organisation-ally shaped'. Working inside a company you not only had to work to certain rules, you were geared to the pace of the company machine and indeed were surrounded by company decisions on such matters as allowable time-off and on more minor matters such as letter-heading, furniture, office decor. In private practice you eventually gained some control over all of these. More seriously, although infrequent, you were ultimately at the whim of the company as to whether you continued to be employed. 'After all, when a company needs to cut back, services are often the first thing to go' (Manufacturing company lawyer). At least once you had achieved partner status, you had to be bought out. (I only came across one example of a company which had terminated lawyers' employment, although a few had reduced numbers by natural wastage during the recession.)

> I would find it difficult to advise a young man which route to take in the profession. Company work is certainly much more exciting. You're part of the management team in the real world. And you get trips to the USA, Europe, etc. But in private practice there's more freedom eventually. You can arrange your own furniture, choose the paint for the walls, how you're going to look on the letterheads and so on. You can't do that here. It's all laid down as a standard company letterhead or furniture or whatever. Also in private practice you don't keep the set hours and week that we have to keep here. You can go off for the day or work the weekend and take time off during the week. (Manufacturing company lawyer)

'Income not so dependent on effort'

Inside a company you had a fixed salary (plus any general company bonus/share option systems) which rose in line with other staff's earnings. In some companies, you were also tied to a company job grading system. Your income was, therefore, determined for you regardless of the effort you put into your work, whereas effort in private practice was more clearly linked to rewards. You also become more involved with the company's symbols of reward and recognition. 'The company grades everyone and according to that grade you receive certain benefits — higher quality make of car, access to the Executive Dining Room and so on. These things become rather important in the personal politics of work inside a company' (Construction company lawyer).

'More open to challenge'

One lawyer pointed out that younger entrants to in-house work were sometimes taken aback by the fact that they had less status *vis-à-vis* the client than experienced by lawyers in private practice. Your clients were more sophisticated and knew you fairly well so were more ready to challenge your advice or question your legal reasoning. Many in-house lawyers, he said, find this aspect stimulating but some lawyers found it upsetting that they had to earn others' confidence in this way.

> You have to warn whenever you're interviewing young solicitors. They start off really having to earn the confidence of others. Whether you're a solicitor or barrister is nothing compared to you as a person. You're more open to challenge. It's not a bad thing. Whereas when someone's paying money, they treat the private practitioner generally as more inviolate. Also you are dealing with brighter people, people who are more searching in their inquiries — doctors or engineers. It tends to come as a bit of a shock to find that nothing's accepted and you're being questioned on every bit of it and even though you think these are lawyers' aspects. It's fair enough because it works the other way on commercial points. (Pharmaceutical company lawyer)

'Career progression lacking'

In private practice there is a clear aim in mind, of obtaining a partnership with all the advantages that carries, financial or otherwise (or, less clearly in the case of the Bar, Queen's Counsel or judicial rank). The career path in in-house work is not so evident. This aspect clearly deterred the outside lawyers interviewed from considering in-house work. 'What happens to an old in-house lawyer? I've never met any.' (In the interview it later emerged that two senior partners had left this City firm recently for company positions.) Being a lawyer for them implied the supreme goal of achieving a partnership, a share in the business. In-house work seemed to suggest therefore a career 'dead-end', an aspect which also worried one or two of the younger in-house lawyers interviewed who saw little hope of progression within a small legal department. Aiming to be head of a large legal department or moving into management were therefore the only apparent routes to fulfil similar ambitions. (There is a further discussion of this below.)

COMPARING ADVANTAGES AND DISADVANTAGES

None of the lawyers felt that one could confidently tell a young lawyer that one side of the work, in-house or private practice, was to be preferred. It would depend on personality and interests as to which would be the more suitable route. In addition, chance factors played a part in any career so that there were also questions such as which company or law firm you happened to go into, which would determine work satisfaction and career development. Overall, however, it was clear from the interviews that in-house work could be highly rewarding (in both senses of the word) so that it merited at least equal consideration from someone considering a legal career.

CAREER PATHS FOR IN-HOUSE LAWYERS

Nearly all lawyers interviewed felt happy with their current position and did not anticipate any move in the short term. Some thought that there probably would come a time when they might feel restless but did not have any current inclination in that respect. They accepted that there was no obvious career development except to become a Head of Department or work for a different company, but most said it was not an area to which they had given a great deal of thought[6]. Two of the interviewees were considering whether to try to move across to general management; one felt he probably would not; the other was fairly certain of a move to a senior management position.

Although the interviews did not elicit much detailed comment on career progression, it might still be useful to complete the picture by setting out some of the possibilities that may be open to in-house lawyers. The increasing consciousness of in-house lawyers of themselves as a distinct professional branch is likely to lead to more consideration being given to this issue in the future.

Return to private practice

It seemed easier to move in-house from private practice than to move in the opposite direciton. This was mainly due to the fact that normally one could only expect to move into private practice at a basic solicitor level without remuneration reflecting one's experience as a company appointment might. One could not even expect to bring one's clients into the practice as one might when moving from one private practice to another. The only circumstances, therefore, where a move into private practice could be contemplated might be in cases where one had good personal contacts; where a large firm wanted a company specialist in a particular area; or possibly, if one had been made redundant by the company. However, only one 'younger' in-house lawyer expressed interest in such a move (as a later stage in career development) and she had only recently entered in-house work from private practice. Another young in-house lawyer moved into a newly-established private practice on being given an attractive offer (by a friend who had established it) to join and exercise his commercial conveyancing expertise.

'Locals' and 'cosmopolitans'

Literature on organisational specialists categorises them broadly into two types, those who tend to identify with a single company ('locals') and those who have their eye on moving across a range of companies ('cosmopolitans') (Gouldner, 1957). One might expect that lawyers could be a particularly mobile group because they provide a professional service rather than one linked to an industrial specialism. However, in the sample studied, most of the lawyers felt closely attached to their company and had no immediate plans to move. Several had worked for other companies although they had moved mainly for negative reasons (for example, dislike of autocratic management style; salaries blockage) rather than for career development.

Such stability would seem appropriate to a role where there is recognition that some of the advantages of the role are linked to questions of familiarity with the company. However, whether this career stability was linked to basic job satisfaction, lawyer conservatism (they had already taken a major step in moving to in-house work), or lack of career opportunities, is difficult to unravel. The author's impression was that the first two factors were most significant.

Career opportunities within a company were similar to those obtainable by transfers to other companies, namely becoming Head of Department or Company Secretary, or moving into more specialist areas or into international work. There was an impression that younger lawyers would be more inclined to greater mobility, and it may also be that mobility will become more prevalent as in-house work becomes increasingly seen as an important and separate legal career, or as younger lawyers become more influenced by greater integration with the management function (see below).

'Super locals'

Most in-house lawyers knew of cases of other in-house lawyers who had progressed in their company by moving into non-legal managerial positions — Personnel, Contract Negotiators, Chief Executives, and so forth. This was said to occur when managerial talent had been spotted and more frequently the jobs had been offered to those individuals rather than their applying for them. Companies with more sophisticated management appraisal and development systems and which recognise lawyers as part of the management team (and therefore can more easily assess their performance in commercial situations) are perhaps more likely to offer this career opportunity. A number of those interviewed felt that legal background provided a very good training for a potential manager. 'Because they can see through to the essential questions, they can step outside the superfluous parts and make a decision on the important points. That's what they're trained for' (Manufacturing company lawyer). Also the contact with senior management was a help. The same senior lawyer went on to say:

The great advantage of being in industry is that you are in

close contact with senior management from an early age, in your twenties as a lawyer. You're watching senior management from that time and how they behave and operate. By the age of 40 you have a lot of business experience behind you. Compare the engineer who may come in from the field at the age of 45 before he gets his feet under a desk for the first time. He's lost and he's not sure how to tackle things but the solicitor is already there with 20 years' experience behind him.

Again, however, few in-house lawyers expressed much interest in this route. Of those that did, it was more of a 'wait-and-see how things develop' attitude rather than an anticipated and worked-for career option. In contrast, another small group felt in any case that lawyers were not particularly qualified for management positions. One of the lawyers who expressed interest in management work felt that it was best to be a law graduate with a postgraduate business qualification rather than a professional lawyer. In the latter case, one identified more strongly with the profession and felt one might be risking too much in crossing over to management with its greater demands for 'making one's 10 per cent every year'. This outlook perhaps neatly sums up the stability alongside conservatism in the career attitudes of in-house lawyers. Compare the following career outlook of a younger Australian lawyer who had been offered an in-house post after being spotted by the company executive in his capacity as a litigation solicitor:

I wrestled with it very hard but I think it was the best thing I ever did. For example, I've had a recent visit to Hong Kong to get us out of a TV company we're in which was a disaster. It's whetted my appetite for the business side. I see myself less and less going back to being governed by time sheets. If I wanted to stay in law I think I should be in a large firm in private practice after a few years in the corporation. . . . I wouldn't want to be an in-house lawyer for 40 years. It's mainly a young profession, though having said that General Counsel of a very big company could be very exciting. I suppose as law departments develop there will be more scope to skip jobs and get a bigger role. [At the end of the interview he announced that he was likely to be offered a senior management position in his present company which he intended to take up.]

FUTURE CAREER PATTERNS IN IN-HOUSE LEGAL WORK

The future of in-house legal work is likely to be affected by a number of trends, although it is a matter of speculation as to what the overall effect of such movements may be. First of all, there is the question of developments in the profession in general. The increasing competition in private practice may drive more lawyers into considering a shift to in-house legal work, thereby strengthening yet further the awareness of in-house legal work and its significant numbers in professional debates. At the same time, the likely strengthening of the larger commercial law firms, and the shortages of commercial lawyers, may provide a better economic base and incentive for commercial firms to attract experienced in-house lawyers in order to bring greater commercial background to their practices. In addition, there is the likelihood that the 'private practice' and 'in-house' distinction itself may become blurred if, as seems likely, solicitors (and possibly barristers) move into mixed-profession partnerships or into businesses providing, amongst other services, legal services (such as conveyancing). The legal profession in these respects is at a critical period in its history, an issue which is examined more closely in chapter 13.

As regards developments within industry, the position is likely again to move in-house lawyers into more 'dynamic' career paths. Most companies seem to be responding to a more 'entrepreneurial' culture, and expecting more innovative and more integrated service from their specialists. This is likely to bring in-house lawyers even more closely into commercial decision-making, circumstances which in turn would seem inevitably to stimulate greater career flexibility for in-house lawyers both within and across companies. At the same time companies will be faced with needing to identify more carefully the career paths and incentives they can offer to their specialists, particularly where such specialists are in short supply.

There is therefore a convergence between in-house and private practice developments which point again towards a more 'integrated' lawyer, integrated both as between lawyer and client, and in the career options within the 'business' branches of the legal profession. The paradox of this for the lawyers involved is that they are therefore even more likely to be confronted with career diversity and possible moves outside law into management positions either within a company or within a 'law and financial services' business. There was already some evidence of this, more so in Australia with its aspirations to United States business practices, in comments by in-house lawyers on the usefulness of advancing their qualifications at any stage of training, whether towards joint Law and Commerce degrees, MBAs or expertise in foreign languages. Developments towards flexible life career patterns are therefore likely to affect the world of the in-house lawyer just as they are affecting other occupations in society.

NOTES

1 For a recent survey of the field, see Dingwall and Lewis (1983), and chapters 12 and 13 below.
2 The issue of earlier choice of career direction (that is, barrister versus solicitor) for intending in-house lawyers is also relevant to career path in terms, for example, of the range of industries one is likely to obtain access to, given the preference for solicitors in certain spheres (see chapter 4). The AGCAS (1984) survey concluded that qualifying as a solicitor is likely to offer a quicker and more certain route into in-house work. Current debates on fusion of the profession or a common professional training may of course also affect the issue.
3 Note, however, the important relationships between the two lists. For example, 'familiarity' suggests better legal advice but also provides for the individual a greater sense of involvement with the client.
4 Compare the comment of an IBM in-house lawyer: 'It's like having a series of private tutors for fifteen to twenty minute periods throughout the day' (Townsend, 1970: 50).
5 An academic lawyer who had spent six months on secondment to a company legal department said she had expected to find a trade-off between income and security for in-house lawyers, compared to the possibly higher rewards but insecurity of private practice. However, she left thinking that in-house lawyers had perhaps the best of both worlds with high incomes and security, at least for the first major period of their working lives.
6 The AGCAS survey (op. cit.: 14) noted the lack of response to a question

as to how the careers of new entrants might develop. Also that no one referred to a move back to private practice as a goal.

Part II
The Law Business

10 Business Regulation and Business Ethics

A frequent issue which arises in discussions about the position of the in-house lawyer is the question of 'ethics', although there are two different expressions of this interest. First, there is the interest *within* the legal profession in the concept of the 'independence' of the lawyer. The attitude of outside lawyers to in-house legal work is quite important in this respect, and chapter 12 devotes some attention to this aspect of professional ethics. There is also a second area which is related to, but not identical with, the first.[1] That concerns the role of a legal professional within a business organisation in terms of the debate about government regulation[2] of business and of business 'morality'. How do in-house lawyers perceive the value of such regulation? Do they have an additional ethical role inside the modern corporation by reason of their training in the law? The first half of this chapter provides a brief introduction to the concepts of business regulation and business ethics. The second part relates these to the perceptions by in-house lawyers of their companies' standards of conduct, and their views on the role of the in-house lawyer in relation to these standards, and concludes with a redefinition of the in-house lawyer's role.

Where governments intervene to control business activities or to use corporations to fulfill wider social purposes the concept of 'behaviour within the law' may become critical (in terms of costs and/or public relations) for the success of companies affected. As we have seen, this background has been said to explain much of the rise in numbers of in-house lawyers. The 'technical' role of in-house lawyers in helping companies 'translate' law into organisational behaviour or in responding to, or preventing, regulatory controls has already been discussed. But what are the wider implications of this day-to-day work for concepts of regulation and public policy measures? How did in-house lawyers view government regulatory controls on business? How did they see their own role inside companies in relation to business 'morality' or 'business ethics'? And what links did these

169

attitudes have to their professional values? The implications of these questions have some importance for social policies in the business field and for understanding the ethics of the legal profession. Much discussion of regulation and business ethics is of a highly theoretical nature. An analysis, therefore, of an occupation which has a central role in company standards of conduct, should provide an important empirical contribution to the debate as well as further evidence to elucidate the nature of this branch of the legal profession.

THE RISE AND FALL OF REGULATION?

There is little disagreement in society about the fact that major companies, private or public, are important constituents of public life. However, there is considerable disagreement (particularly from free market economists) about the need for, or value of, government intervention in the workings of the business sector,[3] a disagreement which came to a head in the early 1980s with the election of governments in the UK and US committed to 'deregulation'. Prior to that the post-war period, and in particular the 1960s and 1970s, had seen an extensive development of attempts to regulate by law the conduct of industrial and commercial organisations, partly in terms of *economic regulation* concerned with the health of an industry or industries (competition and pricing policies, licensing requirements to enter the industry and so on), but more publicly in terms of *protective regulation* concerned with the social impact of business both externally in fields such as consumer and environmental protection, and internally, in the areas of health and safety, job security, employee involvement, sex and race discrimination.

The political tensions in this debate are mirrored in those experienced at the level of regulatory agencies, caught between the conflicting demands of 'social activist' critics for stronger 'policing' emphases, and the 'business' public emphasis on non-interference with the economic 'basics' (Hawkins and Thomas, 1984). This bipolar model should not, however, obscure the fact that business itself sometimes seeks regulation and regulation enforcement for reasons of self-protection or to avoid competitor undercutting on 'unfair' grounds, nor the fact that the form, substance and procedural characteristics of regulation in any particular sphere are the outcome of a complex matrix of interest groups and political processes (Wilson, 1980). However, the triumph of the deregulation movement in the 1980s reflects the political stances in the broader debate and the influence of an increasingly sophisticated political leadership within the business community created by the pressure of the regulatory and economic difficulties faced by business in the 1960s and 1970s (Useem, 1984). As was seen in chapter 5, in-house lawyers play a significant, if limited, role on behalf of business in the prevention and refinement of regulatory controls on business.

It is worth making an initial observation that a majority of in-house lawyers interviewed did not see a significant change in the amount of regulation under the 'new-style' government, a view supported in some management surveys over the period.[4]

I don't see any possibility of regulatory growth declining: rather of it expanding. . . . Because of the general desire to regulate everything. If there's a scandal, the government has to be seen to be doing something. (Manufacturing company lawyer)

Deregulation is a myth. It's a political joke. Deregulation will start to come when we start to dismantle public servant numbers. (Australian oil company lawyer)

It is, of course, possible to point to areas where the UK government has deregulated, as in the field of employee rights — for example, quadrupling the period of employment service necessary for an employee to claim unfair dismissal (from six months in 1979 to two years by 1986). However, support for the above comments can be derived even from an examination of the employment sphere, where European policies or government policies inconsistent with deregulation have led to increased regulation (as in the fields of sex discrimination and equal pay, largely EEC-driven; or the transfer of responsibility for payment of employee sickness benefit and maternity allowance from government to employers in an effort to cut back on public expenditure). Other in-house lawyers, however, did detect a difference in the extent of regulation, or at least, in acknowledging that regulation had not been reversed, did suggest that the pace of regulatory growth had slowed down or that there was a 'psychological' shift because of a new government emphasis on 'wealth-creation'.

Certainly, the UK government had begun by 1986 to sift legislation systematically in an effort to repeal 'unnecessary' restrictions on business.[5] On the other hand, the issue of regulation of the financial services sector, an issue not so far advanced at the time of the interviews, seems likely to emerge as the major focus of government concern in the late 1980s following the 'Big Bang' (ending of restrictive practices in Stock Market dealings) with the 'scandal-to-control' sequence perhaps again a likely postscript to events.[6]

Nor should this brief introduction to the topic ignore the fact that dissatisfaction with regulation has not been solely the province of conservative governments. Concern with the efficiency and effectiveness of regulation as a method of influencing business practices has also influenced other political parties. Labour governments in Australia and New Zealand, for example, had also chosen by the 1980s to embark on a process of legislative deregulation in significant areas, although more in the field of economic regulation than in that of protective regulation[7] — with the adoption, for example, of systems to monitor the costs and benefits or regulatory proposals, and 'sunsetting' provisions on subordinate legislation, whereby the legislation expires at the end of, for instance, ten years, unless renewed by Parliament. (And even trends in Eastern Europe in this era have indicated movement towards ending some constraints on business enterprise.) This tends to suggest that the 'deregulation movement' is perhaps less a belief system than an era of return to a pragmatic concern for efficiency and effectiveness after an era which devoted more attention to *ends* than to appropriate *means* of control of business conduct. The experience of regulatory controls has in many spheres been as disillusioning for social radicals as for free market theorists. However, the tensions in the intimate relationships between business activities and the community make it unlikely that one can anticipate the 'withering away' of regulation any more than one could predict an end to 'politics'. It seems safer to predict that future governments will be characterised by *selective* regulatory concerns and a concern with *optimising* the efficiency and effectiveness of particular forms of regulation ('re-regulation') according to their particular belief systems, rather than by a belief in deregulation or regulation as such (albeit the terms will continue to carry symbolic political weight). In this debate, there is considerable room for argument around the technicalities of regulatory controls, for example, around the appropriate degrees of 'mix' of self-regulation and statutory control (as in the case of the Financial Services Act 1986 which establishes a system of quasi-regulation of investment advisers). Such a trend, incidentally, is likely to enhance the role of lawyers.

As well as appreciating the complexities of government practice underlying the political symbolism of deregulation, it is also important to recognise the cultural dimensions to this issue, and the possibility of future intermingling of distinct national approaches to business regulation. This latter effect can be predicted from the trends towards global markets and the internationalisation of business operations (reflected in my research in legal departments of a number of companies which had regular 'review meetings' on international developments usually on a Europe-wide basis). The outcome is likely to be one of business pressures for 'equitable' regulatory standards across markets between business competitors, that is, the growth of international legal regulation (or deregulation). Britain's membership of the European Economic Community, for example, has been a significant factor in the degree to which the pace of business regulation in the UK has continued despite an allegedly deregulatory domestic government. However, several lawyers commented that they felt the EEC reflected more of an 'anti-industry' view than did the current UK government. This was reflected in the increasing number of regulations being imposed on industry, the costs of which these lawyers felt exceeded the benefits to the consumer. (Correspondent with this view, these same lawyers commented on the EEC tendency to see in-house lawyers as being in conspiracy with their employers to evade legal regulation, a tendencey exemplified in the decision of the European Court in the *A.M. & S* case (see chapter 13), reducing the claim of in-house lawyers to professional privilege for their advice to employers in issues where European law is relevant.)

A second important cultural factor lies in the difference between UK and US approaches to regulation, despite a current emphasis by both on deregulation. It has often been noted that British regulation is based on an assumption that companies

largely seek to comply with regulation, US regulation on the
opposite assumption, reflecting a more individualistic, material-
istic culture where companies are seen as more likely to 'offend'
(legally and morally) without regulatory constraints.[8] Indeed,
there is a considerable US literature on 'regulation' and its
effectiveness or lack of it, a literature which does not really have
a strong counterpart in the UK,[9] with such issues raised, for
example, as the problem of 'regulatory agency capture' (the
tendency for industry to take over any external agencies set up
to control it in the public interest). UK emphases, although
echoing American literature in vague complaints of 'too much
government intervention', have more often been linked to specific issues of employment legislation, or of debates around
privatisation as an effective form of deregulation.[10] Again,
however, there is some impressionistic evidence that British
business may be picking up some American themes[11] (including
a tendency for greater resort to litigation in business disputes)
because of a more competitive market situation and the
increasing links between the two countries' business structures
and personnel.

Such differences in cultural background have led to more
attention in the US on the role of lawyers in business regulation
(or rather their lack of a role) including that of in-house lawyers
(for example Smyser, 1976; Westin, 1981), although usually as
part of a more general critique of the decline in the traditional,
independent small-town lawyer. In the earlier part of the
century, US objections centred on the development of 'corporation lawyers' (see Levy, 1961). This referred not only to in-
house lawyers, but to an increasing trend for all lawyers to act
on behalf of 'Big Business'.

> Specialised service to business and finance has made the
> learned profession of an earlier day the obsequious servant of
> business, and has tainted it with the morals and manners of
> the market place in its most antisocial manifestations. (Chief
> Justice Stone, quoted in Swaine, 1949)

Later concern shifted to the new business forms of corporation
practice, the shift towards organisation into 'law factories', law
firms with massive numbers of staff, devoted to the service of
business interests (see Smigel, 1969) rather than to their control,

and beyond that into 'mega-law' practice matching the gigantic form of business enterprise (Galanter, 1983).

Disillusionment with the ability of external agencies and traditional legal frameworks to control business activities effectively has led some critics to offer alternatives of regulation based around greater 'in-house' accountability, whether through changing the rules on the liability of company directors, or ensuring greater 'exposure' of internal operations by means of information disclosure provisions, legal audits, non-executive directors, supervisory boards or special shareholder protection audit committees.[12] The in-house lawyer has been picked out in some of these debates as a potential candidate (Stone, 1975:45–6; Smyser, 1976), alongside others such as Company Secretaries, to conduct 'legal audits' of their company's operations or to disclose information to shareholders.[13] The likely reactions of in-house lawyers to such proposals can be gauged from the views outlined in the second half of this chapter. First, however, it is necessary to explore further some of the conceptions of business behaviour which underlie the drive for regulation.

BUSINESS MORALITIES

The historical, cultural and political complexities surrounding concepts of regulation reflect some of the difficulties of analysing the 'morality' of business behaviour. There is, for example, no commonly accepted definition of business ethics, nor could one expect one to emerge easily given the major social changes which surround, and are created by, business activities. The problem is confounded by the absence of helpful models of company *misconduct* or non-compliance. Criminologists have generally assigned corporate wrong-doing unhelpfully to the field of 'white-collar crime', where 'corporate' or 'economic' crime (a concept itself covering a range of types of misconduct) merges with other, more personal, types of unlawful acts and actors.[14] It is at any rate arguable that it is unhelpful to regard traditional criminology as an appropriate discipline with which to analyse corporate wrong-doing in respect of regulatory concerns, a more appropriate form of analysis being that of *political economy*, that is, analysis of the nature and actions of social groups in establishing social control within a society (Jones, 1979; and see Snider, 1987). But that does not take one much further than reinventing the notion of a political system. On the other hand, organisation theorists have usually eschewed questions of values or morality in favour of more value-free 'functionalist' analyses which concentrate on describing internal processes rather than on evaluating them or studying organisational interactions with the environment (Pfeffer and Salancik, 1978).

Nevertheless, there are some models to consider that relate to these issues and provide assistance as background to in-house lawyer views. Kagan and Scholz (1984) suggest that there are three different popular 'images' of corporate non-compliance which serve to guide differing political emphases to regulatory policies on the control of companies. In the first image business firms are pictured as *'amoral calculators'* who deliberately flout the law where they see appropriate benefits by way of profits and who comply only where costs exceed likely profits. A second image pictures the business firm as a *'political citizen'*, ordinarily inclined to comply with law, in part because of a belief in the rule of law, in part as a matter of long-term self-interest. However, such obedience is contingent on laws being perceived as neither arbitrary nor unreasonable; where they are perceived as such, firms are likely to retaliate in some manner. In the third image the business organisation is seen as law-abiding but is *'organisationally incompetent'* — managers fail to monitor employees adequately or fail themselves to keep abreast of legal changes.

Beaumont (1983), in the more specific setting of an examination of the introduction of health and safety committees under the relevant regulations, finds also three types of response to regulation. The *'leaders'* are those companies whose practices provided the model on which the legislative rules are based,[15] the *'fast-movers'* those who act quickly to comply with any new regulations, while the *'slow-movers'* bring up the rear and have to be prodded into action by regulatory agencies. One should add, perhaps, a fourth category recognised by regulatory agencies under various titles such as 'bad eggs', 'bad apples' or 'cowboy firms' — those companies which will quite deliberately flout legal control so long as they think they can get away with it. Regulatory concerns would derive from the latter when compared to the 'leaders', then require action from the others — the 'scandal-to-control' sequence.

It is difficult to find helpful models from organisation theory for the reasons mentioned earlier, the avoidance of questions of values or of environmental variables, and the exclusive attention to internal factors in organisational behaviour. (For critiques of this approach, see Pfeffer and Salancik, op. cit.; Hall and Quinn, 1983). In management literature (apart from political objections to regulatory control) discussion of company wrong-doing tends to be set in terms of the debate on corporate 'social responsibility'. Lee Preston (1980) has suggested three managerial views of the corporate social role. The first management view centres around *economic individualism*, the belief that the pursuit of individual economic self-interest is sufficient to ensure social welfare. A second view perceives law-compliance as necessary in the long-term interests of business, a view that business must be successfully *integrated* with its society and its values in order to survive. Finally, Preston suggests a more active role for business, *social performance as management practice*. In this view business in complex modern social systems is required to institutionalise a management leadership role in social responsibility that goes beyond a merely passive response to external legal pressures.

The significance of these differing models of business morality lies particularly in the fact that they share a recognition of the diversity of business types and the complex motives and outcomes of control processes. The impetus creating regulation is, as in-house lawyers noted, derived particularly from political pressures arising around the groups which are most likely to offend (the 'scandal' sources), the very groups which are also unlikely to be controlled by systems of self-regulation. Because of the difficulties inherent in trying to devise and implement 'offender' controls, the regulatory controls which are eventually generated out of political processes are likely, in a number of respects, to demand *new* actions and different types of procedure from those currently maintained by the original non-offenders. Thus, all are drawn into a regulatory response. For example, although in-house lawyers often claimed that their companies had not resorted to 'unfair' dismissals before the legislation on the topic in 1971, few of them could say their companies were unaffected by the legislation. They, too, had remodelled their procedures to meet standards which quickly took on a life of their own in tribunal practice.

'Optimal' regulatory solutions are therefore extremely difficult to achieve against this background of business and political community diversity, quite apart from the 'technical' questions raised within any regulation enforcement system. Undoubtedly this is a major factor in the degree of discretion normally afforded to regulatory agencies, and in the well-established tendency for regulatory officials to move towards 'education and persuasion' as preferred strategies for influencing the regulated (Kagan, 1984). They are, after all, dealing with a community the majority of which seeks to be law-abiding, although they may have fought the birth of the regulation. This background also lends weight to a system for introducing regulation which relies heavily on prior consultation and negotiation with the regulated in the manner of collective bargaining in industrial relations (Dunlop, 1976), although such systems assume a degree of consensus which may not always be present in a political community.

IN-HOUSE LAWYER PERCEPTIONS

There was little doubt amongst the in-house lawyers interviewed of where their companies stood in respect of corporate wrong-doing. They clearly saw their employers as law-abiding in intent, often more than law-abiding in their approach to business activities ('social performance as management practice'), and more likely to be among the 'leaders' of legislative standards. Non-compliance with regulation of any kind was attributed to failures of control or communication, usually at lower levels of management, or possibly to misinterpretation of regulations (that is, 'organisationally incompetent' in Kagan and Scholz's terms, although at the same time 'political citizens' in intent). In making this point, they also recognised that the political environment and the public did not always take the same view.

> We're here because the organisation perceives the need to keep itself straight. We are the law officers of the organisation. No self-respecting company would admit to being [anything] else but ethical. . . . No, I don't know of any particular

instances of unethical conduct [by lawyers]. (Manufacturing company lawyer)

They [critics in private practice and in the EEC] seem to think we are in danger of being corrupted by links to private companies. That's a load of rubbish. It's based on the assumption that company directors are somehow less moral than solicitors. It's just not the case. It's the reverse if anything. (Manufacturing company lawyer)

Frankly it's offensive to most businessmen to be told their lawyers are the keepers of the company conscience. They are equally concerned. (Consumer products company lawyer)

However, while in-house lawyers regarded the *company* (that is, directors) as law-abiding in intent, they did experience more problems with lower levels of management. These problems reflected a tendency among managers to work by expedience, for short-term objectives linked to other organisational goals, rather than any desire to confront the law or company policy. Therefore there were rarely occasions where lawyers felt any need to take the matter higher in the organisation. Recognition of this background contributed to the in-house lawyer's anxiety to be 'positive', to send someone away with a solution rather than block their commercial objective. Other aspects of this approach came out in relation to the stress on being 'accessible' and sympathetic. They avoided for the most part any suggestion that the in-house lawyer had any 'policing' function over management on behalf of the Board or senior management — 'Otherwise people would stop talking to you'. (This did not, however, preclude acceptance of a 'silent footpad' role — see chapter 5.)

We shouldn't act as policemen. I had an up-and-downer with the Chairman over one incident. 'You're my eyes and ears' he said. I told him I'm not going behind the Managing Director's back. It's not my job to report any manager if he comes to me for advice. So what I do in these cases if they come to me is say — 'Have you told your boss about this?' I would usually go through the problem with them and then go along with him to see his boss and say what the problem

is, what happened and how, if it could or should be put right.
You provide the solution, not a problem, for them. You have
a loyal friend in the company then. (Manufacturing company
lawyer)

[Do you check if they follow your advice?] It's not my duty
to go and hound them. Unless it was vital, if we would be
liable for prosecution, perhaps I'd chase them up. A different
lawyer might take a different approach. Some are very
'touchy' about their advice. But you have to be careful about
it or people won't ask you questions if you come down on
them. (Manufacturing company)

In most cases they follow your advice. If they don't they
don't, that's all. (Oil company lawyer)

Am I a lawyer working for the company or a law enforcement
agency? With a private client, after all, there is no need to
drop the client if you know of an unethical practice. You just
don't become embroiled in that specific issue. (Retail
company lawyer)

Compare the above views with the statement of the managing
director of a medium-sized engineering company which had no
in-house lawyer department but used lawyers in City firms:

Yes I know plenty of cases of moral people in high walks of
life doing things to defend their company in the marketplace,
even if they're to be found guilty. The lawyers don't like it
much. They pretend they didn't hear you. But they will help
you up to the point of illegality. Especially in tax law with
all its international connections. There are all sorts of devices
they use.

Despite the reluctance to go over someone's head, most
lawyers nevertheless valued the formal access to the Board
normally available to legal departments as a protection against
major conflict in a particular case. Another factor which made
such a remedy a rare occurrence, however, was the problematic
nature of legal judgements (see chapter 6). It was often in the
nature of a legal opinion that it provided only an assessment of

risk rather than a definite warning of illegality. Therefore, it was open to managers to take a different view of the risk equation on commercial grounds, as they could with an opinion from a lawyer in private practice.

> It's not the job of a senior manager to accept our advice that we are on a loser any more than he should accept the advice of any other technician. If he wants something and the technical report says it's impossible, he rightly would subject him to pressure to get round it so it's not impossible. I'm not suggesting there's any improper pressure, unlawful use of accomodation vehicles on the North Sea or anything like that. But cases where we advise we are on a loser, we expect to be put to the test. These people can be quite sophisticated, contract negotiators say. It arises quite frequently. They put their own views and interpretations to us — 'doesn't that make a nonsense of it commercially?' or 'that doesn't reflect the intention of the parties'. (Oil company lawyer)

In-house lawyers were also aware that companies resisted regulations which they regarded as unnecessary or which interfered in major ways with their commercial interests as against competitors, but such resistance took the form of arguing over interpretation of regulations, fighting a point in court, or lobbying for changes in legislation, rather than deliberate defiance of law.

> There are not many cases where we are in breach as we usually know about the regulations in advance. There is one practice where we know we are vulnerable . . . [because of a recent decision on trading standards with respect to double-wall glass jars]. But it makes commercial sense and when we looked at it, we decided it was within European standards. So we would fight it if we were prosecuted. (Consumer products company lawyer)

Thus there were, as far as this sample of in-house lawyers were concerned, few practical ethical issues for them to face, so much as questions of the exercise of political judgement and influence inside the company in order to steer it along a path

of least damage. A similar position was found in Australia,
although one in-house lawyer there added a further element:

> Corporate ethics is a big issue with our companies here
> because most of them have an overseas base, so they are very
> sensitive to criticism because of their public image in this
> country. (Consumer products lawyer)

The absence of any major issues of *professional* ethical
concerns, however, was again apparent, and evident from other
sources. A survey of Australian lawyers found that amongst
the various legal groups surveyed (country, suburban and city
practices), corporation lawyers were the least likely to have
consulted a professional association over ethical concerns or to
have observed breaches of ethics by other lawyers (Tomasic and
Bullard, 1978). These findings also confirm American evidence
that the greatest pressures to break ethical standards tend to be
on lawyers with 'low-status' practices and clients (Carlin, 1962).
Compare this observation with the following statement from a
lawyer working as secretary of an in-house lawyers' professional
association:

> I have not come across any cases where there has been a
> conflict between an in-house lawyer and his client over the
> legality of an action. If it happens at all, I'd say it's in the
> small company — the succesful builder, say, who says 'I must
> get myself a lawyer'.

While finding ethical concerns to be of little practical importance in in-house legal work, the 'political' element described
was, however, clearly a powerful factor, evident in the manner
in which in-house lawyers resisted strongly any notion that their
role should be to act as internal 'policemen' or as the 'conscience'
of the company. There is likely to be at times, one suspects, a
fine line in the relationship between 'advising' and presenting
oneself as a conscience of the company. Inevitably, in their
technical role lawyers would be involved frequently in the translation and application of legal standards inside their organisations. Thus, many acknowledged the need to avoid being seen
as 'no' advisers, thus implying that there were many areas where
a particular interpretation of the law could impinge on company

actions. However, it should be stressed that this was seen most frequently not so much in relation to legislation as in the proper formulation of protective devices in commercial contracts, an area where company sales staff, in the desire to clinch sales, were prone to act with some *risk to the company's future liability under the agreement* rather than risk to the *legality* of the company's actions under regulatory controls.

REDEFINING THE IN-HOUSE LAWYER ROLE?

It is tempting to conclude from the evidence of my research that the question of the in-house lawyer as the conscience of the company is a non-issue. Most of the lawyers I interviewed seemed to find this question a rather unreal one, other than in a literal sense that they advised on the terms of the law. All[16] of them felt their companies were law-abiding in intent and in many cases would do more than the law recommended if it was company policy to do so (as it often was, particularly where employee or customer relations were prominent in the matter). Thus, one company had paid for double glazing for all the houses in the vicinity of one of its transport depots in the interests of ensuring that its lorries could unload one hour earlier in the morning. The representative of the small employers' association echoed these sentiments:

'Deemed-to-satisfy' requirements. That's all they're interested in. They just want to push out the goods with the least trouble. And they'll do even more than the law requires — if they're told by the local Department of Employment that such-and-such is the law but we'd recommend X, Y and Z, they're prepared to do X, Y, and Z in order to satisfy local people and local conditions.

Several lawyers also felt that their companies were, if anything, too 'delicate' with the law.

The directors are far more fearful of the law than solicitors. The're like a load of old women actually when it comes to the law. (Manufacturing company lawyer)

> There are very few questions of cases where we would say it's 'legal but dirty'. In fact, in this company we are more often frustrated because management are too decent in their dealings, and expect others to behave likewise when our inclination would be to take the kid gloves off and start proceedings — they're simply stalling you. (Oil company lawyer)

> It's surprising how worried some senior managers are by the law and lawyers. (Food production company lawyer)

Only one lawyer quoted to me an instance of an unethical request by a colleague who had asked him to backdate a letter. He had refused to agree to it.

Of course, it should be borne in mind that the companies studied are large concerns and therefore may have more interest in compliance with legislation for public relations purposes (they have a great deal to lose if their name becomes associated with sharp practice) and can do so at lesser relative cost than the small firm (Reiss, 1984). Nevertheless, the comment quoted earlier by the small employers' representative is typical of the attitude. As one in-house lawyer remarked, 'Businessmen only want to know what they have to do and they'll get on with it . . . they don't want the hassle of fighting legal actions'.

The reaction of lawyers and companies to regulation is merely a reflection of their acknowledgement of the supremacy of the political forum. Morality in the business sphere is neither absolute nor constant. Most unlawful business activities are labelled as such by complex socio-political regulations reflecting experience of 'imbalances' of some kind in the marketplace or in the tensions between community and business practices. Questions of restrictive trading practices, trading standards, consumer credit arrangements, and so on, do not immediately strike the man in the street as horrendously immoral practices. The small businessman is, in other words, 'more likely to be ignorant than to be evil' with regard to the bulk of legal regulations while, for the larger company, the in-house lawyer will help reduce the excuse or likelihood of ignorance. The difference between the small employer and the large employer is that the former is more likely to be managed *by* his legal environment (the 'slow-mover') while for the large employer the presence of an in-house lawyer should help the organisation to be more proactive in *managing* its legal environment (fast-mover), including not only early identification of regulations but involvement in translating them into organisational practice. (The differing sizes of the organisations, however, might diminish the slow-fast distinction, since 'translation' in a large organisation may be a more cumbersome process.)

The easy distinction often drawn, however, between acts which are morally wrong (*mala in se*) and those which are socially inconvenient (*mala prohibita*) (the bulk of regulatory controls) ignores the fact that many of the latter can come to take on a *moral* force although they begin as restraints on semi-acceptable practice, whether tax evasion, parking restrictions or sex discrimination. Social change can lead to a long-term acceptance of new standards of business practice in health and safety and other fields, although such changes ostensibly add to the cost of carrying on a business. At the same time, some rules, for various reasons, retain more of an 'administrative' character and are easily amended or reversed, while others develop greater moral force. Thus sex or race discrimination would seem likely now clearly to offend the conscience of many in-house lawyers and companies, but a far different role as 'conscience' of the company would have been held even 30 years ago. Equally, there were obviously areas where in-house lawyers felt free to indulge in more legal 'gamesmanship' over questions of liability and prosecutions, where regulations had more of an administrative character. The crucial point, however, is that *business morality is thus evolutionary.* Business standards are inevitably conditioned by the wider social context, at local, national and international levels. *The meaning of 'civilised business practice' in the public arena has to be created and sustained at each of these levels.* It is this factor which makes unlikely the decline of regulation (social control) of business conduct, although the mechanisms of social control may take different forms. It is also this factor which throws into question the in-house lawyers' assertions of their negligible role as the conscience of a company, since it may be argued that the lawyer *is in a unique position of observing how 'public policy considerations' enter case-law and legislation,* of how narrow commercial goals may have long-term repercussions in community perceptions of business and in business liabilities.[17]

As we have seen, however, in-house lawyers are closely integrated with their clients. Companies were likely to accept legal change as much as the lawyers who advised them and therefore it is difficult to envisage an occasion where in-house lawyers will step outside that ambit where they 'share conscience' with their clients. However, such a 'leadership' or 'weather-vane' role (Gossett, 1963) has been suggested by some US writers on the subject, again reflecting the stronger US tradition of the campaigning, 'public service' lawyer (as well as the innocence of the early days of the regulation explosion).

In the light of hindsight, the corporation lawyers of the previous generation might well have given greater thought to the economic and social consequences of many of the transactions in which they did the legal engineering to affect the lawful attainment of their clients' objectives. (Swaine, 1949)

[He] . . . usually is in the councils of power when decisions are made. He more than any other understands explicit corporation law; but he also knows that beyond its limits there is an inchoate law waiting to become explicit when crisis comes. Understanding the corporation's business as well, he is increasingly likely to enter the business situation as legal and economic statesman as well as corporation employee. More consistently so, perhaps, than the businessman executive. (Berle, 1964: 471)

[It is] . . . his opportunity, his right, indeed his duty, to counsel and encourage good corporate citizenship . . . the importance of an acceptable corporate citizenship in our delicately balanced capitalism cannot be overemphasized. Corporate freedom of action extends only so far as there is at least public acquiescence, and preferably public support; and the public is fickle. It is the corporate counsel's prime function to work towards maintaining the public's support and consent for the existing and evolving corporate form . . . a corporation can proceed into this difficult area with much more effectiveness if its corporate counsel is also alert to the problem. (Hickman, 1964: 480–1)

Hickman goes on to argue that this sensitivity to the corporation's public image does not mean the corporate lawyer must only seek to appease. Rather, it involves an appreciation of when to fight,[18] when to yield and how to prevent battles arising in the first place.

While there were elements of these conceptions in some of the concepts and activities of the in-house lawyers studied (as in their role in trade and industry associations described in chapter 5), the evidence of this study suggests that such conceptions of lawyers are unlikely to dent the more humble view of UK lawyers that they are merely specialists, no more qualified or entitled to pronounce on business morality than their equally concerned management colleagues. Hickman was also writing at a time when it was acceptable to emphasise a more detached, 'staff' role for the in-house lawyer than an 'integrated' one.

> Like the abbott in the ancient monastery, the clerk to the feudal baron or the chancellor to the king, the corporation counsel is in a position to wield a unique influence. (482)

Nevertheless, although rejecting the notion of 'moral *superiority*' over businessmen, in-house lawyers may underestimate the potential 'moral *influence*' implicit in their work. While the debate about in-house lawyers as the 'conscience' of their company tends to have polarised between the 'visionaries' and the 'technical specialists', the real issues, like those of regulation itself, are more subtle and more complex. First, there is the paradox within the work of a lawyer that, in translating and interpreting legal standards, they will inevitably have some grasp of the 'inchoate' law referred to by Berle in order to anticipate judicial interpretation of legislation, particularly the element of 'public policy considerations'. Similarly, they will often have the opportunity to play a significant role within a management team in examining and contributing to the 'corporate policy' or corporate 'social responsibility' statements which are increasingly found in modern business. Third, unlike their colleagues in private practice, they are more likely to be in touch with the continuing situation subsequent to any advice they give, and thus to exercise continuing influence within the company.

Alongside this last 'silent footpad' role, lawyers also have other organisational means of influence of some importance. The tendency for lawyers to act as 'record-keepers' for the company, their experience of working with senior management from an early age, their ability to cross departmental boundaries in their work, all of these give them an exceptional opportunity to be experts on the broader corporate culture (the 'internal law') of their organisation and to utilise this expertise in their translation of law into practice. Insofar as this culture itself reflects the desire to be law-abiding, and perhaps more than law-abiding, as many claimed, lawyers have a particular opportunity to maintain and raise the standards of conduct of business organisations. This is not to attribute a higher moral role to them, nor a leadership function, nor is it to say that this is a frequent or major activity within their work. Rather it is to say that at times as a part of their decision-making choices in their 'management of legal practice' inside the company *they have the opportunity to manage the gaps between business practice and business policies in line with the ideals of their organisation in its community*. The fact that they have rejected a 'policing' *style* of management in order to achieve this result does not gainsay the fact that the nature of their occupation and their self-identification as professionals are intricately bound up with this integration of social and business values, and the influencing of business practice towards that end. An 'integrated' style may work towards the same *ends* as a 'policing style', but its value lies in a recognition of how to achieve effective influence inside an organisation.

Apart from any personal inclinations, a critical factor in the *degree* to which lawyers are called on to play this 'integrative' role between social and business values, and business practice, will inevitably be the *culture of their organisation* — whether they work for a 'leader', a 'fast-mover' or a 'slow-mover' (or, exceptionally, a 'bad-apple') in the regulatory field. Such organisational cultures will in practice be likely to carry great weight in determining how far an in-house lawyer is able or willing to deal with 'inchoate' law. However, in all of them, the fusing of business practice with social ethics will demand some degree of managerial skill from the lawyer, by which he can exercise his professional expertise and standards in an influential way inside the organisation. He should, in other words, be able to anticipate what 'needs to be anticipated' in managing the legal environment, and should be able to identify the 'appropriate' level of management at which a legal risk should be accepted. At its 'lowest' level, the lawyer in this area will be playing 'organisational politics'. But in some companies, it may come closer to 'statesmanship' (Murphy, 1968):

This is not a concept of morality but it is a plain recognition that large organizations, be they major corporations or labor unions or even large government-corporations, occupy such a status in this country that their relationship with various governments must involve not alone strict legal technicalities but also a very high degree of good judgment and diplomacy. One comes very soon to the analogy of international law. However precise its rules and interdictions, its practice includes a shrewd appraisal of public opinion, of future trends and political dynamics and a kind of leadership in the area of intellectual principles that cannot always be framed in terms of present legal precedents. ... I am not sure the quality we are describing can best be labeled statesmanship; it may be only a Machievellian sense of planning the corporation's affairs in a way that will deal effectively with power, politics and human cussedness.

NOTES

1   The professions can be regarded as a special case of business ethics. How special may depend on how much one sees them as a distinct form of social activity as against a form of social status (see chapter 12). In either case, one can still effectively use the analogy of business ethics as a fruitful source of comparison. Clearly the law business has won for itself a great degree of self-regulation. Much of the current debate about the legal profession concerns whether this is overall to the benefit of the consumer (Bartlett, 1982).

2   There are a number of possible definitions of regulation, there being little precision in the literature. Here I have adopted the simplest, which equates it with an increase in legislative control of business activities, particularly (although not always) associated with subordinate legislation.

3   See Bardach and Kagan (1982), and more recently Utton (1986)

4   See the Institute of Directors' surveys of its members (1986). The UK government, more intent on trade union regulation and privatisation as a form of deregulation, took six years from first coming to office before embarking on a systematic campaign against regulation in general with the publication of the White Papers *Lifting The Burden* (1985) and *Building Business . . . Not Barriers* (1986). Also, despite such efforts, the pace of legislation goes on to the extent that the government are seemingly intent on increasing their use of subordinate legislation to bypass the lengthy parliamentary processes involved in statutory law (see Richards, 1986).

There are now around 4000 Acts of Parliament and 14 000 statutory instruments arising from them. Over a ten-year period from 1974–83, six government departments alone produced almost 5000 statutory instruments.

5 See n4 *supra*.

6 The phenomenon of 'scandal-to-control' was further in evidence at the time of completing this book, over the issue of City self-regulation following various allegations of insider trading and major sums of money being used illicitly to support a takeover bid. Without going into details of the 'Guinness affair', the case makes a fascinating case study of the mix of individual and corporate wrongdoing, and the problems of control within and between companies, as well as the dilemma for government of how to sustain policies of self-regulation in the political atmosphere of scandal. It arose too late, however, for detailed comment in this work but it does raise some question marks over in-house lawyers' images of corporate conduct.

7 The Labor governments in the State of Victoria and in the federal capital of Canberra, for example, had established regulation review units in response to business complaints. These aimed to alert government departments to the cost-benefit nature of new legislative proposals and to implement sunsetting provisions in subordinate legislation. See, for example, *Victoria, The Next Step: Economic Initiatives and Opportunities for the 1980s*, April 1984, Government of Victoria.

8 See Kelman's (1984) comments to this effect in his comparison of US and Swedish Health and Safety regulations. Faucheux and Rojot (1979) detect a parallel distinction between the Anglo-Saxon and Latin cultures in Europe, that is an assumption of trust and consensus in the former but not found in the Latin context.

9 See Wilson (1980), Bardach and Kagan (1982), Hawkins and Thomas (1984).

10 See, for example, Daniel and Stilgoe (1978), Utton (1986).

11 As in the case of the 'insider trading' scandals of 1986, which, beginning with the Ivan Boesky affair, stretched across the Atlantic to involve cooperation between British and American government investigation agencies, culminating in the revelations of illicit share dealings in the Guinness takeover of the Distillers Company.

12 For one of the most stimulating accounts of the gap between regulation and organisational behaviour see Stone (1975).

13 Stone rejects this idea, however, on the ground that in-house lawyers have insufficient trust and influence amongst their business colleagues; Smyser argues, in keeping with my own findings, that in-house lawyers have no interest in such a role.

14 For a useful attempt at separation see Leigh (1980).

15 Other writers in the field of employment law have also suggested that much legislation is based on the example set by 'advanced' companies (either unilateral management practice or arising from standards set in collective bargaining between trade unions and management). The extent to which, or the manner in which, such legislative 'modelling' takes place

is far from clear and worthy of more research. It is clearly applicable to some of the companies in this sample.

16 I have met several in-house lawyers (in smaller companies) since completing the interviews who have been less positive about their companies. They have expressed disquiet about their companies' 'sharp practices'. Again, however, these actions, although dubious morally, fell short of illegality. However, their situation brings them closer to the model outlined in this final part of the chapter of a lawyer who is proactive in the area of 'inchoate law'. Other in-house lawyers present at these discussions have generally advised them either to leave for a better company or fight for long-term change of policy.

17 For an example of a limited perspective leading to later difficulties for the company (a disclaimer and indemnity clause for sale of a chemical used by a steel company to a cosmetics company without medicinal trials), see Rosen (1984) and the comment on a similar hypothetical case by Maddock (1968).

18 It is a common finding, of course, that business tends to resist initially most new forms of regulation. In this respect, one can argue that law as a force for change is always a secondary or subsidiary factor in the evolution of business controls (Snider, 1987). However, this leaves the in-house lawyers and business leaders with the same dilemma of how to handle 'inchoate law'.

11 Beyond Litigation: Mega-Clients, Mega-Law and Mini-Trials

THE RISE AND RISE OF LITIGATION

The extraordinary size of modern corporations literally means that big business takes place at virtually every level of commercial operations, whether in terms of contracts with other businesses, consumer disputes, health and safety concerns or dealings with public authorities and agencies. Add to this the modern tendency to diversify business operations and engage in highly competitive strategies involving frequent acquisitions, divestments, joint ventures and other complex arrangements, together with an inexorable internationalisation of business activity, and one is provided with a context where the potential for dispute is quite vast, and considerably complex. The inevitable corollary it seems is that dispute-resolution itself becomes a growth industry.[1] Companies are faced with situations where litigation reaches 'mega-levels', not only at one end a *frequent* activity in terms of repeated small-scale disputes (as with consumer claims), but also, at the other end of the dispute spectrum, the potential for individual disputes and litigation which are of *mega-* proportions in terms of their business or financial implications,[2] or in terms of their complexity (whether over a major product liability issue or a major business agreement or arrangement breaking down or a significant regulatory challenge).

The large amounts at stake provide an incentive also to invest a great deal of money in resolving or winning disputes, although the extent of the incentive will vary according to the type of dispute and its potential to harm the company's operations. This enlargement of the dispute by reason of the amounts at stake is further exacerbated in inter-business disputes by the often complex organisational processes — within and between the parties — which led up to the dispute, in turn requiring an equivalent scale of research to trace the historical positions and justifications of the parties. To this existing 'goulash' of disputes, one turns to the legal profession and the legal system for the final touch. Or does one? In this chapter, we will consider the views of in-house lawyers on litigation and the legal system as it relates to the resolution of business disputes, and consider the effect the trends outlined above are having on the dispute-resolution industry.

Lawyers have long been at the heart of dispute-resolution processes: 'The traditional function of lawyers is to assist in the control and operation of the community process of authoritative decision, a process essential to the maintenance of an orderly society' (Johnstone and Hopson 1967:3). The crucial word, however, in this picture of lawyers is 'authoritative'. It would be naive to consider that most business disputes are, or can be, resolved by litigation or indeed any other third-party system of intervention. Most business disputes are settled by agreement between the parties. Whether or not such agreement represents the authoritative legal position of the parties to the dispute is often of secondary concern to parties who are more often anxious to keep the business going, to maintain good customer, supplier or buyer relations, or merely to simplify a problem by treating it as a business loss (Macaulay, 1963; Beale and Dugdale; 1975). The exercise of economic power, whether expressed formally in standard form contracts which limit liability or in other pressures (such as potential loss of future business from the other party) to achieve a settlement favourable to one of the parties, is also a highly significant factor: ' . . . the interplay of power determines the overwhelming majority of business disputes' (Coulson 1968: 129, currently president of the American Arbitration Association). Additionally, agreements may be reached (and later form the basis for a new dispute) under pressures of time constraints, of uncertainties arising from the complexity of the issue or the difficulty of covering all eventualities, particularly in complex negotiations over acquisitions or joint venture arrangements (by means of a clause such as 'profits to be shared according to the relative contribution of the parties').

Nevertheless, many disputes cannot be solved by these methods, and one or both parties may choose to resort to litigation, whether because they see no alternative, because of the amount or precedent at stake, or in response to legal advice. A growth in litigation business is thus ensured if only to accompany the numerical growth in business transactions. 'We can't stop work coming into our litigation department. It just keeps on growing.' (A senior partner in a leading Australian commercial law firm.) However, there are also wider social trends at work towards 'juridification' of social relationships with the breakdown of more traditional and shared community norms (Rueschemeyer, 1973). This process itself intensifies trends to seek 'authoritative' rulings on appropriate rules of conduct. The growth in formal disputes in the business sector is therefore likely to be even more pronounced in reflecting (as well as contributing to) these broader trends. Conditions of recession or fierce competition may further exacerbate such developments.

An immediate effect of this expansion of disputes is therefore to add to the work of lawyers and the legal system. However, the outcome is not a mere quantitative expansion of legal business. The corporate sector has also played its part in transforming the legal profession and legal system, as part of its wider impact on social change (Rueschemeyer, 1973). Not only has the corporate sector encouraged a growth in legal business, but it has also inevitably furthered a division of labour within the legal profession (Heinz and Laumann, 1982). Beyond that, and this is the main theme of this chapter, business may also come to play a part in the reassessment and restructuring of dispute-resolution processes. The reason for this last trend is that the 'community process of authoritative decision' does not necessarily carry the same weight for the businessman as it does for the lawyer. The increase in litigation and its attendant costs in fact come to highlight for companies the gap between the 'normal' outcome of business disputes (agreement) and the processes and outcomes of litigation.

The first and most direct contribution of business to the division of labour in the legal profession concerns the subject-matter of this book, the in-house lawyer. Chapter 3 described the benefits that an in-house lawyer brings to an organisation. In particular, the common business concern with costs is an important factor in the trend towards 'privatisation' of legal services. An inevitable outcome of this must be a drop in legal business for some law firms formerly used. However, the presence of in-house lawyers, as has been described earlier, may help companies identify more legal problems and thus increase legal business for outside lawyers in some areas. More significant, however, is the fact that this restructuring leads to further *specialisation* of outside lawyers. The new division of labour, alongside general growth in litigation, helps channel outside lawyers even further into a litigation-support role. In-house lawyers have taken a greater share of the 'office work' and general advisory role of the commercial firms, leaving the latter more heavily involved either in commercial law specialisation or, more often, in advice and activities concentrating around litigation.

The in-house lawyer is, of course, only a part of a wider trend within the profession towards larger commercial firms servicing major corporate clients, separate from the large numbers of small- or medium-sized firms with smaller business clients or only occasional, small-scale work from the larger companies (*Business Week*, 1986). A principal reason for this is that the major corporations have the resources to pay for a high-quality technical service, resulting in an inequality of income and status within the legal profession itself that has become more and more marked, particularly in the United States (Heinz and Laumann, op. cit.).

. . . one of the chief reasons why competent lawyers go into corporate work is precisely that business clients are willing to invest enough in their lawyers to permit them to develop the highest possible levels of professional skill. Indeed it is not far wrong to say that lawyers for the big corporations are the only practitioners regularly afforded latitude to give their technical best to the problems they work on. The rest of the Bar ordinarily has to slop along with quickie work, or as one lawyer put it, make good guesses as to the level of malpractice at which they should operate in any given situation. (Hazard, 1978:152–3)

Another consequence of this specialisation is that the major commercial firms in turn become more like businesses than the traditional lawyer practice, with a greater employment hierarchy (fewer partners per number of associates), employment on merit rather than on social connections, and an emphasis on rational business systems.

> Although the partnership form is retained, these are modern firms with central direction and rationalised management presided over by full-time professional office managers. Legal services are seen as a product to be sold; clients are charged by the fraction of the hour for the time of each lawyer who works on the matter. The remnants of patrician airs and professional *noblesse* are further dispelled. Lawyers are more businesslike . . . 'law firms are becoming more like businesses and less like clubs' . . . the product is labour-intensive custom work. (Galanter, 1983:156)

Galanter identifies in the US a new type of law practice, 'mega-law', arising out of the resource-base of the law practices which serve corporations and other wealthy clients. Its effects are particularly pronounced in the area of litigation, where the preparations for 'battle' assume gigantic proportions, gathering around a dispute not only teams of lawyers, but also a mass of litigation-support specialists to collect and analyse information arising from the massive documentation gathered for the action from the company and other parties, stemming from and, at the same time, stimulating a considerable 'companion litigation' on discovery and procedural issues.

> The majesty of mega-law is imparted not by wigs, robes and gibbets, but by files, experts and computers massed in assemblages beyond the span of personal experience and beyond the grasp of personal understanding. The evocation of religion is replaced by the evocation of science. (166)

Investment of massive amounts of time, relentless investigation, exhaustive research and lavish deployment of expensive experts imposes on the other side corresponding expenditures, endless delays, and costly disruptions of their normal operations. If not everything is an open question, sufficient investment can make almost any matter sufficiently problematic that it takes considerable money and time to lay it at rest. Pursued in multiple forums, with brazen insistence on extracting the last measure of formal entitlement, and offering little hope of respite — such litigation raises the bluster and strategem of ordinary litigation to lethal proportions. Litigation in the mega-law mode is distinctive in the way that mobile high technology warfare between super-powers differs from the set piece battles of an earlier day. (163)

The litigation partner in a City firm echoed this theme in his comments on the changing nature of commercial litigation.

People are seeing lawyers in a more American style. The nature of litigation is changing. When I was first an articled clerk it had a low status in the City. Now it's very, very strong. Some firms are even litigation-led. It's not seen purely as a debt-collecting function any more, but as a commercial department in its own right. I think people are trying to use litigation more creatively than they ever did, for example, to stop acquisitions and mergers. To a certain extent it's highlighting the inadequacies of the Bar.

Galanter's vivid portrayal of mega-law tends, however, to over-play its distinctiveness from ordinary processes of litigation. One has only to study the progress of personal injury actions in English courts to realise that delay, cost and technicalities are not to preserve of wealthy clients, although it is undoubtedly true that greater resources applied to the process can also emphasise these features of the 'litigation-bargaining complex' and have led to more than one 'twentieth-century sequel to *Bleak House*'.[3] But even for ordinary processes of litigation, it is not uncommon to find the view that 'as a litigant I should dread a lawsuit beyond almost anything else short of sickness and death' (Judge Learned Hand, quoted in Coulson 1968, Introduction).

Similarly, Galanter's observation that mega-law litigation 'usually leads to a prolonged clinch and then to settlement' is equally applicable to most civil litigation, although perhaps there are greater economic pressures on the *lawyers* in the ordinary cases to settle out-of-court (or more often 'on-the-steps-of-the-court') and avoid the time out of the office that litigation demands (Rosenthal, 1974; Joseph, 1985). Mega-law, therefore, is perhaps little more than a demonstration of the traditional process of litigation with greater amounts of money applied to it. It is the logical outcome of standard legal procedures, grounded in tradition-based processes of authoritative decision-making.

Galanter sees the growth of the in-house lawyer as another side of the same coin of the mega-law process, only less costly (quoting consultant estimates that an in-house lawyer costs half as much as an outside practitioner). However, this ignores the potential differentiation between in-house and outside lawyers, particularly in the former's greater understanding of and identification with client goals, which, as we shall see, may signify a divergence of approach to litigation. However, he hints at a central theme of this chapter in his observation that

> Mega-law is ultimately connected with a dual movement of legislation and disenchantment . . . As law becomes omnipresent and elaborated, it is exposed as indeterminate, manipulable and political. Mega-law heightens our expectations of legal vindication while it teaches us to despair of their realisation. (173)[4]

Litigation reform

A common theme amongst the in-house lawyers interviewed was a concern over the delays and inefficiency of the present legal system, particularly in respect of litigation (although a few thought the system was still the best one was likely to achieve). In this they were reflecting the concern of their own clients, and especially the manner in which the faults of the legal system reflected badly on their own profession.

> Businessmen want almost rough-and-ready justice, not high-faluting technicalities. They would prefer a quick decision to the finely-tuned decision you tend to get years after the event. They don't understand the detail you need to get into in court. (Manufacturing company lawyer)

> Once you get to the level of the Court of Appeal and the House of Lords, it's all very abstract and impractical. (Retail company lawyer, referring to employment law appeals experience)

Sensible lawyers ought to be able to get together to solve a problem before litigation. Agreements tend to break down in lawyers' hands. I don't know yet if arbitration is any better. My first one is coming up soon. Lawyers could play a significant constructive role if they were prepared to compromise. ACAS [Advisory, Conciliation and Arbitration Service] are very helpful in those type of cases [conciliation in employment disputes before they go to an industrial tribunal]. I once suggested that industrial tribunals could be used for commercial law cases. Something has to be done about litigation in this country. It's too expensive. I don't know exactly what has gone wrong, but the system's wrong. The judges are too important. And a divided legal profession can't help. There are too few specialists. (Consumer products company lawyer)

Some of the outside lawyers also commented on the crisis in the system.

The system at the moment is absolutely mad. There are too few judges and too much depends on oral evidence at the trial. [He explained that there were too few judges because of the effect of the selection of judges from the limited numbers at the Bar.] We were involved recently in a trial that took over nine months. The opening speech of the plaintiff's counsel took six weeks. If he had put it down in writing and the judge had read it beforehand it would have saved six weeks instantly. But because there are too few judges, they don't have time to read any documents beforehand, so you have to spend time explaining what it's about. He should read the evidence and take the initiative in saying 'These seem to be the issues. One, two, three.' In the end most people settle, which is desirable but not for the correct reasons. It's ludicrous that there are really only five judges to deal with the mass of commercial work in this country. If I went now with all my pleadings, I'd be given a trial date in [nearly three years' time]. (Partner in City firm)

The Australian in-house lawyers were, if anything, much more outspoken. The first quoted was perhaps the most blunt in his views and is worth quoting at length for his articulacy on the subject:

I think generally the legal system is very ill-equipped to deal with complex commercial cases. Judges can't understand the complexities in modern commercial cases and they are often very limited in the remedies they can give. . . . The worst aspect of the courts is that you go to a lawyer, he briefs a barrister and you perhaps get an opinion that you have a good case so the solicitor advises you to go to court. What most lawyers will never admit at that stage is that a QC's opinion is no better than tossing a coin. Your chances are only 50–50 — because at that stage he's only heard one side of the case. Then you have years of discovery and interrogatories. Perhaps four, or five years later, or more, it comes to court with witnesses who now have only hazy memories of what exactly happened. Only then do the lawyers get round to seeing the full picture. Therefore you've wasted a lot of costs, executive time, etc. And often when the lawyers see the full picture, they then advise you to settle. . . . The system is too black and white. There has to be someone right, someone wrong. It's not the truth normally. Also, I find obscene the whole business of putting someone under pressure in the witness box, subjecting them to intense examination on issues that they hardly remember and are not black and white in any case usually.

I'm not certain that the court system is a system that's viable for the year 2000. We ought to be working out now what is viable. It's not that the system is in difficulties. Simply that it's failed. . . . If 'justice delayed is justice denied', then justice is denied every day in this State. The trouble with the courts is that they seek absolute justice. In doing so, they create other injustices of delay and costs. Law is simply a way of getting a decision. Lawyers in private practice tend to believe it's the only way. There are other ways, many better. We've got to try to get back to the Japanese concept. You've got to try and settle your own disputes compared to the Western philosophy which is legalistic. Third parties are still useful if it's the right sort. But they're damned difficult to find. A quasi-negotiator come marriage broker . . . Negotiation is far more flexible. Lawyers get combative, feel they have to win to the nth degree. The negotiator who wins all points is just not a good negotiator — for future relations. It's flexible in solution, too, there are no end to ways of resolving a dispute; you can innovate, whereas law offers only limited solutions, nearly always damages. Compare the case of a mineral buyer with a poor market suddenly and who doesn't want to take your shipment. A lawyer would say sue, but if you've any sense you want to keep him as a customer. You realise he's got a point of view, genuine problems. Therefore you defer some tonnage, allow him to re-sell, split the loss between you, come to a barter arrangement which suits you better — there are various options. They keep the arrangement intact whereas the legal process tends to pull it apart. (Insurance company lawyer, with earlier minerals company experience)

My recent experiences with litigation have been disasters. I'm just not happy with the legal profession . . . The courts are a lost cause. It's the unreality of the Bar and the Bench. The one leads to the other. They haven't got their feet on the ground. No concept of time and space, the time to get things done. It's really an arrogance. So people vote with their feet and avoid disputes. The two areas of litigation I have at the moment are rank disasters. But it's a typical experience with lawyers. No wonder the commercial people are on the ceiling. [He outlined the two cases. One had taken two years to settle a technical point of whether there was a cause of action or not in a case of construction plant failure costing the company a million dollars (on an older contract 'put together by accountants and engineers'). In the other, lawyers had failed to file a notice in time which had resulted in the need for a new, more complex legal action.] . . . Let's sweep away all this nonsense of pleadings, all the preliminary crap we have to go through, the theatricals of barristers. I don't know how to do it frankly. I don't see the system changing, until there's a crisis. (Resources company)

Like the last lawyer, few others were very specific about what could be done to improve matters. (Some of the Australian lawyers had developed an interest in 'Alternative Dispute Resolution' — see below.) It was not something to which they had given much thought. And surprisingly few had had any experience of the standard alternative to litigation, commercial arbitration, although most knew by repute that it had also become

'litigious' in style as a result of the extensive use of legal representation. The lawyer quoted above who had suggested an industrial tribunal-type approach had also commissioned a report on
the French commercial court from his company's French
lawyers. Hermann (1983) has also commended the French style
of operation (for a brief account, see 22–4), and has severely
criticised the failure of reform in the English system, together
with the failure to recognise the need for commercial arbitration
to offer a distinctively different dispute-resolution system.

The English machinery of justice is of medieval design, embe-
llished by a few Victorian improvements. Its last major over-
haul took place in 1873. The many committees and Royal
Commissions appointed since then to pacify discontent have
produced a mountain of paper but hardly a mouse of reform.
Commercial arbitration, as well as the numerous tribunals
created in response to the new needs of an industrial society,
has been invaded by lawyers and imitates the anachronistic
and costly ways of the High Court.

Neither Parliament nor the legal profession have so far had a
strong enough incentive to reform the system. The profession
has delighted in its ancient ways, not only because they are
picturesque but also because they have been profitable. The
point has now been reached, however, when resistance to
reform may kill the goose that lays the golden eggs. The
solicitors will be the first to suffer . . . (17)

Built into the system, however, are organisational forces for
conservatism. Parties do not litigate often enough to build up
any real pressures for reform; legal education and training are
still strongly fixed on the appellate court model and on litigation
as the 'typical' substance of the lawyer's work (thus incidentally
laying the foundations for ignorance of arbitration, never mind
of negotiation, compromise and settlement which are the overwhelming outcomes of disputes handled by lawyers); the
judiciary hear in court mainly other lawyers like themselves who
are happy with the system, and indeed mainly barristers who
under the English system are deliberately shielded from extensive contact with the public by the rules of etiquette founded on
the division of the profession. The specialisation created in the

wake of regulatory and corporate development adds to the intricacies of the confusion in the system.

You can't get away from the fact that law is inherently complex and lawyers are making it even more complex. One of the effects of the rush to specialisation is that specialists have a self-interest in justifying their own specialism and extortionate fees. I grew up in an ethos of problem-solving without litigation, whereas the first thing you get presented with today in the City firms is an expert and their natural tendency is to dive into the deepest part of the pool. They come up with some refinement that's fiendishly complicated. You get a six-page letter back and say to yourself 'thank God I consulted Mr X. I didn't know it was so complicated.' There's some really lousy lawyering going on. But the combination of complexity and consumer demand means it's a growth industry. It's a function of a very selfish, de-communalised, materialist way of life, all this resort to litigation. So my tendency is to try and go back to reinforce the consensual aspects of people's lives. (City firm lawyer)

Business concern with the inefficiencies of litigation, however, particularly its escalating cost, has gradually been surfacing into public debate, to the extent of business conferences being held on the theme of 'Controlling Legal Costs'.[5] In-house lawyers are likely to hear this message very strongly in a much more cost-conscious business climate.

Neither inside nor outside counsel have absorbed this basic fact [of a need to settle early]. Outside counsel really don't have the fundamental incentive and inside counsel simply haven't paid enough attention. Too often inside counsel have been content to ship off a complaint to whatever outside lawyers they used in the jurisdiction, with a general exhortation to fight like hell and to occasionally report back. There may have been some discussion of what the time rates would be (and only recently at that), but seldom an attempt to predict up front what the litigation would actually cost. A basic factor in the settlement equation remained an unknown. . . . Litigation cost is becoming a major focus of client concern and whether we like it or not, hard economic reality is changing our profession. . . . For some kinds of cases, at least, an effort should be made to establish a budget or projection of litigation costs, on a monthly or quarterly basis. The decision to litigate or to settle can then be made by management with some appreciation of the real cost of alternatives. (Leary, 1982: 447–8)

Nor are direct costs the only concern of business. The loss of executive time and attention on litigation and pre-litigation preparation can be considerable, not to mention the stress and emotional factors involved. And all this to end up with what is often inconclusive or unhelpful or over-costly compared to an effectively negotiated outcome — 'almost every litigated case is a mistake' (Fisher, 1985).

However, it would be wrong to say that pressure for reform is entirely outside the legal profession. Re-examination of the efficiency of litigation as an instrument of dispute-resolution has been forced on the Lord Chancellor in the UK not only by public complaint, but by the paradox of the ever-increasing workload of litigation facing the courts, both in the civil and criminal jurisdictions (see *Judicial Statistics*, 1986). A number of reforms have been undertaken (apart from an intensified court-building programme and appointment of more judges), such as more use of written evidence on appeals, pressure on the Bar to reduce the presence of junior counsel appearing with Queen's Counsel, and so on. Also, a thorough study of the system has been initiated, based on management consultants' investigations of litigation (see the *Consultative Papers*, 1–6, Civil Justice Review). Suggestions for reform from these sources — 'documents-only' personal injury actions for claims below certain monetary limits, minimum amounts for Commercial Court cases, fixed-fee declarations — are already causing a degree of concern and controversy within the legal profession. Similarly, awareness of the need to make arbitration an effective alternative to litigation rather than a copy of it (or prelude to it) has led to attempts at reform both nationally and internationally, and to a lively debate within the arbitration world.[6] However, my concern in this chapter is less with the details of this process than its relevance to the business community and to the in-house lawyer within that community.

Clearly in-house lawyers' professional training had led them to identify with the processes of the legal system. Yet at the same time their involvement with their clients led many to question its relevance to the nature of business disputes. However, here there was the difficulty of envisaging alternatives to the system (their training also made them less ready to turn to the unfamiliar practice of arbitration), and in any case such developments were easily shrugged off as outside their direct work roles. The predominant tendency amongst in-house lawyers was therefore not directed at reform of the litigation system, so much as at trying to manage litigation for their company in a more efficient manner. In this respect there is evidence that they could be eminently successful. One company reported hiring an in-house lawyer when they discovered they did not know the number of product liability suits pending against them at any one time. 'The difference was like night and day' (*Business Week*, 1984). Fischer (1984), general counsel for the Alcoa company, writes that an in-house self-examination led them to *increase* their in-house costs in order to make savings overall in their budget. The reason they could do this was because litigation costs were such a major part of their budget.[7] The method they used to save on these costs was to recruit an additional two in-house lawyers, both litigation specialists, and to rely less on outside lawyers. One of the companies in my own study which had conducted an efficiency analysis had taken the same route of cutting back on outside legal services.

Fischer also comments on his department's new interest in Alternative Dispute Resolution[9] (ADR) processes, not only arbitration but other conciliation and mediation techniques including 'mini-trials'. The consequences of the mega-law described earlier, together with the popularity of litigation in the United States, and the heavy costs this has imposed on business, have led many other companies to explore alternatives to the existing legal service industry. One of the more recent developments, mini-trials, has attracted particular interest as a method which is more apt to the real nature of many business disputes. Promulgated by the Center for Public Resources in New York (Henry, 1985), the mini-trial operates by promoting voluntary agreements by companies to adhere to a code of practice for disputes whereby senior managers from companies in dispute sit as 'judges' on the dispute, usually with a 'neutral' adviser (an expert or lawyer). Lawyers and/or staff from the respective companies present their case and are questioned on it. After this information presentation the managers attempt to reach agreement, with the neutral adviser providing an expert view on legal or technical aspects, or sometimes acting as a mediator (making active efforts to help the parties reach a solution). The process therefore formalises the practice of informal dispute resolution which is already common in business disputes, and prevents the escalation which can occur once a dispute moves out of the parties' territory, leaving control of the process in the parties' hands. It is 'structured to reconvert a legal dispute back into a business problem.'

Mini-trials are only part of a wider movement of exploration of alternative dispute resolution techniques (Henry, op. cit.; Edwards, 1986) of conciliation, mediation, arbitration, 'rent-a-judge', and others, a movement which is also affecting non-business areas of family law, neighbourhood disputes and criminal law (Tomasic and Feeley, 1982; Goldberg *et al.*, 1985). The breadth of the reaction to the rigidity of the 'authoritative dispute resolution' process of litigation, has led some to see an analogy with the historical development of equity in reaction to the common law in England in the 15th century, ADR as a 'New Wave' equity. 'The reasons for the emergence of equity were lack of appropriate remedies, lack of access to the courts, cost and rigid adherence by the courts to the legal rules. . . . Equity came to fill those gaps in the common law. It was free of the procedural formalities. It could sit anywhere. It dispensed justice according to 'conscience' and the merits of the case. It provided swift and inexpensive justice' (David, 1986:27).

In-house lawyers expressed a great deal of interest in ADR, although few, and none of my UK sample, were actively involved. Some saw it as a more natural development in the United States because of the emphasis on litigation in that society. Given the limited direct involvement in litigation of in-house lawyers, and their concerns with intra-organisational processes, one might expect ADR to require some form of leadership activity by opinion leaders. Corporate counsel have certainly been prominent in the mini-trial movement in the US. In Australia the first Secretary-General of a new Australian Commercial Disputes Centre, formed to help resolve commercial disputes by conciliation and mediation techniques, was an in-house lawyer formerly active in the New South Wales Corporate Lawyers' Association.

None, however, saw the movement as a panacea or as a total replacement for litigation. Where the issues at stake were important or involved an intransigent party, litigation was still the obvious alternative for achieving an 'authoritative' decision. In addition, a number pointed out that if the movement did expand, many lawyers had the skills to adapt themselves to the new climate and would eventually play a substantial role as they had done in most administrative tribunals. To some extent this depended on whether the courts and lawyers could 'raise their game', whether reform of litigation and the 'law business' could adapt quickly enough (see chapter 13). In comparing the historical development of equity and the common law, the process of fusion understandably took somewhat longer to achieve. But one can observe already an increase in attention to court-based arbitration schemes (see, for example, the Civil Justice Review, Consultation Paper no. 6, chapter 5, Lord Chancellor's Department). Also, one must note that the status of the profession is a significant factor in maintaining lawyer influence. Thus, eminent lawyers and judges have also been actively associated not only with the 'traditional' form of ADR, arbitration, but are evident on the panels of mediators and advisers used by the Center for Public Resources and the Australian Commercial Disputes Centre, a fact those centres highlight in their publicity. (And in the case of the latter, the initiative for the Centre arose from, amongst others, a member of the judiciary and was initially guided by a partner in a leading commercial legal firm. Similarly lawyers were closely involved with another new development, the Australian Centre for International Commercial Arbitration.) This continues the paradox of the legal profession, the gap between the often critical public image of law and lawyers (and amongst lawyers) as outlined earlier in this chapter, and the status and respect accorded to lawyers and legal skills (see chapter 14).

Of course, alternative approaches to dispute resolution which emphasise a limited role for lawyers have a long history. Trade and professional associations in some sectors, such as construction, already play an important role in dispute resolution or managing legal conflicts through systems of arbitration, providing procedural rules, facilities, and advocates, as well as shaping attitudes on issues. This tradition has extended in the UK in recent years into the adoption (encouraged by the Office of Fair Trading) by a number of industries of rights-to-arbitration contract clauses to deal with frequent small consumer claims. (Other sectors have opted for 'ombudsmen'.)[9] Similarly, collective bargaining disputes between employers and trade unions have long been conducted by means other than litigation, such as conciliation and arbitration (Mackie, 1987), reflecting the normal fact of an enduring relationship (although in these disputes, it is also easier to see the more public manifestation of the exercise of power to assert interests). That has still not prevented cases where the parties are too entrenched or too determined on the principles at stake, to be able to settle the dispute without outside intervention, to the limits of the legal process. However, such cases have been the exception rather than the rule (although more frequent at times when the legal rules are themselves subject to major innovation). There is in the field of collective bargaining also apparent an increasing recognition of the range of techniques available for dispute-settlement, and increasingly sophisticated mechanisms, not only of conciliation, mediation and arbitration, but, for example, of 'final-offer' arbitration[10] or even more sophisticated models combining several options (for example, setting time limits on negotiations, which, failing agreement, trigger a time period for the parties then to agree to conventional arbitration terms, followed by a further period after which, failing agreement, final-offer arbitration is triggered — Ashenfelter and Bloom, 1983).

CONCLUSION

The important general moral to draw from these old and new developments is the potential flexibility of structures for dealing with disputes. For some time now the legal service industry has tended to be dominated by a 'one-product' model, where the lawyers largely control a process in which perhaps perfectability of law and of legal technique, and the traditions of the 'producers', take precedence over the objectives of the 'consumers'. The variability that already exists in types of dispute-resolution techniques, alongside the need to find new forms of dispute-resolution suitable to commercial decision-making needs, and which avoid some of the imperfections of the traditional processes, suggests that the coming decades are likely to see the search for effective innovations in dispute-resolution continue. Nor would it be fair to lay the responsibility for the current deficiencies in litigation, and the failure to promote alternatives, entirely on the lawyers. Business has been equally slow in inventing, or giving attention to, options other than the traditional processes of negotiation and litigation. Rather the increased frequency of disputes has tended to expose more intensely the gap between the two extremes.

It is not inevitable that in-house lawyers will play a significant role in developments in this area, and there are signs that the courts and other lawyers are becoming more alert to customer needs in this 'legal service industry'.[11] However, there are few groups which are better placed to represent 'the consumer', to unravel the complexities of law and practice necessary to the new forms of business dispute-resolution, and few groups with better access to the corridors of power and to the machinery which would ensure a concerted approach to new forms of dispute-resolution agreements. Such elements would seem prerequisite to any fundamental change taking place in the approach of business to its disputes. One might also add that the in-house lawyer is in an ideal position to perform the adviser/judicial officer role in such inter-company negotiation resolutions (although US experience suggests that leading outside law firms are soon involved in such developments). An emerging system of 'community-based' justice within the business sector should not therefore be beyond the horizons of the in-house lawyer.

NOTES

1   Outside inter-business disputes, probably the most common disputes are in family matters, partnership differences, personal injury settlements, debt collection, professional fees, consumer complaints, home improvements and construction. In each of these areas one can find a similar questioning of litigation as the appropriate technique for resolving disputes, although in line with the general argument of this book about the differentiation of legal practice, each area can be said to be developing

along a somewhat different route. For an alternative view that the growth of alternative means of dispute resolution could usher in an era of not courts as we know them but Dispute Resolution Centres, see Bartlett 1982, 89, who bases this view on a need to end the monopoly of the legal profession over litigation: '. . . the court system is too often inward-looking. The dispute that the litigants wish to settle often seems only an excuse for the appellate courts to peer into the judicial machinery' (Bartlett, 1982: 11).

2 The litigation arising out of the recent Guinness takeover of the Distillers' company is one such example. For an even more dramatic recent example, see the *Texaco* case, where a major oil company has come close to bankruptcy in a legal action over economic damage to another corporation (reported in the *Financial Times*, 'Legal Blunders That Could Kill', 8 April, 1987).

3 Chief Justice Burger's comment on a marathon anti-trust action, *Hughes Tool Co.* v. *Trans World Airlines*, 409 US 363 (1972), quoted by Galanter: 164.

4 Again, the process of disenchantment may not be exclusive to mega-law. McBarnet (1981) charts the progress of a sociologist confronting the actuality of the criminal process with its gap between legal ideals and daily practice of case-by-case law. 'Weber's description of a move to 'rational' law for the sake of certainty traces the development of an ideology of law rather than a description of either its practice or its form' (163).

5 The title is taken from a conference run by the Confederation of British Industry in 1983. A booklet was later published under the same title. For an account of the rising cost and scale of litigation in the United States, see Kolvenbach (1979: 88–9); Stichnoth and Dolan (1982). See also the comment of Ralph Nader, quoted in Chapter 3, and the perceptive analysis of a chief executive's frustration in Fisher (1985). Also, Leary (1982). One can, of course, argue that the disillusionment with litigation is merely a recognition that it has become such a common occurrence for business compared to its unusual character in the past, that business has been forced to treat it merely as another operating expense (Johnson, 1978) with the ensuing pressure for cost containment that implies.

6 The elements of the debate can be followed in the columns of *Arbitration*, the journal of the Chartered Institute of Arbitrators. The most important aspects have been the attempt to reduce the number of cases going on to trial under the old 'case stated' procedure (the Arbitration Act 1979), and the attempts to forge an international code with similar effect (the UNCITRAL rules). For a national case study of developments in dispute-resolution, see Mackie (1986) 'Commercial Arbitration and Dispute-Resolution in Australia', Research Report to British Academy.

7 Fischer notes that 60 per cent of his department's budget was going in outside legal costs, 76 per cent of that in litigation in 1983 (53–4).

8 Note incidentally how the expression 'Alternative' suggests that litigation is the *norm* for dispute resolution when in fact it is still only used in a minority of disputes. Similarly, law firms have 'litigation departments',

not 'settlement' or 'negotiation' departments, although that is the typical outcome of cases (Fisher, 1985)

9 See Ferguson (1980) for a brief account of the sectors where there was an attempt to absorb the coercive power of the law into a 'lay' system (of arbitration or standard contract forms). Ferguson makes an interesting contrast between these business sectors which sought to 'master' the legal environment (because of frequency or scale of disputes) in this way, others such as engineering (described by Beale and Dugdale, op. cit.) where there was a bifurcation of contracts and commercial norms, with use of law-avoidance techniques.

10 The 'final-offer' system of arbitration in industrial relations refers to the practice where the arbitrator is forced to choose between one party's claim or the other's offer, but has no leeway to award any other terms of settlement. The system was introduced as it was claimed that it led to parties coming closer to agreement before arbitration, so that their final offer was as close as possible to the arbitrator's likely conception of reasonableness.

11 This is an analogy often adopted by the judges of the Commercial Court, a court which has its own committee of users. A recent report by a working party of that committee (set up to tackle some of the issues referred to in this chapter of the increasing tide of litigation) recommended reforms in many of the standard practices of lawyers in the court, such as ending lengthy opening speeches and protracted reading aloud of documents and legal authorities, handing down typed judgements rather than reading them out, and so on (reported in *Business Law Review*, March 1986, vol. 7, no. 3: 76–7).

12 Lawyers and Lawyers: In-House Lawyers and the Legal Profession

A NEW BRANCH OF THE PROFESSION OF LAW

In-house lawyers in Britain[1] see themselves as a part of the legal profession, and are recognised as such by private practitioners. This broad statement, however, conceals some intriguing tensions within the relationship in relation to such matters as the division of the profession into solicitors and barristers, and in terms of debates on professional independence and professional ethics. The analysis in this book of the workings of this 'organisational' branch of the legal profession also suggests comparison with the organisational setting of the profession at large and prompts some thoughts too on wider issues of the organisation and delivery of legal services in society — what lessons are there for the business of law from a study of lawyers in business? This chapter concentrates on the in-house lawyer as a case study on the sociology of change in the professions — what are the issues raised for one of the most traditional of professions by the advent of the salaried lawyer in business (bearing in mind that similar considerations will apply to salaried lawyers in other organisational settings)? The question of legal services and organisational features of the legal profession will be dealt with in more detail in the next chapter. However, it is worth stressing at this point the importance of the concept of 'profession' in understanding why legal services take the form they do in society, and why it is relevant to discuss the issue at all in relation to the in-house lawyer's position. The argument around the word is no sterile theoretical debate but, from a sociological viewpoint, an integral part of power and status conflicts and achievements within our society. In that sense, a discussion of how lawyers use the concept of a 'profession' is inextricably bound up with any debate about the nature and organisation of legal services in a society.

212

The arrival of the in-house lawyer was not universally welcomed within the legal profession. Among the less likeable features traditional to the public stereotype of lawyers are tendencies to pomposity and arrogance. The characteristics can be found in the reception some gave to in-house lawyers. The American literature suggests that epithets such as 'tame lawyers' and 'kept lawyers' were not unknown in the early days as part of the denigration of the in-house lawyer by colleagues in private practice (Hickman, 1968). Others criticised the growth of the in-house lawyer as an example of the trend away from law in its traditional form (or myth) of the fiercely independent, small-town lawyer towards a profession corrupted by the growth of big business (see the comments on this by Swaine, 1949). Vestiges of these attitudes remain today,[2] although perhaps the dominant element of the relationship remains not so much any feeling of hostility or superiority as one of indifference. Legal education and training, public debate, and professional literature are still very much geared to those in private practice, thus fuelling the notion that in a sense the lawyer in private practice is the 'real lawyer'. The attitude is illustrated in a story described by a lawyer working for an employers' association:

> There has been a long history incidentally of coolness between those in private practice at the Bar and the employed Bar. They tend to look down on the employed Bar. They have no idea what company work involves. I remember one example. I was meeting a friend in private practice for lunch and we bumped into the Company Secretary of [ ]. I introduced them. My friend said afterwards to me how surprised he was to hear he had taken silk when he was only a company lawyer. I had to explain he had to know more than one legal system in that company and to be a Company Secretary there you were no slouch! He was dealing with massive company issues whereas in private practice you may be spending your time on only small-scale crimes, park 'flashers' or drunken drivers.

Against this background of marginality, the in-house lawyers' search for recognition can be seen as in part a search for acceptance and in part an expression of a growing confidence in themselves as an *equal* branch of the legal profession. As with other social movements, the claims of this new branch of the

legal profession are forwarded by its 'opinion leaders' in calls
for group cohesion and self-advertisement. These claims are
furthered by the establishment of specialist professional associations while, in the literature and otherwise, such opinion
leaders explore the boundaries of effective in-house lawyering or
describe the 'arrival' of the in-house lawyer as much in order
to educate their lawyer colleagues (inside and outside business)
as to educate management. Others more assertively see the
growth of the in-house lawyer as of a 'better' kind of legal service
which could in turn 'wake up' the more dated world of private
practice. To those beginning to get a sense of this development,
there was at times a special exhilaration in what was
happening — 'We're part of an international movement', an
Australian lawyer remarked on returning from a convention of
corporate lawyers in the US.

The 'arrival' of the in-house lawyer, however, is not merely
a matter of opinion leaders or of consciousness-raising. It rests
on the actuality of the growth in their numbers, the confidence
and competence achieved with experience and specialisation,
the resources made available to them inside their companies,
the power they hold as purchasers of outside legal services —
all in turn feeding back into the mainstream of the profession
in terms of the career choices of younger lawyers (and, of course,
general growth in the choice of law as a vocation), improved
quality of applicants, recognition by the wider profession of their
significance in the practice of law and reputation of lawyers.
Such changes in consciousness either amongst in-house lawyers
or amongst outside lawyers are nevertheless not achieved in a
uniform or consistent manner. Different aspects of the relationship emerge at different periods and in varied forms. Nor can
such a process take place either in isolation from wider social
trends or from those in the profession generally. And equally, it
in turn contributes to those changes. In particular, the arrival
of the in-house lawyer has implications for the essential 'image'
of a profession as it has been commonly understood and perpetu-
ated by the opinion leaders among the profession at large; implications, too, for concepts of the lawyer-client relationship and
for questions of ethics and professional practice.

LAW AS A PROFESSION

It is important to stress in the account of the in-house lawyer movement not only the historical process of how a new branch of a profession comes to be formed, but also the fact that the concept of being part or seen to be part of the 'profession' is so salient for the parties involved. It is a claim not only that the nature of their legal tasks are similar to those performed by lawyers in private practice but also that they are deserving *of similar status* to lawyers in private practice.

It is hardly surprising that lawyers in business should see this status issue as important. The fact of being a 'professional man' (recently also embracing 'woman') has been a cherished concept in the public pronouncements of the legal profession. It is a concept that is repeatedly used in debates about the nature of legal services and who should provide them. It has also been used repeatedly as a shield by the professional bodies to answer criticisms of restrictive trade practices, or of failure to provide adequate and competent service, or that they should be subject to more outside intervention in these areas. After all, a member of a profession was already subject to the profession's ethical rules, training and self-discipline which took him outside the bounds of mere employment (Napley, 1983).

Sociologists have been equally fascinated by the same concept and have devoted much literature to analysing it, somewhat less to seeing how it is achieved in practice (see Dingwall and Lewis, 1983; Johnson, 1972; Freidson, 1986). The element of status attached to the concept is again an important theme, demonstrated in the frequency with which it has been noted that emerging occupations seek to win the status of a profession by public assertions, credentialism, or political activities. (Leading to one of the experts in the field (Wilensky, 1964) writing an article entitled, not entirely whimsically, 'The Professionalisation of Everyone?') One can summarise these studies, albeit a little crudely, by suggesting that they fall into two camps. First, those which emphasise the use of the label of professionalism as a form of power, over the client and/or over the market for expert services in society, professionalisation as a means to acquire economic and political privileges and influence that would otherwise be unavailable (see Abel, 1982). Second, those which reflect the professions' self-assessments, which 'have been inclined to see professions as honoured servants of public need, conceiving of them as occupations especially distinguished from others by their orientation to serving the needs of the public through the schooled application of their unusually esoteric knowledge and complex skill' (Freidson, 1983: 19).

Of course, law is one of the archetypal models of a profession, along with medicine and the church. The case of business lawyers therefore makes for a fascinating case-study, not only for the insight it throws on how the profession operates in practice, of which there have been few studies, but also by the fact that it is a case of a struggle for professionalisation by a new branch of such an ancient profession.

But what is a profession? An intriguing feature of the debate is that there is no satisfactory definition of a profession, despite the myriad studies of the subject by social researchers (Freidson, op. cit.). Indeed students of the subject are now tending to argue that perhaps the concept should be abandoned in favour of such notions as the use and control of expert knowledge in society (Rueschemeyer, 1973). The same writer also points to the fact that the emphasis on the concept is distinctively Anglo-American, that it carries little weight in other societies outside the ancient professions, more attention being given to educational status and expertise. If such studies have some degree of justification, what is the professionalism that lawyers are referring to? A position common to social researchers and to lawyers (see, for example, Napley 1983; Schein, 1972; Freidson, 1986, ch. 2) is to accept that there is no single, inclusive definition, but that there are a number of features which together can be used to identify a profession, although one will not necessarily find all of them together in any one professional group — the 'trait' or 'inventory' approach. Consider, for example, the submission of the Law Society to the Royal Commission on Legal Services (repeating a definition given ten years earlier in the context of an inquiry into legal services by the National Board for Prices and Incomes):

When a profession is fully developed it may be defined as a body of men and women:
(a) identifiable by reference to some register or record;
(b) recognised as having a special skill and learning in some field of activity in which the public needs protection against

incompetence, and standards of skill and learning being prescribed by the profession itself;

(c) holding themselves out as willing to serve the public;

(d) voluntarily submitting themselves to standards of ethical conduct beyond those required of the ordinary citizen by law;

(e) undertaking to accept professional responsibility to those whom they serve for their actions and to their profession for maintaining public confidence.

The portrait of a professional man which emerges from this definition is of one who has knowledge of a particular field of learning which he will place at the service of any person who wishes to instruct him, subject to obedience to rules of conduct designed to ensure that the service is performed honourably and that the interest of the client is pre-eminent, subject always, in the case of a lawyer, to his duty not to mislead the court. (Response to Question 29 to Law Society, Law Society Memorandum to the Royal Commission on Legal Services)

If one examines these characteristics in any depth, however, problems of circularity of definition remain. When would we recognise a new field of activity as deserving professional status and what stages are there before it is 'fully developed'? Whose criteria do we use to assess such achievement? If we took the occupations of, plumber, undertaker, computer consultant, manager, ambulance driver, for example, is it really correct to say that they do not require special skill and learning in fields where the public needs protection from incompetence?; that the standards of skill are not in effect prescribed by the occupation itself?; that they are devoid of ethical standards beyond those required by law?; and if they don't have codes of conduct or a register, couldn't they invent them? (Nor does the classification problem in such approaches only apply 'downwards' — see Paterson 1983, on judges as a 'third tier'.)

Nor is the problem merely one of definition. One can also ask, if these are the distinguishing characteristics of a profession, *what effect do they have in practice?* Are the standards of the legal profession higher than of other occupations by way of competence in their special areas of expertise, or of effective self-regulation, or ethical conduct and control by way of internal disciplinary committees? It is difficult to answer such questions in the affirmative other than as an act of faith; there is little comparative research on such claims. Indeed, some writers go further and argue that the privileges granted to the legal profession by virtue of this professional mantle have acted as a cloak for almost the converse conclusions, namely that the monopolies and self-regulation granted to lawyers have acted *against* the public interest in many cases, have led to *less* competent service, to corrupting restrictive practices and to inadequate control by the professional bodies of the errors, negligence (and worse) of their members.[4]

In the face of the strong undercurrents of public feeling in these matters, and more crucially in the face of legislative reforms, the legal profession itself, particularly the solicitors' branch, now seems finally ready to acknowledge publicly that the profession is in need of reforms to bring itself more into line with the public interest. In a number of areas changes are under way — the introduction of mandatory continuing education (Page, 1985), acceptance of the practice of advertising by solicitors and of new practice rules in response to the threat to conveyancing income (Professional Code of Conduct, 1986), and the reform of internal disciplinary proceedings arising from public complaints about solicitors in the direction of a greater element of independence from Law Society control (Administration of Justice Act, 1985). One can argue over whether the changes go far enough but in themselves they represent radical changes in existing practice.

Nor are these winds of change merely affecting lawyers *vis-à-vis* the public. Within the legal profession, there has been increasing and public evidence of struggles between opposing factions of lawyers seeking to determine the manner of response to the social and economic pressures on the profession. Both the Law Society and the Bar have been faced with internal opposition to their style and structure of governance, moving the Bar Council closer towards what was widely recognised in press reports as a move to establish more of a 'trade union' to represent barristers' interests (Blom-Cooper, 1985); both bodies also fought a public battle with the Lord Chancellor, extending as far as an initial court hearing, over lack of consultation on levels of increase for Legal Aid fees; finally, tensions between solicitors and barristers have surfaced over, on the one hand, the failure of solicitors to pay fees promptly (traditionally a taboo subject for barristers, a non-contractual matter based on 'professional' understanding), on the other the claims by solicitors to be equally worthy of rights of audience in the higher courts and elevation to senior judicial office, currently still the preserve of the Bar (see Law Society Contentious Business Committee, op. cit.), a claim barristers alleged to be a product of a search for work following the loss of solicitors' lucrative conveyancing monopoly by legislative reform. In an attempt to resolve these differences without a damaging public debate, a joint committee of the Law Society and the Bar (the Marre Committee) was set up in April 1986 to examine and report (within two years) on the future structure of the legal profession.

The decline of formerly accepted professional practices, such as the ending of restrictions on advertising and the erosion of the principle of self-regulation, tend to confirm the view that the use of the word 'profession' obscures rather than reveals the processes involved in social control and application of expert knowledge, and indeed supports the case of those who have argued that this has been a primary motive in the way the concept has been so heavily used by lawyers and other professions and would-be professions. Substitute the term 'trade union' for 'profession' and a very different view would have been taken by governments, public and media, as well as the judiciary, of the various restrictive practices which have been the privilege of the legal profession to exercise. The late Sir Otto Kahn-Freund, a distinguished labour lawyer of German origin, writing from another perspective, suggested that the professions *and* the trade unions in Britain reflect a peculiarly British tendency in their jealous pursuit of guild interests in a manner frequently to the detriment of the wider public interest (Kahn-Freund, 1979).

Developments in the legal profession coincide therefore with a new sociological understanding of the concept of a profession, a readiness to 'demystify' the attributes of a profession (along with a secularisation of other social rules and morals), to see it as a culturally relative concept which serves mainly to cover the pursuit of status and class distinctions in the interest of member advancement or protection, or a concept which derives its main value not from any objective characteristics but from social perceptions and attitudes — a 'folk concept' (Freidson, 1986) used by professional elites to establish social positions of power, 'market shelters'.

However, reducing professional identification to a case of mere rhetoric to conceal material interests of status and class may help explain some of the activities of professional associations, particularly defensive reactions to proposals for change. Nevertheless, one must distinguish between a cynical observer's view of social processes and the psychological reality of the concept for its holders. The economic explanation of professional identification ignores the positive aspects of the concept, particularly what one might describe as its symbolic value or 'aspirational' character. As one City firm lawyer expressed it — 'My thesis is that there is something to being a profession so long as you take it seriously.' The fact of feeling oneself part of an esteemed profession is perhaps as much a factor in inducing internalised standards of conduct and aspiration as the formal machinery of rules set out by the association. Debates on change in the profession are couched in terms of the professional ideals to which allegiance is owed, choices have to be consistent with the integrity of the professional, colleagues are judged in terms of their adherence to professional norms. In other words, the concept of a status has both enabling and disabling aspects. Which is dominant at any one time, or in any one individual or group, is more a matter of specific circumstances than of any general rule. More concretely, it *would* make a difference if lawyers regarded themselves as 'merely' a business or as merely a trade union. But how *much* of a difference? And *what kinds* of difference? Such questions go to the root of the argument about whether the concept of a 'profession' carries any real significance other than its classic capacity to separate the holder from those engaged in 'trade' or as 'labour' — the concept of profession arose after all at a time when it was not socially respectable to engage in either and when employment relationships were governed by Master and Servant concepts.

It is also pertinent to point out here that the assumption of many lawyers about a profession being something distinct from business or a trade union itself is revealing about their own negative concepts of these social institutions. Rejecting the cynical observer's view of the professions, they in turn take on the role of cynical observer of other social institutions, at once confirming their identity and rejecting alternative and threatening models as being predominantly directed by self-interest (see, for example, the comments on business by Napley, op. cit.). Yet just as the notion of being a member of a profession has a psychological function which both extends and limits individual capacities and moralities, equally one can argue the same process occurs for those who identify themselves with business or a trade union. Both of these latter institutions have self-seeking and self-serving aspects to them. Yet they also achieve more. Membership of a trade union also traditionally carried with it connotations of solidarity, of sharing and of helping the underdog, of democratic organisation. (Because of this last factor, unions can be criticised for failure to hold ballots, while the question of 'democracy' in companies or the legal profession is seen as a separate issue — see Mackie, 1984). The early trade unions in fact grew out of skilled trades which like the professions decreed their own training and standards of workmanship and provided benefit schemes to assist members in difficulty. Equally, the modern literature on business emphasises the need for *professional* management, including attention to the need for continuing learning and for dealing with customers and employees with integrity (as reflected in in-house lawyers' perceptions of business ethics; see, for example, Lippitt's comments on ethics in organisational consultancy, 1982: 363–77; and Kozelka, 1962).

One can in fact detect a trend towards a *convergence* of public policy towards these different sectors, subsumed under a more diffuse and difficult political notion of the 'public interest' dimension in all 'social estates' and occupational practices. In each case there have been past (and present) claims that these social institutions are capable of self-regulation — business in terms of its economic imperatives, trade unions and the professions in terms of their essentially autonomous nature and inherent integrity. In each case the regulatory trends of national governments have begun to establish more detailed rules of conduct, to 're-regulate' not only in relation to that institution's impact on public affairs, but also in terms of its internal workings, although the extent and direction of trends have been influenced by the particular nature of the government of the day as well as by the contemporary political influence of the social estates involved. Some of the complexities of understanding this process of regulation have already been outlined in chapter 10 in relation to business conduct.

In summary, if the concept of a profession is being 'secularised', the way becomes clearer, too, for more open debate to take place about the role of experts in society, about the use of, and access to, expert knowledge and skills, unhampered by the traditional prejudices of, and towards, sectional interests. The legal profession's status in turn will derive more closely from its special *expertise* in the community, not because of its *social* status. Nonetheless, some see these trends not as opening up the professions to a more rational sense of status, but as leading to the destruction of professional value systems (Napley, op. cit.), a professional equivalent perhaps of moral nostalgia for an era of non-secular social values. In this debate, the in-house lawyer's position is a significant one.

IN-HOUSE LAWYERS AND THE LEGAL PROFESSION

Lawyers in business are required to obtain the same professional qualifications and standards of training as lawyers in private practice in order to carry out similar legal functions for their client in areas of *exclusive* professional competence — conveyancing, advising counsel, appearing on behalf of the client in the lower courts, preparing documents for legal proceedings, and so on. Of course, an employer, as any other client, can choose to use unqualified assistance to check on legal matters, advise appropriate actions, draw up contracts and so on, and two managers interviewed in my study were employed in this manner — as legal/personnel manager, and as a legislation monitoring adviser, the latter a law graduate.[5] The lawyers working in business clearly regarded themselves as lawyers, although working for a single client. (Those who had shifted over to a position of Company Secretary, however, felt their work had become more administrative with less legal content.) Their training, experience of private practice, and continuing contacts with other lawyers working inside and outside business organisations, reinforced this and gave expression to it in terms of the terminology they used in interviews of 'advising the client', 'taking instructions', and so on. (There were signs, however, that this terminology might come to be seen as inappropriate for a more integrated business lawyer, as it signified a distancing of the lawyer from the business.)

This status was echoed in managers' perceptions, most in-house lawyers admitting to having to cope with sections of management who sought to avoid involvement of the legal department in case it restricted their freedom over their business dealings. Accepting a degree of banter by other employees about the legal profession was a common experience. The fact that they saw themselves as lawyers was also confirmed in their views about the limits on their career options in the company. Many saw a need to break down such barriers, but this does not alter the basic fact of their professional identification, by themselves and others.

It is in the relations with their colleagues in private practice where one finds the most intriguing illustration of the intricacies of professional legal practice. I have already referred to the way the profession initially disparaged the concept of the employed lawyer. This neglect of the role of the employed lawyer meant that it is only recently that more attention has been given to detailed aspects of their professional practice which do not fit closely with traditional 'ethical' rules[6] (Fletcher Rogers, 1968; Gow, 1968). The restrictive practices employed by the legal profession have also led to certain tangled matters of detail in the professional character of the work of in-house lawyers. I have singled out three aspects of the professional situation of in-house lawyers as significant indicators of the complexities of professional practice — the division of the profession, the independence of the lawyer, and the definition of the client.

A DIVIDED, FUSED PROFESSION

The division of the legal profession in England and Wales into two branches, of barristers and solicitors,[7] has been mirrored in the associations representing business lawyers. The Commerce and Industry Group of the Law Society (the C and I group) and the Bar Association for Commerce, Finance and Industry (BACFI), represent respectively solicitors and barristers employed in business. Both associations rely on voluntary membership, and both are closely attached to the main professional bodies, the Law Society and Bar Council.[8] The C and I Group was formed in 1960 and now has just under two thousand members, BACFI in 1965 and now has just under one thousand members. Both groups form only a small percentage of the total population of lawyers in the professional bodies (although BACFI forms a more significant proportion of barristers in private practice, almost ten per cent, than the C & I Group of solicitors, under five per cent), a fact in itself which accounts for some of the difficulties they have in achieving changes in professional rules. Both associations hold regular meetings, seminars and conferences for their members, issue bulletins, and campaign within their wider professional bodies for reforms relevant to their memberships.

Some of the tensions in the relations between the two branches of the profession referred to earlier in this chapter also spilled over into some of the comments made to me. However, such intra-professional criticism, as with criticism of fellow lawyers in private practice, was made with a certain amount of reserve, a wish not to be quoted or seen as undermining what were generally good relations between the two groups.[9] The main point made by solicitors was that the fact of being an employed lawyer made a nonsense of the distinction between barristers and solicitors, since an employed barrister had not the same rights of appearance in court as a 'practising barrister', even for his own client (on this see below), could not do conveyancing without a special certificate of qualification, and as a barrister, generally had had less training than a solicitor and less experience of direct dealings with clients (these latter points also applied to barristers in general). Sometimes, these attitudes were reflected in the fact that a company did not recruit barristers to its legal department, particularly where recruitment procedures were under the direction of existing legal staff who were solicitors. In most companies, solicitors and barristers worked side by side and the difference in initial qualification was forgotten for most purposes except insofar as it affected initial assumption of work responsibilities, such as conveyancing duties. Solicitors are probably in the majority in all business sectors[10] (other than newspapers perhaps), barristers most prevalent in advisory bodies in keeping with the traditional role of barristers outside their advocacy specialisation.

The barristers interviewed were less vocal on this issue. It was accepted as an inevitable and common feature of this branch of the profession that most barristers did not pursue life at the Bar either because they were unsuitable for its rigours or could not afford the period of penury forced on aspiring barristers, of an unpaid pupillage and early years of struggle to build a successful practice. (The economic factors were the most common reason given by interviewees as to why they had left practice at the Bar.) Most young barristers therefore went into other forms of employment including that of business. (One Head of Department, himself a barrister, admitted to a preference for recruiting barristers on the grounds of 'character', that is, barristers were more forceful, in his view.) They did not feel criticism of their position as employed lawyers was justified given their legal qualifications and the accepted practice of the Bar, and saw any criticism of their position as on a par with solicitors' resistance to the ending of the conveyancing monopoly, a job protection reaction.

The debate over the value of the divided profession has been a long-drawn out one, the system last receiving an official seal of approval from the Royal Commission on Legal Services in 1979. It is not necessary in the context of this study to revive the arguments over costs, specialisation, independence (see Hazell, 1978; Reeves, 1986), merely to note the resurgence of the debate with the recent threats to the conveyancing work of solicitors and the establishment in England and Wales of a salaried Crown Prosecution Service. There have also been calls for a common training for both branches, with specialisation thereafter (Law Society, Contentious Business Committee, 1986). Whatever the merits of the arguments for division on grounds of specialisation, it has no evident justification in the context of in-house legal work other than as an inevitable side-effect of a divided professional training, *particularly since employed barristers lose the rights of audience available to their colleagues in private practice.* Employed barristers are prevented from representing their client in the higher courts (the case must be taken by a barrister in private practice) and only recently (through the campaigning work of BACFI and with the support of the Royal Commission on Legal Services) won the right to represent their client in the lower courts (county and magistrates' courts) and to advise counsel in non-contentious cases (a practice normally reserved for solicitors). Conversely, the Bar's ethical rule of only dealing with clients indirectly through the medium of a solicitor does not apply in the case of employed barristers.

While the division of the profession *inside* business legal departments seems an irrelevance, only made necessary as a consequence of the external profession training arrangements, there was no doubt that in-house lawyers at least welcomed the tradition of access to outside lawyers of both branches, for the reasons mentioned in chapter 7 — access to second opinions, divestment of difficult or demanding cases, political support in intra-company debates. (Similar reasons are sometimes given to justify a divided profession as such although it has been argued that the same results would be achieved by specialisation within firms of solicitors.) Only a few companies aimed to keep all work (other than that solely the jurisdiction of the Bar) in-house. The in-house lawyer therefore benefits particularly well from the structure of the profession, having access not only to other firms of solicitors but also to counsel, without arousing client objections (at least where cost questions do not arise). It is possibly more difficult for a partner in private practice to suggest to a client that they seek additional advice from other firms of lawyers, partly because of the cost and partly because it may lead the client to wonder about the competence of the lawyer the client has consulted (Rosenthal, 1974), although the use of other firms as agents in certain areas of legal practice is well-established, for example, for work in another locality.

There were cordial relations between the two professional bodies in the area and a number of joint activities. My overall impression was that my questions about the division of the two branches raised an issue which was little considered in practice but was a source of annoyance to some solicitors if they thought about it. However, of the two groups, barristers were placed in a more awkward position because of professional rules arising from a divided profession.

THE INDEPENDENCE OF THE LAWYER

The stance taken by the Bar in relation to in-house barristers may derive partly from unquestioned tradition (an important and often underestimated element in the creation, maintenance and defence of professional norms). However, insofar as it is based on policy, that policy gives us an insight into another important word in the debates of lawyers in relation to the practice of law, one closely allied to lawyers' understanding of the term 'profession', namely that of the 'independence' of the lawyer.[11] In-house lawyers, in keeping with their professional identification, use the expression frequently in their professional literature. Yet one finds that, like the term 'profession', the word has more than one connotation (Zander, 1976). Being 'independent' seemed to be used with two separate emphases. In-house lawyers most frequently used the expression to refer to their need to remain 'objective' in their analysis of the application of legal rules to management practices, rather than lose sight of the possible judicial interpretation of an 'outsider'. On the other hand, it referred sometimes to the need for the in-house lawyer to avoid undue pressure from any manager to follow a particular line of reasoning when the lawyer's judgement clearly called for a different evaluation of the situation. The former could arise from a self-induced element of bias, and demanded an ability largely related to thinking skills, which depended on the lawyer's training and continued vigilance over his own judgements. The latter was externally focused, and required firmness, a sense of organisational 'politics' and, on a rare occasion, the ability to appeal over another manager's head for support from the head of the legal department or from the Board. As we have already seen, the latter was seen as an uncommon occurrence, few ethical problems being posed in practice. It is in relation to the second part of this issue of 'independence' that one finds a subsidiary debate within the profession on the status of in-house lawyers, closely linked to the question of the organisational form of legal services.

The position of the Bar in relation to employed barristers provides the first evidence of the argument around independence. As we have seen, access to the privileges and restrictions on practice at the Bar primarily depend not on training, nor on specialisation (since a large company could probably justify employing a barrister full-time for its cases in court) *but on the organisational structure of legal service*. It is *self-employment*, and therefore public access to the Bar (although only, of course, via a solicitor as intermediary), which is the litmus test of independence for this branch of the profession. It is not training, knowledge, specialisation or qualifications (all of which an in-house barrister may have) which ultimately determine the right to exercise fully one's profession, but the *business form* in which it is exercised.[12] This traditional stance is taken even further than that held by solicitors, in that the rules of the Bar also prevent barristers going into partnership. Barristers share chambers, paying individual contributions towards the cost of running the chambers. Also, additional employment while practising as a barrister is prohibited, with certain limited exceptions. The arguments for this position are primarily based on the notion of the need for 'individualism and independence'. Other business arrangements, it is claimed, would begin to erode these traditional qualities of legal practice amongst this branch of the profession, and lead to conflicts of interest between client representation, duties to the court, and business needs.

Such arguments have been largely accepted by official inquiries into the legal profession, the most recent[13] that of the Benson Royal Commission (although see Reeves', 1986, comments on this). Whatever the merits of these arguments they still leave open the question of in-house employed barristers. They did not doubt their own independence, nor were they seeking to set up in general practice. But what is the strength of the argument against their representing their own employer in court? The argument in this case seems a weak one, and indeed this fact was recognised in the Royal Commission's findings. Since then, the Bar has made some further concessions under pressure from BACFI, so that it is now possible for an employed barrister to act for his employer in certain limited circumstances of non-contentious business or lower courts or tribunals. Such a limited degree of concession of rights to members of their own profession suggests perhaps that the practice has more foundation in job-protection concerns than on principle. (In any case, most in-house lawyers felt they would not wish to spend the time necessary to follow a case in court, suggesting that reform of the rule would have little effect in practice.)

Criticism of in-house lawyers' independence by some solicitors in private practice has followed a similar, but separate, emphasis, again based on the question of *organisational* constraints and on the identification of independence as self-employment (in partnership form and with allowance for salaried associates). Solicitors employed by organisations are

alleged to be more open to undue influence because of their
employment status (and hence job security pressures), a view
in-house lawyers have resisted vigorously.[14] In-house lawyers
have suggested that they are no more open to influence than an
outside lawyer dependent on important clients for his fees, that
the accusation contains a misunderstanding of business practice
and business attitudes and of the in-house lawyer's role inside
a company (see chapter 10). The issue of independence is also
emerging over questions of restructuring legal services, particularly the question of whether lawyers can be employed by banks,
building societies and other organisations to offer legal services
(conveyancing) to members of the public rather than act for
them directly as employer, a distinction which in some circumstances may be a little ingenuous. The Law Society has opted
for opposition to such developments (see the new Rule 4 in the
Professional Code of Conduct, 1986 — an employed lawyer shall
not do professional work for anyone other than his employer).

Finally, the question of independence and in-house lawyers
has arisen also in the courts, on the topic of legal professional
privilege, and brought to light yet further differences of
emphasis, this time between countries, in the resolution of the
independence versus employment debate. The normal rule of
evidence is that communications between a party and his legal
adviser are protected from discovery by the other side, if they
are made for the purpose of obtaining or giving legal advice and
assistance. In England the point was expressly decided in the
Court of Appeal in the case of *Alfred Crompton Amusement Machines*
versus *Customs and Excise Commissioners* [1972] 2 All E.R. 353
where Lord Denning M.R. said (at 376) of employed legal
advisers:

> They are regarded by the law as in every respect in the same
> position as those who practise on their own account. The only
> difference is, they act for one client only, and not for several
> clients. They must uphold the same standards of honour and
> of etiquette. They are subject to the same duties to their client
> and to the court. They must respect the same confidences.
> They and their clients have the same privileges.

The other judges, Karminski, J. and Orr, L.J., expressly agreed with Lord Denning on this point and the point was conceded on appeal to the House of Lords [1974] AC 405.

A similar legal position has been established in Australia (Jones, 1985) and in the United States (Coombe, 1985, f.23): the question of a lawyer's independence, of whether a lawyer can be said to be under the undue influence of a client so as to deny the lawyer access to confidential documents of a third party (competitor), is a question of fact in each case. However, the position has been complicated for in-house lawyers in Europe and for non-EEC lawyers by a decision of the European Court (*AM & S Europe Limited* versus *Commission of the European Community* [1983] 1 All E.R. 705). In its decision the court held that legal professional privilege protecting communications from disclosure was only available to practitioners in private practice, not to in-house lawyers, on the grounds of the latter's lack of independence. The judgement, which can be seen as an attempt to find a common baseline for varied European practice with regard to the professional status of in-house lawyers (Boyd, 1983), has caused not a little difficulty for such lawyers. In cases where there might be a European element, care would have to be taken with sensitive advice to ensure that it was given by outside lawyers or communicated in a less sensitive form. While the judgement has been a blow to the status of in-house lawyers, my impression from the interviews (where the issue was not raised unless the interviewee mentioned it) was that it has as yet had only a limited effect on practice, perhaps because of the limited occasions where this issue arises in proceedings. However, more research would be necessary to establish the accuracy of this conclusion. At a professional level, in-house lawyers have taken the decision very seriously and are engaged in a campaign to have the position re-assessed.

What the case does illustrate for our purposes is not only the importance of the issue in lawyers' understanding of their professional position, but exactly how closely once again the concept of the 'independence' of the professional has been equated by lawyers with a business or organisational form of practice, that of self-employment. The exact impact of this on the practice of in-house lawyers varies with the extent of their development and status not only in different countries but, as we have also seen, even with relation to different branches of the profession and different aspects of professional practice.

Thus, the position of the in-house lawyer is proving a testing ground in practice for the boundaries of this concept. If in-house lawyers can claim that, despite their close economic relationship with the client, their professional standards are equally high and that the 'proper test of independence is the paramountcy of the lawyer's duty to observe professional and ethical standards' (Jones, 1985) (that is, whether the lawyer is subject to professional rules of conduct which override any economic relationship), then it calls into question the paramountcy of the *economic* form in which law is practised. It makes conceivable alternative business forms for the delivery of legal services, subject to appropriate safeguards of the professional standards of independence (such as mandatory liability insurance policies, special employment protection rules, and so forth). This issue is considered more fully in the next chapter.

Finally, one should note that the salience of the concept of independence for lawyers rests on the particular nature of law as a profession, with the role of the lawyer as the prime defender of individual rights against other social interests, assisted by, and hence with appropriate responsibilities to, the courts. The notion of independence takes a different form in other professions, thus usually allowing other organisational forms of practice, for example, hospital doctors as employees of local health authorities.[15] As with other aspects of debates about the legal profession, one can conclude that the field would merit far greater detailed research. The author has been a little surprised to find that, in countries so firmly attached to the 'common law' tradition of proceeding to develop law case-by-case, the debates within the legal profession on independence and professional ethics are almost invariably devoid not only of systematic analysis or a research base, but also of much by way of precise definitions,[16] concrete instances[17] or case-law[18] (Zander, op. cit.).

This confusion was reflected in the varied comments and differences of opinion amongst the outside lawyers interviewed in response to questions on in-house lawyer independence. However, even amongst those who perceived a problem, there was generally a readiness to accept the principle of the case-law referred to earlier, that some lawyers in private practice were also vulnerable to excessive client influence.

We're never dependent on one client. As an in-house lawyer

if you think that what they're doing is improper, you can't walk away. Your car and mortgage are owned by the company. All you can do is quit. Here you can say I will not work for that client and neither should the firm. Whether the senior partner would agree is the next question. . . . You turn down work for all sorts of reasons, you're too busy, conflicts of interest, the size of transaction is not cost-effective. (City firm lawyer)

Ultimately it's a question of commercial judgement as to how lawyers argue whether a question's ethical or not ethical – whether it would be good for your practice. . . . I genuinely have never perceived any ethical problem for in-house lawyers. If there is an ethical problem, I think it makes them *more* concerned about their company image, whereas an outside lawyer would tend to say 'we have our strong points, let's move forward.' An in-house lawyer would see the awkwardness coming. . . . There are not many ethical problems in private practice either, outside of conflict of interest questions. . . . I don't see standards dropping. There are a lot of horrible, nasty, shitty firms but there always have been. Always the opportunistic ones. It's not so much that they're unethical but they behave badly. Writing snide letters, serving documents at the last moment, taking cheap points. Not exactly lying but coming close to it. That's always been the case. (Litigation partner in City firm)

You've got to be a very strong person to stand up to the powerful bullies you can have in business. I think there's a certain amount of self-selection, if you're an independent-minded person, you tend not to end up as an in-house lawyer. . . . You can come under tremendous management pressure. A big department would provide its own shell. Or if the lawyer's straight, the company would just go outside. . . . There's a general rising tide of amoral and immoral dealings, and most of the transactions need lawyers involved. And generally there are large fees involved so who can resist. Your moral autonomy comes under maximum pressure. It comes to the fact that the big law firms and the big accountancy firms are now out of control. They don't have any clear moral guidelines . . . The modern lawyer is at the coalface of ethics.

Law is more and more intrusive and business more and more competitive so you're constantly coming up against the frontiers, the cliff-edge of what's permissible. Because the guy who goes one inch more wins. (Partner in smaller City firm)

The pressures are different for an in-house lawyer. He's got to take a stand on principle. It puts an enormous burden on a person's professional integrity. And the other factor – it's true for solo practitioners as well – is that there's no one to talk it over with in a professional sense. It's easier for us to resist. . . . [Later, discussing the issue of mixed-professional partnerships . . .] for some reason, solicitors are extremely gullible when it comes to people standing up at meetings and making grand statements about independence and integrity. What it actually comes down to is very difficult to unravel. (Former in-house lawyer, now partner in provincial commercial firm)

The in-house lawyer's in no different position from the small firm with a large client . . . You always have to be that little bit more careful with a client in private practice. They may go to another solicitor's down the road. (Former in-house lawyer, now partner in provincial commercial firm)

As with the definition of the word 'profession', the imprecision of the debates on independence (used at times to refer to freedom from state control, at other times from client control or from 'extraneous' considerations) and professional ethics, and their lack of a proper research foundation, may paradoxically be an advantage for the legal profession in its endeavours to defend itself from outside regulation. However, public disquiet about professional services and restrictive practices, and the changing role of law in society which earlier chapters have referred to, point towards likely changes in the business structure of legal service (see chapter 13). In such circumstances the profession can gain little from asserting values and terminology which have such a tenuous foundation of research or case-law. The independence of the lawyer, most lawyers would agree, is a vital aspect of legal services. It therefore deserves more systematic analysis and more attention to the balance of public and private interest. If the legal profession is indeed becoming, as other

professions,[19] increasingly differentiated and specialised, both in
the content of its work *and* in the organisational forms by which
services are delivered, such analyses would assist the development of professional codes of practice which give appropriate
recognition to this differentiation, to the fact that there are
'lawyers and lawyers', and that the concept of independence
therefore needs refinement if it is to be meaningful in these
varied contexts.

ORGANISATIONS AS CLIENTS

Finally, in relation to this outline of the in-house lawyer as a
case study of intra-professional practice, it is worth pausing to
note that the term 'client', like the other expressions discussed
in this chapter, has a degree of flexible ambiguity to its use in
professional practice. The fact that corporations have been given
legal personalty, that they can sue and be sued in their own
names, means that both in-house and outside lawyers can act
for a fictional entity. The corporation does not exist in any
individual but is an entity in its own right, to which directors
have a fiduciary duty. Essentially, of course, it is the body of
owners of the company, the shareholders, to whom this duty
is ultimately owed. However, lawyers deal normally with the
corporate officers of the company and assume, for most
purposes, that these officers are acting within the scope of their
fiduciary (and contractual) duties. There are theoretically, and
in practice, many occasions where one might doubt that the
theory works exactly along these lines, since the interests of
the different constituencies of a company, directors, managers,
employees, shareholders may have varied interests and influence
over the direction of the company. However, this approach to
companies as clients seems to have worked reasonably successfully in practice and will no doubt continue to do so unless there
is a major reappraisal of corporate structures, either in the
direction of European concepts of supervisory boards, or towards
more personal American notions of corporate responsibilities or
more explicit recognition of the rights of the various 'stake-
holders' in company structures (see, for example, Stone, 1975).
    As mentioned earlier, in-house lawyers had little practical
difficulty in acting out their role within the company. The client

was the company, and the requests for advice and legal action from the directors and senior management could normally be taken to represent the interests of the company. This position is no different from that taken by outside lawyers. However, it is perhaps worth making the point that there is an extended understanding of client service for in-house lawyers. The in-house lawyer's assistance to the client is in practice much wider than that likely to be undertaken by outside lawyers. While an outside lawyer most commonly liaises with one or a few corporate officers on particular purposes, *the in-house lawyer's function was to be available to a range of managers*, depending on the extent of department specialisation and the lawyer's accessibility, in order to fulfill the role of making company practice legally effective. The 'client' of the in-house lawyer is therefore more accurately described as the *'community of management'* in the organisation, the in-house lawyer as 'community lawyer'[20] within the organisation assisting the community (corporate) decision-making process. This is, in sociological terms, equivalent to the fiction of the corporate entity as client because the psychological reality of a business is that the purposes of the organisation permeate all management decisions either as a result of hierarchical directions to lower management, or through self-directed adherence to those same purposes (or self-justifying rationalisations of these). This is not to deny, of course, that such corporate purpose is subject to differing interpretations, to deviation and personal manipulation of the overall aims (the concerns of much organisation theory), just as the actions of directors can not always be said to be entirely in line with shareholder interests in practice. It is, however, a ready approximation to the legal theory.

In keeping with this basic organisational ethos, the in-house lawyer's practice created not so much ethical problems – the accusation levelled at them by some outside lawyers – as problems related to 'organisational politics'. In-house lawyers talked not of the problem of being asked to assist in corporate wrong-doing, but in terms of the need to be seen as accessible, 'not going over people's heads', 'giving them solutions, not problems', and so on. The key emphasis was winning friendship and respect in that community by furthering business aims, not one of resisting attempts to corrupt lawyers in the pursuit of profit. At the same time the hierarchical nature of the business was, for lawyers, as influential as for other employees. A higher level of management was, other things being equal, entitled to priority in requests for advice:

> One has to consider the 'jumpability factor' I suppose. In private practice, the jumpability factor is money, if the client pays, you jump. Whereas in in-house work, I suppose it's a question of who asks you to do it, that is who in the management structure – and probably the possible consequences in the long run if you don't do it and as it leads to potential embarrassment. (Oil company lawyer)

NOTES

1 The statement also applies to lawyers in Australia but I have focused my discussion on UK lawyers as the division of the profession is less rigid in Australia and the position varies between states.

2 For a discussion on some of the tensions, see the panel discussion at the annual conference of the Corporate Lawyers' Association of Victoria (1985). Note also Cohen's (1984) comment that questions of the second-class status of in-house lawyers are still a live issue in the UK and US (146ff.).

3 And particularly are affected by cultural settings – see Kolvenbach's (1979) discussion of the variety of the extent of professional recognition of in-house lawyers in different countries.

4 See the severe indictment of lawyers by Joseph (1985), and the more restrained but equally telling account by Reeves (1986), both solicitors. Both writers have little faith in the findings of past public inquiries into the profession, arguing that they have been over-influenced by the powerful status of the profession (or parts of it) in their analysis and perceptions. Some justification for this viewpoint may be found in the very fact that the issue of professional restrictive practices keeps returning despite these expressions of support for the system, although this time under a more 'radical' government perhaps. See the Office of Fair Trading Report on the Professions (1986) and, for debates within the profession, 'Lawyers and the Courts: Time for Some Changes', Law Society Contentious Business Committee, January 1986.

5 Many other law graduates are, of course, employed in large companies but normally in capacities which do not have any or any major legal function. (Whether a law graduate who does have such a role falls within the ambit of the legal profession is another difficult borderline issue for the definition of profession – after all many academic lawyers are not

professionally qualified but usually regarded as part of the legal profession in some sense. For example, in several countries, it is accepted practice to appoint academics to appellate courts, in recognition of their expertise. The idea has been mooted in the UK but so far firmly resisted.)

6 Gow (1968) distinguishes between three types of ethical rules – general principles of decent behaviour (arising from the traditions of lawyers as gentlemen); rules to facilitate the fair administration of justice; and rules designed to regulate competition between lawyers for the benefit of all (lawyers?). Barristers in employment are particularly affected by the third type, but both branches of in-house lawyer have suffered to some extent from attitudes and practices derived from each category.

7 See Reeves (op. cit.) for a bibliography and brief history.

8 The C & I Group is a division of the Law Society, while BACFI by contrast is independent of the Bar Council although it has close relations with it and is given official status in the structure of the Bar Council, and voting rights which have recently been extended in the newly-formed General Council of the Bar.

9 For a tactful reference to the 'superiority' of solicitors for in-house work that some solicitors alleged, see the evidence of the Commerce and Industry Group to the Royal Commission on Legal Services (Law Society, 1977, paras. 3.5, 6.5).

10 See the AGCAS (1986) survey. Solicitors were found in larger numbers across all sectors (almost 80 per cent of the sample), the highest proportion of barristers being found in the professional/advisory bodies (36 per cent), approximately one in four lawyers being barristers in commercial, engineering and financial sectors (and in oil/chemical/coal excluding the effect of one major company in that sector). In building and civil engineering, only 5 per cent of the lawyers in the survey were barristers.

11 Sexton and Maher (1982) see this issue of how to accommodate in-house lawyers in the traditional notion of the independence of the profession as the major issue raised by the development of the in-house lawyer. They suggest there is as yet no accepted view in Australia of how the in-house lawyer is to maintain professional independence yet look after potentially conflicting interests of management, directors and shareholders. (The position of the outside lawyer representing a company is, of course, little clearer in this respect.)

12 Barristers working in Law Centres are also an allowable exception to the rule.

13 The Office of Fair Trading (1986) more recently was asked to consider the position with regard to the restrictions on business structures in various professions. It describes the position of the Bar, then refrains from comment (p84) because of the wider issues regarding legal services the question raises, and the fact that a joint committee of the Bar Council and Law Society, with independent members, is to report in two years' time on the subject (the Marre Committee, expected to report in 1988).

14 The most outspoken article on the subject was written in the Law Society Gazette by a leading solicitor in private practice, Sir David Napley (1983). The article led to a vigorous correspondence on the subject in subsequent issues.

15   In this connection, it is of interest that Napley (op. cit.) appears to take the view that the move to employee status by doctors has led to a deterioration in their professional standards. Some examples of restrictions on business practice by other professions – architects and accountants, are outlined in the Office of Fair Trading Report (1986).

16   See Gow (1968), n6 for a useful starting point.

17   Stereotyped or defensive reactions to broad questions of ethics in lawyer interviews have been noted by other researchers (Smigel, 1969; Rosen, 1984).

18   For example, the Office of Fair Trading report notes (45, para. 4.13) that the Senate of the Inns of Court and the Bar does not keep any systematic central record or statistical breakdown of complaints against barristers for professional misconduct. The Royal Commission on Legal Services had similar difficulties.

19   Freidson (1986) in fact stresses that independence is not specifically linked to business form for the majority of professions as most professionals are now employees. ' . . . the serious issue for theorising and descriptive analysis is not some trend toward the loss of independence through entrance into employment but rather the conditions of employment . . . and whether they are changing sufficiently to be worth comment. . . . In a market economy one's labor is a commodity whether one sells it to an employer or a customer . . . when one is self-employed, one is not independent but rather operating a franchised trade, the terms of the franchise varying with the institutions that structure one's place in the market. The task is then to trace out the direct and indirect set of independencies created by the franchise' (124–5).

20   A minor addendum to this 'community lawyer' approach is found in another aspect of in-house legal work, informal advice to employees of the company on legal questions arising outside of employment. (In two companies this practice was apparently approved, although not publicised, by the Board as a company policy.) The range of employees given such advice varied from personal acquaintances to advice to any employee who happened to have been advised to have a chat with the company lawyer. The most frequent requests covered such matters as vehicle accidents, family problems, probate and problems with outside solicitors. Such an advisory role was not frequent nor encouraged, but was normally given out of courtesy. It was also very limited, amounting usually to no more than a ten minute interview giving general guidance or advising someone to approach an outside lawyer.

13 The Law Business and the Business of Law: A Crisis of Direction?

ORGANISATIONAL FACTORS IN PROFESSIONAL WORK

It is a common tenet of management literature that types of organisational structure and process do make a difference to the character, effectiveness and efficiency of a business, over and above any influence of individuals' characteristics (Handy, 1985). Much of this book has already dealt with organisational issues in the context of the in-house lawyer's role. It is also evident from this discussion that it is important to retain notions of *purpose* or *values*[1] to understand the individual's contribution to organisational directions. We have seen how the *integrated lawyer* notion has arisen as an image of effective service, of purpose, for the in-house lawyer's role. Purpose is also an important concept in explaining how the 'single client' legal fiction has a degree of psychological reality, founded on the hierarchical structures of business organisations dedicated to particular aims. (Although in each case such aims, whether that of the integrated lawyer for the individual or those of profit maximisation/organisational survival for the company, are never 'pure' but influenced and channelled by individual, organisational and environmental factors.)

If we take this analysis a stage further and apply it to the legal profession in general, the same factors of structure and purpose are equally important in understanding the nature of the 'law business', as well as in analysing aspects of the differences in the service provided by in-house lawyers and lawyers in private practice. The legal profession has readily spoken of its *professional* purposes in the past (service to the public and to the client), but there has been only limited research into the organisational or *business* structure of legal services, and the organisational characteristics which might give them best effect.[2]

Yet, as we saw in the last chapter in the discussion of the concept of 'independence', this essential professional standard of independence has been, and is, closely allied for lawyers with particular business structures, particular organisational forms of service (self-employment for barristers, partnership for solicitors, and a rigid division between their services). Lawyers have been fiercely jealous of this purpose of independence to the extent that they have been for the most part reluctant to explore alternative forms of organisation for legal services. Reform has been difficult given the united opposition of the two branches of the profession, as well as of the judiciary. This traditional distaste of the profession for public discussion of its business aspects has impeded more open consideration of the range of organisational forms in which the purposes of legal service might be, and have been, achieved. While it would be unfair to the professional bodies to say that they have not explored some of these questions with their own members, in their public stance the professional bodies have tended to defend the *status quo* rather than to acknowledge any need to restructure the profession to meet changing social needs (see Reeves, 1986). The in-house lawyer ideal of being 'proactive rather than reactive' has hardly been a characteristic of the profession as a whole, although there are now signs of change in this respect.

The signs of change in the profession's stance on these issues have been largely precipitated by wider political pressures. Most organisations, public and private, have in recent years gone through a degree of restructuring and re-evaluation of their 'business strategy' in the face of heightened competition and a renewed emphasis on consumer rights and on 'consumer-led' business. The same broad social currents of active consumerism and political inclinations towards 'free market' solutions to organisational effectiveness are also now confronting the professions; thus the importance of more openly examining the business structure of legal services. The ending of the solicitors' monopoly over conveyancing business has already stimulated this process within the profession (although some solicitors argue that the heightened consumerism of clients had already altered lawyers' pricing of conveyancing services). This is likely to have flow-on effects in other aspects of legal services. In particular, changes in the regulation of conveyancing and government pressure to reduce public spending (and thus the real value of

Legal Aid), have both led to the legal profession acknowledging more publicly the *commercial* side of legal services, whether one describes this in terms of a 'business organisation' question (Office of Fair Trading, 1986) or as a 'trade union' response (Blom-Cooper, 1985).[3] Lawyers have traditionally been very sensitive to comparisons of the professions with the world of business (see Faulkner and Saunders, 1985). However, the pressures of modern practice are increasingly exposing the underlying business issues in legal services practice, suggesting that such comparisons may at least help as a creative analogy in analysing and clarifying the nature of the pressures and the alternatives available to lawyers in providing legal services. It may be that the status of the profession allowed lawyers traditionally to work on the assumption that '[a] professional man does not work in order to be paid, he is paid in order that he may work.' (Napley, 1983). However, such an assurance of outside beneficence is hardly likely to sustain the legal profession in the future. The 'law business' (the organisational structure of legal services), the 'business of law' (the purposes to guide this structure), and the relations between them, need therefore to be re-examined.

Such a re-examination requires an initial recognition of the differentiation that has taken place within the legal profession, of which the in-house lawyer is only one example (Podmore, 1980a). Generalised avowals that 'service to the public' is the overall purpose of the business of law, fail to acknowledge that there are a variety of publics with different legal needs, different resources to pay for those needs, and different degrees of influence over the structure and purpose of legal services. Equally, there is now the prospect of a variety of forms of organisation of the business of law, in each of which a different approach can be envisaged to legal work. The 'law business' of the sole practitioner in a rural area demands a business strategy and structure that differ from those which can be envisaged by a major City firm. Additionally, there are different 'business competitors' in different sectors, and even the prospect of lawyers being driven out of areas of legal service as principal providers. In the area of public service, there are suggestions of lawyers' 'social welfare' business being absorbed by a base of less well paid, or even voluntary, paralegal staff (in terms of a government proposal to extend the role of the Citizens' Advice Bureaux[4]); lawyering work in the field of property and financial

242   *The Law Business*

services, on the other hand, is threatened by competition from accountants, banks and building societies (as a result of the conveyancing monopoly disappearing and of a growing 'aggressiveness' in the financial services sector).

Within the limits of the research underlying this study of in-house lawyers, it is not possible to explore questions of business form and strategy in depth.[5] However, a start can be made by highlighting some of the issues around the question as a pointer to future research directions and theoretical analyses. First, as an example of the impact of structure on services, we return to a theme which has underpinned much of the commentary of earlier chapters, namely, that the differences between the in-house and outside lawyers in terms of the business structures within which they operate explain much of the distinction in attitudes and approach between them. The second part of the chapter contains a more speculative analysis of current developments in the structure of the 'law business', referring briefly to some current trends in the organisation of legal services and pointing up their relevance to a search for a 'business strategy' for the legal profession.

IN-HOUSE AND OUTSIDE LAWYERS; ORGANISATION AND PURPOSE

The growth of the in-house lawyer branch of the profession must be taken in part as a failure of the legal profession in its traditional form adequately to service business needs, or at least to do so in an efficient and effective manner. Having the money to 'privatise' this already private service, business has exacerbated the trend to 'mega-law', to law even more out of the reach of the citizen (although this should be set against the fact that business has been stimulated to respond in this way partly as a result of previous government efforts to redress this imbalance between business and the individual by increased regulatory controls). The fact that this growth has also accompanied a growth in the size of the private practice sector which services major business clients, should not lead one too glibly to see the in-house lawyer and the 'law factory' lawyer as two faces of the same coin, although they are more likely to interact with each other than with other sectors of the legal profession. The motives, organisational structures, and loyalties of the two branches are quite distinct. Lawyers in business are salaried employees of their client organisation, part of a larger body requiring to sell its own services and products; the law business is legal service as a revenue-producing concern in its own right, servicing usually many clients. Further, the two branches have a particular relation to each other, which is in itself of special significance, namely the fact that the lawyer in business, acting as the agent of his or her employer, *becomes the purchaser*, the *de facto* client, of the legal services offered by the lawyer in private practice. In a few cases, it is true, I encountered companies which used law firms on the basis of links between individual managers and the firm concerned, either on the basis of geographical autonomy (local managers who required regular small-scale legal service) or personal contacts between a senior manager and a partner or law firm (for instance, through a traditional 'family' connection). However, these were in the minority and acknowledged by both in-house lawyers and private practice lawyers to be diminishing in significance.

> I've noticed big changes. Virtually every company on our books is no longer the client. Our clients are now the lawyers who direct whether work goes to us. Some Managing Directors still may say 'I want you to use . . .'. In these cases, the in-house lawyer only has discretion to go to the specialists there. In the old-fashioned company with that sort of relationship, everything went to their solicitors and they briefed barristers. These days, solicitors have lifted their specialism and commercial understanding till they've outstripped the barristers except on highly technical legal questions. The paradox is that our work is now more closely scrutinised by in-house lawyers. It's a sort of Catch 22. (Australian partner in leading commercial firm)

The fact that in-house lawyers are placed in this position inevitably increases their power in the relationship in an objective sense, although they might have neither the confidence nor the desire to treat the relationship in this way. It was clear, however, that as in-house lawyers became more established as a professional group and more self-confident in their status, they began to see the value of exercising this power. What is this power composed of? First, the fact that it is the company which is buying in the service of the law business. Second, if it is not satisfied with that service, whether on the ground of its cost, its efficiency or effectiveness, it is open to the company to go into the marketplace to seek other suppliers of legal services. Third, it is the legal department of the company which often translates this legal service, giving it communication power inside the organisation in terms of company evaluation of outside legal service. Fourth, it is the legal department which itself increasingly comes to act as the evaluator of the quality and cost of legal services. And it is important to note here that the business lawyer is in a unique position to develop this competence since, regardless of any initial lack of expertise in an area, the access he obtains to repeated and varied legal advice ensures he is able, if he so desires, to become fairly expert in the fields of activity of his company. Since legal service is very much knowledge-based, the in-house lawyer, already skilled in legal work, can learn from outside lawyers faster perhaps than purchasers of other company services can learn the intricacies of those areas. Finally in-house lawyers, if sufficiently confident and if there are enough of them, can dispense with outside law service altogether and, as already reported, a few aimed to do this. (The restrictions by the Bar on rights of audience in the higher courts prevents this option being taken to the absolute, but this is in any case not a frequent area of a company's legal activity, nor one that most in-house lawyers would have wanted, given their unfamiliarity with it and its time-consuming nature.) Given these areas of power, the image of 'in-house' lawyers and 'out-house' lawyers may be less whimsical a contrast than might first appear.

The fear of loss of work to company lawyers was one that had been expressed by the private profession in the past. There was less public acknowledgement of how the subtler processes of power influence could come to alter the division of work and of power between the two branches. Nevertheless, some accepted that it had occurred, but the general feeling was that the increasing numbers of in-house lawyers had altered the character rather than the amount of work available for private practice. It was acknowledged that much of the routine work of drafting and checking contracts had disappeared, but it had been replaced by the increasing flow of specialist requirements (for example, mergers and acquisitions) and of litigation work (although this growth reflects wider social trends rather than a re-direction for which the in-house lawyer is responsible).

There were still many advantages for in-house lawyers in being able to 'sub-contract' legal work in this manner (see chapter 7). Additionally, the limited size of many legal departments, professional loyalties and the free flow of personnel between the two branches are likely to counteract any tendencies to a 'split' between the two sectors. Moreover, the outside lawyer has the complementary strength of dealing with a variety of companies and hence being more likely to be in touch with varied options for tackling a problem, with new developments or emerging legal requirements. Nevertheless, the lawyers in private practice were learning the lessons of this loss of work and decline in consumer confidence by increasingly showing concern for cost-effective services, for being 'proactive', for example, keeping themselves informed of developments in the work of the industries with which they dealt. Thus the comments made to me by partners in two major commercial practices in Australia — 'We are being more proactive in relations with our clients, keeping up-to-date with developments in the industry'; 'we are developing a "client awareness" programme — collecting information on clients on our files and keeping in touch with developments in the industry, visiting new developments and so on.'[6] Also evidence of this was the increasing acceptance of the practice of 'beauty contests', where several major commercial firms made a presentation to the client of how they would conduct a case in order to bid for the work (in the process providing an increase in the sophistication of any in-house lawyers' involved). One of the City firm lawyers noted that his firm now made a habit of inviting in-house lawyers to their client seminars, and sometimes asking them to give a talk on what they looked for from the outside lawyer. 'We like to know how they think, and it helps to let them know we care how they think.'

Given the in-house lawyers' familiarity with legal work, their use of outside lawyers to provide legal services makes them a particularly interesting case-study on the more general issues of the competence and cost-effectiveness of lawyers in private practice, issues normally reserved for the views of the public who are less well equipped to judge standards of service. What views did they hold of their fellow lawyers?

The most interesting aspect of their replies is the fact that they do not differ significantly from most public surveys.[7] They were generally reasonably happy with the service received, but all felt that one had to be very careful which practice one chose or more precisely which partner, and nearly all had experienced what they regarded as poor service, although this was more often a question of annoyance over delays, cost and poor communication than of technical incompetence. Choosing one's lawyer is perhaps after all no easier than deciding on which builder or plumber to use. There are in every occupation the competent and the incompetent, the variation in value for money. (A significant minority, however, agreed with those critics of the legal profession who argue that it is even more dogged by incompetence than plumbers because of failures in the organisation of legal services, particularly the outdated traditions around litigation — see chapter 11.)

Variation in quality will in turn apply to the in-house lawyers. However, in this area, too, there was an implied criticism of the legal profession generally. Some of my interviewees described poor quality in-house lawyers less in terms of individual differences than in terms of an understanding of the occupational role. In other words, they felt the business lawyer's standing might be undermined if too many lawyers brought with them the narrow concept of the lawyer's role held by many lawyers in private practice into a business environment which demanded a more active, integrated and rounded approach. Outside lawyers who acted in this way were losing business for the profession.

> Our profession is too prissy. Too cautious. We're losing business hand over fist to accountants, estate agents, merchant banks. Our profession is getting narrower and narrower. We're not looking forward, we're looking backward. Protecting family matters, workers' compensation, the solicitors in the suburbs. People like us are chafing at the bit. The large corporate firms are trying to keep abreast of business as well. (Australian oil company lawyer)

Both groups of lawyers are lawyers by training, by socialisation, by self-identification. What distinguishes the in-house lawyer most clearly from his or her colleague in private practice? The central difference is, of course, that the in-house lawyer is salaried and working inside a large business organisation; the lawyer in private practice may be salaried but is working inside an organisation wholly devoted to selling legal services to the public. Less important is the factor of the number of clients dealt with, since the assumption that the in-house lawyer deals with a 'single client' is in fact based on a legal abstraction rather than on the reality of practice. In practice, the in-house lawyer services many clients. More important is the fact that these varied clients are bound together by some form of bond with the company (itself a legal fiction but in this case with a more meaningful psychological reality). This bond may be based on ownership (for example, subsidiary company) or common employment, but it is the organisational unity, the unity of purpose, which creates the difference with private practice, not the fact of a range of clients. (Of course, private practices may on occasion perform a similar role for some clients, but usually retain a greater diversity.)

What are the likely effects of this distinction? The most crucial point to note for the purpose of this chapter's inquiries is the different *purposes* underlying the two forms of service. Whatever the nature of the individuals in a private practice, at the end of the day the lawyer there is effectively providing a legal service which must be directed overall to making a profit or at least ensuring survival of the law business concerned, maintaining a proper cash flow, and so on. Related to this is the fact that even in some of the larger practices the business environment is essentially small (Faulkner and Saunders, op. cit.), based on a personal service product. By contrast, the lawyer in the business organisation is only a working unit within a larger body devoted to profit-making. In-house lawyers were well aware of the profit factor underlying their businesses, of course, but did not need to take on the psychological responsibility for it, and could feel they were contributing to it merely by the service they provided. They also had additional props by way of a range of other expertise available in the company, financial, technical, and even legal (by way of specialists who monitored legal changes in their own areas), thus deepening their knowledge base of law-in-practice. Where the in-house lawyer may lose out in this process is in terms of a loss of objectivity (a fact most recognised) since they are effectively drawn into the cultural thought processes of the organisation, rather than advising a diversity of clients, and may therefore become subject to what has been referred to as 'groupthink'.

The heavy preoccupation of private practice lawyers with the *business* aspects of the provision of legal services was supported by in-house lawyers' comments on their experience of private practice, often reasons for their dislike of it, namely, the element of fee-chasing, routine low-level work, personal aggravation with other members of the practice and with clients, all perhaps more typical of small business activity. The same message emerges from surveys (and traditional stereotypes of lawyers) which have indicated that the public tend to see lawyers as 'money-grabbing'.[8] An in-house lawyer who had moved back into a partnership in a provincial firm, expressed it in these terms.

It's purely the difference between being in a business and running a business. I've just spent a lunchtime talking to the partners about cash flow. In-house you're not as conscious of the money side. [He went on to describe how this difference was reflected in tighter control over staff activities, over who does what level of work in cost-effectiveness terms, and how his wife had noted that he now spent more time talking about the business rather than about the clients.] I think what it comes down to is that in-house lawyering is probably not quite as selfish as private practice. In-house you would send out an overflow. Here it's a decision whether you refer to someone else and risk losing a client, hire temporary help and risk them making a mess of it, or delay it.

A much more serious issue arises out of this than merely thoughts of the applicability of organisational theory to legal practice. Namely, that given that the legal profession has traditionally sought to operate in economic terms within the structure of a small business organisation with limited resources to allow for research, updating or office management, and without the organisational connections to other expertise necessary to the application of law, perhaps this lies at the root of the persistent complaints about the competence of the legal profession, its delays and costliness. Experience of the ranks of small builders is no different fundamentally than that of lawyers, but seen differently because of the status and skill attached to legal practice. (With some clients, this will probably lessen sensitivity to a poor service; with others it may heighten it.)

Given the complexity of modern society, of the law and legal processes it engenders, and given greater consumer sophistication and expectations of standards of service, it may be that the business form of traditional legal practice is quite inappropriate to the demands it must meet. The reasoning behind this leads one to somewhat different reform emphases from the traditional reaction of the profession to public complaints — reforms of disciplinary controls over errant solicitors, increased attention to education in professional ethics, or expanded continuing education. Such reforms reflect the inherent preference within the profession to seek to resolve their problems by reference to *personal* or individual change. It may be, however, that the *organisational structure* of the legal profession in its business manifestation must be altered not only to meet current consumer needs but to answer new ones. Such is a common experience of business in general, but the lack of the tradition and constraints of the rules of professional practice enables business to move more quickly to new organisational forms.

If such an analysis is valid, then perhaps the nostalgic desire for the era of the small practice is misguided. What is needed is organisational reform in which legal service can be provided so as to best meet modern demands for competence and cost-effectiveness, providing the service the modern client is likely to be looking for. In some respects, of course, legal practice is already being transformed by changing social demands but largely in a reactive rather than proactive sense. To assist this process it may be advisable to consider more carefully the options available to restructure and redirect the law business and its purposes.

BUSINESS STRATEGY IN LEGAL SERVICES

An analysis of the nature of the commercial organisation of legal services in order to lay the foundation of an effective 'business strategy' for the legal profession would require a book in itself. However, as a contribution it is worth referring to some discernible trends in the organisation of the law business in order to provide pointers to alternative forms of organisation for legal services. Whether the profession as a whole responds to such developments 'proactively' or 'reactively', change in the organisation of legal services is already taking place. The rest of this chapter seeks to contribute to the debate by providing a brief survey of significant trends in the organisation of the law business, dimensions of business activity relevant to new concepts of legal services and to the strategic choices which face the profession in the near future. These are: size, specialisation, diversification, public subsidy and increased efficiency. Underlying each of these dimensions there are the vital strategic elements of 'customer orientation' (how closely does the business seek to meet client needs?) and 'market share' (is the market for legal services finite or can it be developed?; what competition is there to provide such services, first between lawyers, and second between lawyers and other businesses?; can other products replace current services provided by the law business?). These underlying elements are critical in evaluating the trends outlined below. (Much of the academic critique of the Royal Commission on Legal Services centred on such issues, although without the 'business' terminology — see Thomas, 1982.) It should be said at the outset of this discussion that the legal profession is now acknowledging more than ever its need to respond to client concerns over the standard of legal services. Far more worrying for the profession in recent years has been the second aspect, how to maintain a share of the market in legal services, and how far to compromise with traditional values in the profession in order to do so.

Size
One of the obvious organisational trends within the profession has been in the sector servicing major business clients. In this sector, the affluence of their clients and the demands for a sophisticated legal product, have led increasingly to the establishment of larger and larger law firms. This trend has been evident in the UK[9] and in Australia[10], but particularly so in the US, where ironically there has been the strongest cultural tradition of the small-town, independent lawyer.[11] Warnings of the lurch of the legal profession towards 'law factories' and 'mega-lawyering' (Galanter, 1983), have had little effect on the

growth of the giant legal firms. Thus, the practice with at most several dozen partners is giving way to practices with in some cases several hundred partners (*Business Week*, 1986), and many more associate salaried lawyers and para-legal staff, serviced by personnel, training and research directors, and servicing branches in most major cities as well as major financial centres in overseas locations.

The growth of big business and the internationalisation of business creates a momentum which will add to other economic pressures for growth in law firms. Thus, talk of 'the 200-lawyer firm' in the 1970s (Cantor, 1978) has given way to articles about the 'mega-firms' and the 1000-lawyer target with revenues around the $1.5 million level — six US law firms are now of over 500-lawyer size, and 28 over 300, the world's largest, Baker and McKenzie, having 875 lawyers, of whom over 300 are partners (*Business Week*, 1986).[12] Alongside this is evidence of greater use of paralegals and other employees of the business. The process seems to work in revenue terms although one might think there would be few economies of scale in the personalised services of a legal practice (*Business Week*, 1986: 72). The pace of law-firm mergers (and disappearances) adds to the trend of a growth in business to point to a radical shift in the business structure of legal practice at this level. While the trend has been more marked in the US than in Britain (Reeves, 1986), the special character of 'City firms' within the profession is already well known and recent developments both in London and in the provinces point in similar directions (the largest number of partners in one firm is just over 160). Not only might this be a case of what the United States does today others will do tomorrow. The internationalisation of business means that such firms must develop an active interest in establishing offices in other international business or financial centres (or in absorbing local firms). Hence, not only do such firms act as an example of trends; they will also directly change the nature of the competitive business environment for national firms, forcing them to compete on similar lines or to offer distinctive, specialist services.

With such pressures and growth in size, changes in the philosophy of professional practice also seem likely, with lawyers likely to follow in the steps of the accountancy profession which has seen the development of the 'Big Eight' which dominate the accountancy world internationally, and also moving towards the notion of the incoporated business form to replace the traditional partnership model.[13] Also, in the wake of growth comes an appreciation of the need for more systematic management practices to handle a firm which has outgrown its traditional small business character. The internal workings of the firm have to be managed, but also its complex transactions with the outside world. For example, part of the price for growth will be a greater number of employees and a lessening of the former glamour of partnership to a 'career employee' status with greater problems of motivation and quality control issues. This does not mean necessarily that all partners must also become businessmen, but it does at least mean that the firms are more likely to see the need for some lawyers to adopt this role, and the need to employ business specialists of various kinds, in areas of finance, staffing, work control systems, public relations, research, and training and development.

Most, but not all, of the law firms listed in this study have outgrown the 'shadow of one man.' More often, a consciously established 'representative government' guides the firm as to objectives, client needs, competition, size, rapid growth, specialization, centralization or decentralization, and even sheer survival. These problems are the main determinants of how a law firm establishes or changes policies, structure, management and controls. General Motors and other well-managed enterprises at the same stage of accelerated growth wrestled with the same problems that now beset many of the expanding law firms. (Cantor, op. cit., 219)

The days of collegiality are waning. Once-democratic partnerships are looking increasingly like autocratic companies. (*Business Week*, 1986: 73)

There are fundamental forces at work. We need to be more productive in a more competitive environment and we need to rationalise services in an over-serviced environment. Looked at as an industry, there are too many lawyers. For every successful firm like ours, three or four are foundering — they're static, no growth, no employment prospects, no future. .... This is a very competitive firm. We hire only the best and those with a leading edge such as language degrees.

We spit out recruits if we find they haven't got what it takes, though in a caring way. But we're businesslike about it. Our people count.

Our priority is we must grow as a firm. If we don't, we can't promote people or increase their salary, so they feel they're not getting anywhere. Therefore we must give opportunities. If not, morale drops, productivity and efficiency. It's the top firms which are going from strength to strength. The key is management — size, specialisation, personnel, cost control, etc. Traditionally lawyers were especially good at two forms of management. One, general administration, the other financial management. But they were lousy in personnel and marketing policies. . . . We've got to lift our level of service across the board and get the right people. But to do that we need to grow, therefore we have to look to marketing. And organisational development. We've never explicitly told our staff — it's just crystallising in our own minds now. (Australian partner in a commercial firm)

Such structural change seems to be inevitable, shaped to accompany the growth in size of business and state activities. While the warnings against it perhaps are merely an expression of nostalgia, they do raise serious questions about access to legal services and the competence of the smaller practice (Heinz and Laumann, 1983). If large organisations can afford their own legal departments or can use expensive legal services as provided by the large firms, who does the small man (whether small business or individual client) turn to? And of the practices which remain, how can they ensure they are competent to cope with the cases they have to deal with?; after all, one of the reasons for the growth in the size of the legal practice has been the need to pool resources for economies of scale and to have access to sufficient specialists, libraries, information technology, to cope with the ever-increasing complexity and differentiation of law.

One answer to such questions is to assume that the problem is more apparent than real. While the scope of the major client cases has changed considerably in complexity, that of the small man remains much as before — transferring a small property, drawing up wills or divorce arrangements, forming a business, drafting a simple contract. In most business fields, from retail to construction, one can find large companies and small ones servicing different customer groups and needs, so why not in law? The paucity of research studies of the legal profession as a type of business, means that such a question is difficult to answer with any degree of certainty. To what extent is lack of specialist knowledge a problem for the small practice? To what extent can lawyering achieve economies of scale and in what areas? The traditional lawyer is likely to doubt that the personal service provided by a lawyer is capable of conversion into a 'mass production' industry. Yet if that is the case, why has there been a growth, recently accelerating, in the numbers of mergers and in the proportion of larger practices not only in law but in the related profession of accountancy? Similarly, the legal profession might need to give more attention to alternatives to *single* practice expansion in order to maintain the viability and competence of the smaller practice (and in turn the public reputation of the profession). For example, by developing and clarifying systems for referral to specialists (an issue which would have to be confronted in any case if fusion of the profession was to proceed), or systems for the sharing between practices of certain resources such as libraries, technology, educational facilities, or the further development of specialist legal consultancies offering the services (recruitment, management, and so on) which the larger practices can provide in-house.

Specialisation

Another explanation for growth is the need to house a range of specialists in one firm to cope with the increasing range and complexity of law, thus meeting more capably the demands of the market for legal services. Here again, however, one can ask what limits on this development are there likely to be, and what are the implications for public access to legal services? One of the arguments of the Bar against fusion of the profession has been that a likely consequence would be that specialists at the Bar would quickly be headhunted by the larger law firms, thus depriving the solicitors' profession as a whole (and in turn the public) of equal access to specialists. There is clearly some degree of justice in this point, and it is an argument that has influenced the various inquiries into the question of fusion. However, other systems of access are possible to envisage if it was felt that the balance of advantage was against a divided profession (Reeves, 1986). So far the Bar has resisted such developments but the force of the public interest arguments for fusion (around cost and quality) may yet prove too strong. There has also been a clear development in the solicitors' branch of the profession of a range of specialist groups which might lay the foundation in the future for specialist advocates. Whichever attitude is adopted to this long-standing issue amongst lawyers, there is little doubt that the trend to specialisation amongst solicitors will increase, leaving the Bar with a choice of a limited role in litigation or creating pressure for an expansion of specialists practising at the Bar and of their resource base.

The growth of specialisation also carries with it two important trends. First, the need to make the public aware of who is qualified to practice such specialisation. This pressure in itself, apart from the economic pressures of general competition, leads to requirements for a system by which the public can obtain such knowledge. The simplest course is to allow advertising, a path solicitors have now taken after many years of resistance to the concept. A second set of questions raised by this development are issues concerning the nature of schemes of certification of specialists, and the extent non-specialists are to be prohibited from practising in these areas. There are again clear indications that the trend is towards such developments, but the likely effect of this on the provision of legal services and on the division of the profession, and particularly the ability of law practices to cope with such developments, has been less clearly researched. Again, however, one suspects the impetus will be towards the growth in size of law firms in suburban as well as city contexts, as well as an increase in specialist referral systems and experiments in 'joint ventures' between practices with different specialisms.

Diversification
Once the need for specialists is recognised, why stop at legal specialists, when many client problems have related aspects of financial advice or do not admit of a 'legal' answer at all? Is the current 'product base' of the law business too narrow, either in terms of the financial viability of practices or of customer needs? The logic of this argument has inclined the government and the Office of Fair Trading to re-open the question of mixed-profession partnerships, allowing lawyers to practise in consort with other professions, currently a breach of professional

conduct (unless the other professional is an employee of the lawyer). The most obvious routes for such developments are in the areas of property sales (lawyers and estate agents) or of financial services, such as tax or investment planning or business restructuring (lawyers and accountants). However, there are other areas which might be envisaged — lawyers and surveyors or engineers in the field of building disputes, lawyers and counsellors in the area of family law. Such a development is likely to spawn a range of experiments in service provision, depending on the calculation by individual firms of their existing strengths and contacts and the balance of advantage in any particular case.

As we have seen, for in-house lawyers the advantages of working alongside other experts were considerable in terms of the decision-making process of business clients, not to mention the personal satisfactions such contacts provided. The Law Society Commerce and Industry Group pointed out in 1977 to the Royal Commission on the Provision of Legal Services that in-house lawyers are already working in effect in partnership with other professions, except in legal or financial terms, 'with a common interest and common clients . . . *Commercial activity could not effectively be advised and supported in any other way*' (author's emphasis, Law Society, 1977, para. 3.9). Such advantages could be achieved in the practice of outside lawyers. The real difficulty is not the nature of the legal service this would entail, but what such developments might mean *for the traditional identification of the independence of the lawyer with the economic form of legal practice.* If it can be envisaged that lawyers can work alongside other service-providers (the expression is wider, of course, than the assumption that they will be fellow professionals), what are the implications for lawyer ethics? We have already noted that in-house lawyers saw ethical problems as of a largely hypothetical rather than actual nature. The argument against mixed-profession partnerships on the ground of ethics would equally seem to be largely centred on the economic privileges which lawyers should retain rather than on 'true' ethical questions. The latter concerns are not insignificant, but, given a degree of willingness, could be readily revised by a careful inquiry into the standards necessary for professional conduct in a new working context (with, for example, rules on disclosure of information to clients, to prevent conflicts of interest between disinterested legal advice and other business services offered by the firm, compensation funds, and so forth).

The next stage of this argument, however, poses greater threats to the current economic structure of legal practice and the core concept of independence. Namely, if there are no major obstacles to inter-professional practice, is it any more illogical for legal services to be provided to the public by employed lawyers even where the business itself is not directed by a lawyer? The latter issue has arisen for lawyers over the question of the freeing of conveyancing competition. If banks and building societies can offer conveyancing services to the public, should employed lawyers provide such a service? Or should the legal profession prohibit the in-house lawyer from working as an outside lawyer in a business? Issues of direction such as these are clearly presenting the profession with severe problems of strategic choice[14] in the face of a government which believes in the efficacy of the market mechanism as a primary means of ensuring the protection of the public interest. Again, this study of in-house lawyers suggests that arguments against this development are less sustainable on the issue of the professional independence of the in-house lawyer, than on the problems of economic competition for the profession in its current private practice form. This is not to deny that there are important public interest arguments involved in the prospect of business organisations undermining legal practice (for example, such competition may reduce the range of lawyers in the vicinity who can also offer assistance with litigation or family law). Also, the capacity of in-house lawyers to identify with their profession's values may be based on the fact that they are only a small segment of a larger 'independent' profession. However, in terms of the future of the profession and opportunities for lawyers, the profession should be clear about which are its strongest arguments and whether it is independence or economic viability which is the essential concern. The strategies the profession must adopt to be 'proactive' in the face of such challenges will differ according to the stance adopted. (The comparison with the medical profession in this respect is relevant to such arguments, as are greater precision and information on the 'case-law' of legal ethics.)

Public subsidy

The question of public access to legal services is fundamentally linked to that of the provision of public funding for such services. In this area too, the legal profession has been forced to acknowledge a crisis of direction. The demand for legal services has grown amongst the general public as well as in the business sector. However, the Legal Aid system has grown less capable of responding to such demand, largely because of government desire to restrain the expansion of Legal Aid, both in the amount of funding available to litigants and lawyers (in relation to inflation) and in the areas covered (excluding work in newly emerging fields of law such as industrial tribunals, for example). At the same time, competition is sharpening in areas, such as conveyancing, where lawyers claimed that more lucrative earnings helped cross-subsidise the less well-paid areas of work covered by Legal Aid. The claim that legal services are available only to the very poor or the very rich, becomes increasingly applicable.

The result of such restrictions is again a search for new methods of support for the law business, and again the dilemma of alternative strategies which might be adopted. In its starkest terms the legal profession faces a choice between turning more clearly towards a 'public sector' model of legal services and a 'free market' model. Each has its own opportunities and threats. Since the present political climate apparently favours the latter model, it is to that which we first turn.

Given existing public attitudes towards the level of legal fees, the scope for encouraging greater use of lawyers by the sections of the community which are not covered under the present system seems limited. Amongst past suggestions have been the encouragement of insurance-based cover (which already exists in limited areas but has not proved a popular option), and the adoption of an alternative system of client payment along the lines of a 'contingency fee' system practised in the United States (where the litigant effectively only pays the lawyer if he wins the case). The Law Society has in the past seen little value in the former and has prohibited the latter on the ground that it may undermine the objectivity of the lawyer and his relations with the court. However, a committee of the Law Society is re-examining these and other options (such as a mutual fund) for paying for litigation, in the search to circumvent the difficulties of the current Legal Aid system. Economists who favour a free market approach to legal services, however, would probably wish to question more fundamental aspects of legal service. The answer to why legal services are expensive would be attributed to restrictions on competition in the market. Such an approach would again raise issues which the profession does not feel comfortable with, such as questions of size, division of the profession, and the business organisation of legal services already alluded to. In addition, the workings of the courts as efficient 'dispute resolution centres' would be questioned (Bartlett, 1982).

The public sector model of legal services, such as in the form of a National Legal Service funded and staffed in a manner similar to the National Health Service, where legal services (for certain basic needs such as protection of freedom, property, employment) are provided free at the point of service, is probably an even less acceptable development to many lawyers. Objections to this development have again been phrased in terms of professional 'independence', this time from the state, although again there are clear economic reasons as to why the profession would reject this model. However, since it is difficult to see how a free market model could effectively provide quality legal services at the low-income end of the market, one is once again flung back on the question of whether the existing Legal Aid system can effectively meet the demands for legal services. At present the Legal Aid system can be said to be supporting the legal profession in the form of a public subsidy, rather than representing a committed government recognition of the need to make legal services available to all who need them. If a government were to commit itself to ensuring an effective legal service for all its citizens by means of salaried lawyers working for a public legal service with a network of law centres, 'consultant' referrals, and such like, would there be a net gain in the degree of justice available in society? (It should be noted, of course, that the principle is already accepted to some extent not only with the recent establishment of a public prosecution service but also in the traditional public funding of the services of judges and magistrates. Their independence is protected not in this case by a business form but in special statutory/-constitutional protections.)

While the present government would be ideologically (and in

terms of public spending) opposed to such a model, its possible efficiencies and contribution to the public good have been given some recognition, at least in terms of suggestions from a legal aid scrutiny committee that the Citizens' Advice Bureaux could take on a first-level point of legal advice in many cases. Both lawyers and the CABs have opposed the proposal as a measure which would merely formalise a lower-quality legal service for lower-income citizens. The prospect of full extension of this concept to the workings of the legal profession, however, seems even more unlikely without a radical change in political direction.

Increased efficiency

The most common response in any industry to finding that its competition has become more keen, is to seek to make cost reductions, to make the business 'leaner and fitter'. As an immediate response to one's problems, such an approach has many merits, and most important is perhaps the one which is most readily to hand for the individual business. Clearly, some of the trends mentioned above have involved lawyers becoming more businesslike in relation to cost controls and practice efficiency, for example, by obtaining greater resources in mergers to allow the development of information technology systems. However, the disadvantage of this approach is that it may avoid more fundamental problems, such as the fact that clients are also looking for a very different kind of service, not merely a cheaper one. Also efficiency in legal costs is to some extent restricted by the need for lawyers to work within the current constraints of the litigation system over which they have limited control, as well as confronting again the problem of the division of the profession as a cost factor. While this division is currently under discussion (although change seems unlikely), there has been movement by the Lord Chancellor to bring greater cost-effectiveness into litigation practice. A number of management consultants' reports on civil litigation have been commissioned and a civil justice review committee established to recommend the reforms of civil procedure. While these proposals are at an early stage, a number of developments do seem likely focusing particularly on more simplified procedures for cases below a certain monetary value, greater judicial control over the conduct of cases (to speed up proceedings), greater use of arbitration schemes and written submissions, fusing County Court and High Court procedures (see the *Civil Justice Review: General Issues*, Lord Chancellor's Department, 1987). It is worth stressing that such reforms are likely to have a wider impact on the profession than merely making legal services less expensive or less subject to delay. They may also have the result of altering the nature and distribution of work within and between the two branches of the profession and of creating additional cost advantages for companies in employing extra in-house litigation specialists.

Of course, lawyers in the commercial sector of lawyering have in recent years been faced with competition in an expanding market, rather than a declinging market, a factor which makes for a very different response to efficienty issues, though not necessarily for the quality of the law business in the long term.

It's been like a rush to the coast or a cold rush in the last two years. There's euphoria in the City at the moment. Everyone's jumping on the wagon. There's so much work that there's a shortage of lawyers. But it's not very well thought out. Decisions are *ad hoc*. We've so much work that we just need more people. We have very little time to talk of structure or develop the business properly, although there are some developments. . . . There's a belated recognition amongst solicitors that they're not adept at management. They have difficulty making even intelligent financial decisions. A lot of lawyers still go about their work in the traditional way. So the quality of our work is not that much better but everything is speeded up as though it was on video. We're more competitive, there's more people scrambling around, it's altogether more aggressive. (Partner in City firm)

THE FUTURE OF THE LAW BUSINESS

In the current climate few observers feel able to predict with any certainty the likely future shape of the legal profession. While it is easy to hint at apocalyptic visions of the decline of the law business, perhaps the legal profession has enough of its traditional astuteness and political weight to see that such prospects do not become a reality. Complaints about the profession are nothing new and, given the nature of the lawyer's work, are to some extent inevitable. However, given various market changes and political ill-will, some reforms of professional practices must be entered into, and are already in evidence. Such reforms would include more open advertising (to weed out the incompetent or overcharging practices), adoption of conveyancing as more of a business than a partial legal transaction (in other words, emulate Scottish lawyers by acting as an estate agent as well as a conveyancer), and ensuring that adequate pressure is exercised on the Lord Chancellor to see that Legal Aid income does not decline. Such strategies probably represent the majority position within the profession, although there are differences in terms of how far individual reforms should be taken — for example, with regard to the business arrangements behind property centres, the 'trade union' role of the profession in determining Legal Aid fees, the extent of advertising allowable. Others also would wish to make inroads into the power of the Bar, ending the separate training system, and perhaps even going as far as fusion of the profession, or extending solicitors' rights of audience and rights to take up judicial rank. In exploring these issues, there is clearly room for the profession to make more active use of research into the elements of 'business strategy' identified in this chapter. Experience in the business sector suggests that there are few ready-made strategic formulae. Strategic thinking requires systematic analysis of one's particular situation (whether of the profession or individual practice) as well as intuition, and sometimes painful adjustment, not likely to be made any easier by the partnership form of professional practice.

Outside lawyers are also learning the lesson that in-house lawyers have accommodated to, namely, that they have something to learn about business and management skills in order to run a more efficient and client-oriented practice. Such an emphasis does not imply that all lawyers must learn to be businessmen. The lawyer's skills remain fundamentally rooted in the law. However, they do imply that legal *practices* must be run in a more businesslike fashion, either by developing some lawyer-managers or by bringing in outside expertise in management skills. '[T]he view that the law is a learned profession and that the practice of such has nothing in common with running a business is increasingly untenable today, and it must surely be common ground that sound administration and modern business systems are an indispensable element in the provision of high quality cost effective advice' (Hamilton, 1986: 209). While lawyers are less likely to fall down in the area of financial management since 'money matters act as a "financial aphrodisiac" ', they are, Hamilton suggests, more likely to fail by 'a lack of sympathy for, or understanding of, the point of view of others, a failure to delegate, and a tendency to make arbitrary decisions which are not based on reasoned judgment and consultation' (209). In these areas at least, the organisational situation of the in-house lawyer and the model of the 'integrated lawyer' have lessons for the profession as a whole.

POSTSCRIPT: CHOICES AND STRESS IN THE LEGAL PROFESSION

A final irony of this chapter's outline of the 'situational psychology' of legal practice relates to the study of professional stress. Sociologists, perhaps adopting too readily the professions' definitions of independence, have conducted many surveys into professionals working in bureaucracies,[15] in order to test the hypothesis that they would be subject to greater stress because of the 'role strain' of coping with hierarchical authority, given their professional purpose of providing the best service available (see Donnell, 1970, for such a survey of in-house lawyers — he failed to detect role strain of any significance). The argument of this chapter has turned this issue on its head. Rather one can argue that professionals in *private practice* are likely to experience greater role strain because of attempting to cope with the purposes of law as a service *and* law as a business. The greater the strain on the latter, as in the present era, the more its incompatibility with the former might lead one to predict *greater* stress among outside lawyers, and greater problems of maintaining competence and ethical standards than amongst in-house lawyers, who are more free to concentrate on legal services to their employer without the same degree of direct business pressure. Whether this is in fact an accurate picture would require more studies of the world of the lawyer in private practice, but it was certainly a view shared by many in-house lawyers.

NOTES

1   One of the recent fashions in business, under American influence, has been for companies to adopt 'mission' statements in order to clarify the purposes of the business. (Some legal departments had developed their own.) However, this is a narrower concept than my use of the concepts of purpose and values. The latter are integral to all organisations although their clarity may be affected by the 'political and organisational pathologies' (Rosen, 1984) which afflict all organisations.

2   See Bartlett (1982) and Faulkner and Saunders (1985) for useful insights into this issue. Also Freidson (1986).

3   The difficulty of classifying lawyer campaigns on state subsidies as to whether they represent a business interest or a trade union response supports the case of Freidson (op. cit.) that the question of employment or self-employment is less critical than the nature of the market conditions for selling one's services.

4   See *The Times*, 16 June 1986.

5   For a general discussion of the concept of business strategy, see Porter (1980), a modern 'classic' on the subject.

6   Although, reflecting in-house lawyers' sometimes jaundiced views on outside lawyer fees, one in-house lawyer remarked on these practices: 'At whose expense? If they don't charge for their "proactive" visits, it will still be on the bill the company finally receives'.

7   See the cross-national surveys reported in Gibson and Baldwin (1985); also the findings of the Royal Commission on Legal Services (1979).

8   See the comments in the chapter by Tomasic in Gibson and Baldwin (op. cit.). For recent confirmation of this in the UK, see the report (*The Guardian*, 17 April 1986) of a survey conducted for the Law Society which found that solicitors were ranked second only to estate agents as professionals who were only after their money (although nine out of ten people also said they were satisfied with the service received).

9   See Podmore (1980). Press reports indicate that the trend has speeded up sharply since 1985 (see *The Times*, 11 February 1987).

10 For the growth of corporate law practice in Australia and its American influences, see Sexton and Maher (1982, chapter 5).

11 For a good description of a small-town practice held in this nostalgia and its modern-day corporation lawyer contrasts, see Levy (1961). Compare *Business Week* (1986) for the quantitative leap since Levy wrote.

12 Recognising the human relations problems such size can create, the London office of Baker and McKenzie was emphasising its intimacy in a 1987 advertisement in *The Times* 16 January — 'Tired of Your Mega-Firm?',it asked in bold letters, before describing the pleasures of working in the personal world of its London office!

13 See the Report by the Director-General of the Office of Fair Trading (1986). I have not discussed the other important aspects of moving to corporate status, namely the effect on the ease of raising capital for the business and on liability for professional negligence. Professional indem-

nity insurance premiums are another important reason for consideration being given within the profession to alternative business forms of practice.

14 It appears that the profession has opted again for a more restrictive approach, a new Rule 4 in its Professional Code of Conduct prohibiting employed lawyers from offering legal services to anyone other than their employer.

15 I have not ventured into the sociological discussion of bureaucracy as past notions of the trend to rational systems do not seem appropriate to the more open, fluid system of modern organisational practice and in-house professional work. Similarly, discussions of the 'proletarianisation' of professional labour is based on the notion of independence which I have asserted as misleading, as well as on major assumptions of class relations in industry which would require a lengthy, separate analysis. See Freidson (op. cit.) and Davies (1983) for a discussion of some of the issues, and Smigel (1969) and Murray *et al.* (1983) for an older and more modern approach to bureaucracy issues respectively.

14 Conclusion: Can Lawyers be Liked?

We cannot be popular

The Lord Chancellor, Lord Hailsham, 1985

There's no one out there who really likes us. Their views range from 'they're lazy and get us to do their thinking for them' to seeing us as obstructionist. They sometimes concede begrudgingly that we're useful. (Australian transportation company lawyer)

General management are generally very scathing about lawyers. It's part of the general view of lawyers, of course. There often is a feeling amongst the marketing types that the lawyers are holding them back. . . . a feeling of a nit-picking approach at times. On the other hand, in companies that are integrated units you hear kind words of their lawyers. (Lawyer in employers' association)

In my last company there was a very good in-house lawyer. He was a translator. He put things in a way managers could understand. (Textile company manager)

Business chiefs have given a black mark to solicitors and accountants for the services they provide to business and have called for a 'big bang' in professional services. Of 200 top company chiefs interviewed as part of the Institute of Directors' bi-monthly opinion survey, 58% said that [outside] solicitors had not become more customer conscious and business-like in the way they dealt with their clients' affairs. Twenty-three per cent said they had and 13 per cent either did not know or did not reply. Accountants fared slightly better . . . (Department of Employment Gazette, August 1986: 340).

Nine out of 10 people are satisfied with the service they get from their solicitors, says a survey published today, but people rank them second only to estate agents as the professionals who are only after their money . . . 71 per cent felt they had been charged the right amount or less . . . solicitors were not so highly regarded as National Health Service doctors, but they were looked on more favourably than accountants and estate agents. (Report in *The Guardian*, 17 April 1986)

The long history of quotations, alluded to in the Introduction (and confirmed in the present-day comments above), decrying the motivation and character of lawyers (see Levy, 1961) has equally long been attributed by lawyers to the nature of their professional role rather than to a just judgement. Not only does the lawyer frequently have to be associated with, and act as defender of, a society's 'undesirables', but also the lawyer is often a bearer of bad tidings not only, of course, for the other side in the dispute if there be one, but also as often for his own client. The aggrieved party has frequently to be told there is no remedy or insufficient evidence or that his intentions or actions are unlawful; the litigant has to watch as his (lawyer's) efforts and his (own) money to support his 'just cause' end in a declaration that he has lost the courtroom battle for reasons which frequently may seem mystifying and nearly always by that stage are at least arguable; it is likely too that the loser will in the course of the matter have observed something in the 'system' or the lawyer's efforts to which he can attribute blame for the loss; the happy 'winner' on the other hand may later, or sooner, discover he is also, financially, a loser, but still has to pay for the service he received; the procedures of the battle or of other legal transactions ('inevitably' complex, and therefore slow) are frequently couched in archaic or mystifying technical language and ritual created by the same profession of lawyers who profess to be at the client's service. Little wonder therefore if lawyers, with the former Lord Chancellor, shrug their shoulders and make the best of this familiar public unrest.

Of course, this is not the whole story. There is another side to the evidence, an alternative argument in the case. Lawyers are highly sought after. There is every indication that the more sophisticated a society grows, the more call there is for legal services; the more affluent a person becomes, the more likely they are to employ legal expertise. Business, despite Sir Henry Deterding's warnings (see the Introduction), has embraced the lawyer — in-house, in the City and increasingly in the Provinces. The essence of a lawyer is to facilitate the processes and solutions of complex social transactions and disputes, and modern society and modern business can stimulate these seemingly *ad infinitum*. The law may, on occasions, be an ass, but nearly always offers the chance of someone improving their position in the saddle (often more in terms of 'chance' than lawyers would willingly admit).

Nor do lawyers, nor even the Lord Chancellor, in fact rest content with making the best of it. The ethics of the profession encourage the notion of service, and that is what most lawyers try to give, at least on the level of their day-to-day affairs. They do what they can within their limits, within the limits of the system of law. The research which forms the basis of this book has charted the growth of a new branch of the legal profession and has outlined its evolving efforts to refine or redefine this concept of professional service in the context of its unique position. In explaining the growth of the in-house lawyer we have partly uncovered what business likes from its lawyers, the 'advantages' of the in-house lawyer — familiarity with the business, accessibility, preventive law skills, cost savings, good administrative/problem-solving capacity. Equally, one of the themes which cropped up repeatedly amongst in-house lawyers was the challenge of achieving 'accessibility', a concept which reveals a great deal about the paradox of the law. The lawyer is both valued and feared (or despised). In-house lawyers recognised that in the world inside business, in their client community, the position of a valued adviser does not accrue automatically to a lawyer merely because of a professional status; it has to be won. Especially because of the widespread public images of law and lawyers which filter into the organisation and inevitably cling to any incoming in-house lawyer, it has to be won. The debates within the ranks of in-house lawyers on the direction of the in-house lawyer 'movement', on how to exercise the skills of organisational politics, how to develop their capacity to manage a company legal service, what their role implied in terms of professional and business ethics, how close they should be to management decision-making or to making commercial decisions, all these issues were part of the challenge to establish just what constitutes competence and service for a lawyer working inside an organisation.

Whatever the details of the debate, few in-house lawyers doubted that they had to be what I have described as 'integrated lawyers'; essentially, that they had to be responsive and intelligible to the client, to the business which paid them. They had to be aware of the commercial objectives of the organisation, and had to assist those objectives with advice that was, where possible, both practical and positive, advice that was 'objectively partisan'. (In doing so, they were not always assisted by the rules of law, and sometimes became involved in law reform lobbying if faced with law which impeded commercial objectives.) They would not have referred to this as a need to be liked perhaps, but it was based on the need to be valued, to be seen as effective, influential and helpful.

And what of outside lawyers? Here there are both commonalities and differences with the in-house lawyer, the exact mix of these depending on which sector of the profession one chooses to compare with the in-house lawyer. Lawyers in private practice try to fulfill the same concepts of service, and would in most cases value in principle the same 'advantages' for their clients as in-house lawyers' clients value — familiarity with the client, his context and aims, accessibility, cost. Most lawyers would assert that their advice is always intended to be both practical and positive. Yet increasingly strident public doubts on this score have led to a growing political and economic pressure for the profession to live up to the claim in practice. In a book that is very much about the business world, one might use a business analogy and argue that the legal profession has too frequently failed to live up to the ideal in practice because of the power of the producer, the profession and its work practices and culture, over the consumer. In this respect, in-house lawyers at least have something of an advantage over their colleagues in organisational terms. In-house lawyers are forced into a daily relationship with their client community in which they can readily grasp the client's most pressing concerns, where they can readily compare the practice of other specialists and of professional management in terms of what might be meant by teamwork, by decision-making and advice directed to the practical purposes of the organisation. It is not surprising if they easily accept and seek to implement these values as part of their professional culture. The 'market' which judges the in-house lawyer is not the 'free market' of economic prices; rather it is based on the community of values in the organisation, on the lawyer's reputation and organisational status — as ascribed to a 'lawyer', but even more as achieved. It is, in other words, founded on reputation in the community.

Lawyers in private practice on the other hand usually do not 'live' with their client in the same way. Their 'product' has in a number of important respects been protected from consumer assessment, whether that might have come in the form of free market influences or from effective public sector control systems. In some respects one might say that lawyers in private practice have been hampered, too, by a product which often mistakes the consumer's needs. The 'leadership culture' and 'business strategy' of the legal profession are premised on an adversarial system of litigation which is steeped in tradition and has ensured that the same adversarial process (or anticipation of such) is applied to all disputes that come before it. In this area of its 'products', consumer responsiveness has been even more incapable of influence — the system has even prided itself on shielding the branch of the profession which specialises in litigation, the Bar, from the client through the medium of a divided profession (and drawn the judiciary largely from the same ranks).

There are now, however, many signs of change, at almost every level of the system. While lawyers have managed to live with a 'bad press' from many members of the public and from academic critics, economic pressures induced by the political ethos and public spending cuts are forcing change. Solicitors have begun to explore the question of advertising to the public, have cut conveyancing costs, are devising new business arrangements for property sales, are exploring alternative business forms for their practices, and are approaching practice management and continuing education more systematically. In facing the economic demands placed on them by loss of conveyancing, they have in turn resurrected the debate on fusion of the profession, or on the question of a system of common training for intending lawyers. At the level of the Bar there are perhaps less obvious signs of reform, but the possibility of direct access to the client is being mooted, and in any case barristers are even more dependent on the products of the system, on the formalities of the wider legal system, than are their fellow lawyers. In the Lord Chancellor's Department, business experts, in the form of management consultants, and lay advisers have been used to analyse and assess the need for reform in the interests at least of cost-savings but also of the consumers' needs.

This study of in-house lawyers concerns only a small part of the system. However, it does I hope contribute some lessons in the debate and towards the wider research programme needed on the workings of the law business and the pros and cons of proposals for action. What lessons?

First, the ethic of service is still alive and well amongst the legal profession, despite the more cynical view many might take of lawyer motives, the view in some surveys that legal practice is primarily a money-raising activity, a business more than a profession. However, in-house lawyers could not do otherwise than serve, given the organisational setting in which they function. The profession at large is still in a sense impaled on the dilemma of seeking to combine a service and a business function. Such a combination is, of course, not inherently contradictory, although some lawyers in private practice might say it was, and some economists would say they are one and the same. However, given the changes in the complexity of law, given the range of activities now requiring legal form or advice, from regulation to property transactions, it is more and more clear that the business form in which the profession has traditionally practised is coming to seem inappropriate for many of the tasks it must fulfill. Exactly where or how it must be reformed, from questions of the size of practices to issues of fusion, from alternative dispute resolution to the criteria for independence and avoidance of conflicts of interest — these are substantive issues which this work cannot pretend to do more than highlight.

However, another lesson from this study is that 'employee' status is not in itself a bar to independence, although one might argue that it may need a clear professional identity and external association to sustain it. Also, this work highlights the fact that the legal profession is highly differentiated and in ways not necessarily adequately recognised by the profession at large. For lawyers to be 'accessible' to their many publics and familiar with their concerns, requires a range of more customer-responsive types of legal practice and lawyer, supported in turn by a system of legal training and continuing education, of legal practice, and of dispute resolution methods which allow, respect and encourage diversity and specialisation. Such encouragement need not be blind, but it does call for a legal profession which is more 'proactive', more bold in its analysis of how the 'law business' works as a system, where it is failing its consumers, what criteria it needs to evaluate these issues, how to be responsive to the client whom lawyers have always claimed to serve. In achieving this, lawyers need to recognise the need to synthesise the *professional* ideal of objective advice to one's client in the spirit of advising on the client's best interests, and the *business* ideal of a 'professional' approach to managing its industry to attract and keep its customers. Lawyers should aim to be liked as well as respected. To ask whether a business 'can be liked' is perhaps an inappropriate question. But to ask whether it is serving its members and its customers as effectively as it could, whether it is a valued part of its wider community and, most important, *whether it is perceived as 'accessible' by that community*, are questions that should be at the heart of the profession as much as of any business.

Bibliography

Abel, R. L. (1980) 'The Sociology of American Lawyers: a bibliographic guide', *Law and Policy Quarterly*, 2, 375– 91.

Abel, R. L. (1982) 'The Politics of the Market for Legal Services', in P. A. Thomas (ed.), *Law in the Balance: Legal Services in the 1980s* (London: Martin Robertson) 6–59.

Abel-Smith, B. and Stevens, R. (1967) 'Lawyers and the Courts' in V. Aubert (ed.) (1969) *Sociology of Law* (London: Penguin).

AGCAS, Working Party on the Legal Profession (1984) *Opportunities for Qualified Lawyers in Legal Departments in Industry and Commerce* (London: Association of Graduate Careers Advisory Services).

Anderson, S. D. (1968), 'The Training of the Company Lawyer', in *Le Juriste D'Entreprise* (Belgium: Université de Liège) 387–94.

Ashenfelter, O. and Bloom, D. E. (1983) *Models of Arbitrator Behavior: Theory and Evidence*, Working Paper No. 1149 (Cambridge, Mass.: National Bureau of Economic Research).

Bardach, E. and Kagan, R. A. (1982) *Going By the Book: The Problem of Regulatory Unreasonableness* (Philadelphia: Temple University Press).

Bartlett, J. W. (1982) *The Law Business: A Tired Monopoly* (Littleton, Colorado: Fred B. Rothman).

Beale, H. & Dugdale, T. (1975) 'Contracts Between Businessmen: Planning and the Use of Contractual Remedies', *British Journal of Law and Society*, vol. 2, no. 1, 45–60.

Beaumont, P. B. (1983) *Safety at Work and the Unions* (London: Croom Helm).

Bentham, R. (1978) 'The Lawyer's Role in the Oil Industry', *Proceedings of the Petroleum Law Seminar*, 8–13 January (Cambridge, England, Committee on Energy and Natural Resources, International Bar Association).

Berle, A. A. (1964) 'Review of Levy, Corporation Lawyer . . . Saint or Sinner?', in J. Honnold (ed.) (1964) *The Life of the Law: Readings on the Growth of Legal Institutions* (Free Press of Glencoe: Collier Macmillan).

Binger, J. H. (1968), 'What I Expect from the Ideal Corporate Counsel', in *Le Juriste D'Entreprise* (Belgium: Université de Liège).

Blake, A. (1987) 'Legal Education in Crisis: A Strategy for Legal Education into the 1990s', *The Law Teacher*, vol. 21, no. 1, 3–22.

Blaustein, A. P. and Porter, C. O. (1954) *The American Lawyer: A Summary of the Survey of the Legal Profession* (Chicago: University of Chicago Press).

Blom-Cooper, L. (1985) 'A Cold Wind Blowing Through the Bar', *Observer*, 21 July.

Boyd, J. (1983) 'The Confidentiality of Legal Advice in the EEC', *International Business Lawyer*, September 1983, 35–8.

Brown, L. M. (1965) 'Legal Audit', *Southern California Law Review*, 38, 431–5.

Burns, T. and Stalker, G. H. (1966) *The Management of Innovation* (London: Tavistock).

Business Week (1974) 'How Companies Fight Soaring Legal Costs', 2357, 16 November 1974, 104–8.

273

Business Week (1984) 'A New Corporate Powerhouse: The Legal Department', 9 April 1984, 90–3.

Business Week (1986) 'Megafirms are Taking Over Corporate Law', 17 November 1986, 72–4.

Cain, M. (1983) 'The General Practice Lawyer and the Client: Towards a Radical Conception', in R. Dingwall and P. Lewis (eds) (1983) *The Sociology of the Professions* (London: Macmillan) 106–30.

Cantor, D. J. (1978) 'Law Firms Are Getting Bigger . . . And More Complex', *American Bar Association Journal* February 1978, vol. 64, 215–9.

Carlin, J. E. (1962) *Lawyers on Their Own: A Study of Individual Practitioners in Chicago* (New Jersey: Rutgers University Press).

Carney, W. J. (1982) *The Changing Role of the Corporate Attorney* (Lexington, Virginia: Lexington Books).

Chambers, M. (1986) 'The Cost Advantage of the In-House Lawyer', BACFI Bulletin, *Business Law Review*, vol. 7, nos. 8– 9, iii.

Chan, D. A. and Wilson, C. D. (1983) 'The Rise of the In-House Lawyer', *International Financial Law Review*, May 1983, 4–13.

Choka, A. D. (1969) 'The Effective Legal Department: A Primer of Results Oriented Planning', *The Business Lawyer*, April 1969, 825–75.

Choka, A. D. (1970) 'The Role of Corporate Counsel', *The Business Lawyer*, April 1970, 1011–26.

Cohen, H. (1984) 'Employed Lawyers in England', *The Journal of the Legal Profession*, University of Alabama School of Law, vol. 9, 125–49.

Cohen, L. and Manion, L. (1980) *Research Methods in Education* (London: Croom Helm).

Confederation of British Industry (1985) *Managing Legal Costs* (London: CBI).

Coombe, G. W., Jr. (1985) 'Law Firms and Company Lawyers: The Next Decade', *International Legal Practitioner*, March 1985, 9–14.

Coombe, G. W., Jr. (1985a) 'How to Make Outside Counsel More Productive and Their Services More Useful to Corporate Counsel', *Lawyer Hiring and Training Report*, October, vol. 6, no. 5 (Chicago: Lawletters).

Corporate Lawyers' Association of Victoria (1985) 'Inhouse Lawyers and the Private Profession — Are They on the Same Tram?', Panel session 8 August, 23rd Australian Legal Convention, Melbourne.

Coulson, R. (1968) *How to Stay out of Court* (New York: Crown).

Counter, K. (1986) 'Training Tomorrow's Specialist Lawyers: The Needs of Business', *Business Law Review*, July 1986, vol. 7, no. 4, 210.

Curran, B. with Rosich, K. J., Carson, C. N. and Puccetti, M. C. (1985) *The Lawyer Statistical Report: A Statistical Profile of the U.S. Legal Profession in the 1980s* (Chicago: American Bar Foundation).

Daniel, W. W. and Stilgoe, E. (1978) *The Impact of Employment Protection Laws* (London: Policy Studies Institute).

David, J. (1986) 'Alternative Dispute Resolution: What Is It?', Conference Paper, Canberra, AADRA.

Davies, C. (1983) 'Professionals in Bureaucracies: The Conflict Thesis Revisited' in Dingwall and Lewis, op. cit., (1983), 177–94.

de Butts, J. D. (1978) 'The Client's View of the Lawyer's Proper Role', *The Business Lawyer*, vol. 33, March 1978, 1177–85.

Department of Employment (1985) *Lifting the Burden*, Cmnd. 9571 (London: HMSO).

Department of Employment (1986) *Building Businesses . . . Not Barriers*, Cmnd. 9794 (London: HMSO).

Dingwall, R. and Lewis, P. (eds) (1983) *The Sociology of the Professions: Lawyers, Doctors and Others* (London: Macmillan).

Donnell, J. D. (1970) *The Corporate Counsel: a Role Study* (Indiana: Indiana University).

Dunlop, J. T. (1976) 'The Limits of Legal Compulsion', *Conference Board Record*, vol. 27, March, 23–7.

Edwards, H. T. (1986) 'Alternative Dispute Resolution: Panacea or Anathema?', *Harvard Law Review*, 99, 668–84.

Faucheux, C. and Rojot, J. (1979) 'Social Psychology and Industrial Relations: A Cross-Cultural Perspective', in Stephenson, G. M. and Brotherton, C. J., *Industrial Relations: A Social Psychological Approach* (London: John Wiley) 33–49.

Faulkner, T. M. & Saunders, R. N. S. (1985) 'Are the Professions Entering The Small Business Sector?', *New Law Journal*, 29 March, 326–8.

Fennel, P. (1980) 'Solicitors, Their Market, and Their "Ignorant Public": The Crisis of the Professional Ideal', in Bankowski, Z. and Mungham, G. (1980) *Essays in Law and Society* (London: Routledge & Kegan Paul).

Ferguson, R. B. (1980) 'The Adjudication of Commercial Disputes and the Legal System in Modern England', *British Journal of Law and Society*, vol. 7, no. 2, 141–57.

Fischer, R. L. (1984) 'The Changing Role of Corporate Counsel', *Journal of Law and Commerce*, University of Pittsburgh, vol. 4, no. 1, 45–64.

Fisher, R. (1985) 'He Who Pays the Piper', *Harvard Business Review*, March–April 1985, 150–9.

Fletcher Rogers, D. G. (1968), 'The Company Lawyer Etiquette and Ethics', in *Le Juriste D'Entreprise* (Belgium: Universite de Liège).

Freidson, E. (1983) 'The Theory of Professions: State of the Art' in Dingwall and Lewis, op. cit., 19–37.

Freidson, E. (1986) *Professional Powers: A Study of the Institutionalization of Formal Knowledge* (Chicago: University of Chicago Press).

Galanter, M. (1983) 'Mega-Law and Mega-Lawyering in the Contemporary United States', in Dingwall and Lewis, op. cit., 152–76.

Galuccio, N. (1978) 'The Rise of the Company Lawyer', *Forbes*, September 18, 123, 168–81.

Gibson, D. and Baldwin, J. K. (eds) (1985) *Law in a Cynical Society: Opinion and Law in the 1980s* (Vancouver: Carswell Legal Publications).

Gold, N. (ed.) (1982) *Essays on Legal Education* (Toronto: Butterworths).

Goldberg, S. B., Green, E. D. and Sander, F. E. A. (1985) *Dispute Resolution* (Boston: Little, Brown).

Gorman, R. E. and Brown, J. K. (1969) 'Legal Organization in the Manufacturing Corporation: a survey of business opinion and experience', *Conference Board Record*, vol. 6, August 1969, 42–7.

Gossett, W. T. (1963) 'Corporation Counsel and Social Responsibilities' *New York State Bar Journal*, vol. 34, February, 21–7.

Gouldner, A. W. (1957) 'Cosmopolitans and locals: towards an analysis of latent social roles', *Administrative Science Quarterly*, December 1957, 1281–306; March 1958, 444–80.

Gow, M. H. (1968), 'The Ethics of the Company Lawyer', in *Le Juriste D'Entreprise* (Belgium: Universite de Liège).

Hailsham, Lord (1985) Speech to Judges' Dinner, *Arbitration*, vol. 51, November, no. 4, 500–2, 517.

Hall, R. H. and Quinn, R. E. (eds) (1983) *Organizational Theory and Public Policy* (New York: Sage).

Hamilton, J. (1986) 'Lawyers as Businessmen', *Business Law Review*, vol. 7, April, no. 4, 104–5; vol. 7, July, no. 7, 208–9.

Handy, C. B. (1985) 3rd ed. *Understanding Organisations* (London: Penguin).

Hawkins, K. and Thomas, J. M. (eds) (1984) *Enforcing Regulation* (Boston: Kluwer-Nijhoff).

HAY-MSL (1986) *Survey of Pay and Benefits: Solicitors in Commerce and Industry* (London: HAY-MSL).

Hazard, J. C., Jr. (1978) *Ethics in the Practice of Law* (New Haven: Yale University Press).

Hazell, R. (ed.) (1978) *The Bar on Trial* (London: Quartet Books).

Heinz, J. P. and Laumann, E. O. (1983) *Chicago Lawyers: The Social Structure of the Bar* (New York: Russell Sage Foundation).

Henry, J. F. (1985) 'Mini-Trials: An Alternative To Litigation', *Negotiation Journal*, January, 13–17.

Hermann, A. H. (1983) *Judges, Law and Businessmen* (Deventer, Netherlands: Kluwer).

Hickman L. E. (1964) 'The Emerging Role of the Corporate Counsel' in J. Honnold (1964), *The Life of the Law*, op. cit., 473–82.

Hickman, L. E. (1968) 'The Emerging Role of Corporate Counsel', in *Le Juriste D'Entreprise* (Belgium: Université de Liège).

Honnold, J. (ed.) (1964) *The Life of the Law: Readings on the Growth of Legal Institutions* (Free Press of Glencoe: Collier Macmillan).

Hoskins, R. (1978) *Lawyers in Commerce? Employer Attitudes Towards the Employment of Law Graduates* (Sydney: The Law Foundation of New South Wales).

Houle, C. O. (1980) *Continuing Learning in the Professions* (San Francisco: Jossey Bass).

Johnson, T. J. (1972) *Professions and Power* (London: Macmillan).

Johnson, W. B. (1978) 'A Businessman's View of Lawyers', *The Business Lawyer*, vol. 33, no. 2, 826–30.

Johnson, D. L. (1982) 'Economic Regulation, the Corporation and Corporate Counsel' in Gold, N. (ed.) *Essays on Legal Education* (Toronto: Butterworths) 97–116.

Johnstone, Q. and Hopson, D., Jr. (1967) *Lawyers and their Work: An Analysis of the Legal Profession in the United States and England* (Indianapolis: Bobbs-Merrill).

Jones, B. F. (1985) 'The AM & S Case: An Australian View', *International Legal Practitioner*, March 1985, 15–21.

Jones, K. (1979) 'The Crimes of the Powerful and Beyond: An Essay Review', *Contemporary Crises*, 3, 317–31.

Joseph, M. (1985) *Lawyers Can Seriously Damage Your Health* (London: Joseph).

Kagan, R. A. (1984) 'On Regulatory Inspectorates and Police' in Hawkins and Thomas, op. cit., ch. 3.

Kagan, R. A. and Scholz, J. T. (1984) 'The "Criminology of the Corporation" and Regulatory Enforcement Strategies', in Hawkins and Thomas, op. cit., 67–95.

Kahn-Freund, O. (1979) *Labour Relations Heritage and Adjustment* (London: British Academy).

Kelly, D. P. (1978) 'A Businessman's View of Lawyers', *The Business Lawyer*, vol. 33, no. 2, 830–32.

Kelman, S. (1984) 'Enforcement of Occupational Safety and Health Regulations: A Comparison of Swedish and American Practices', in Hawkins and Thomas, op. cit., ch. 5.

Knowles, M. (1978) *The Adult Learner: A Neglected Species* (Chicago: Gulf).

Kolvenbach, W. (1979) *The Company Legal Department: Its Role, Function and Organisation* (Deventer, The Netherlands: Kluwer).

Kozelka, R. L. (1962) 'Business — the Emerging Profession', in National Society for the Study of Education *Education for the Professions* (Chicago: University of Chicago Press).

Laughton, D. S. (1968) 'The Company Lawyer's Supply of Information' in *Le Juriste D'Entreprise* (Belgium: Université de Liège).

Lawrence, P. R. and Lorsch, J. W. (1967) *Organization and Environment* (Cambridge, Mass.: Harvard University Press).

Law Society (1977), The Royal Commission on Legal Services *Memorandum On the Commerce and Industry Solicitor* no. 3, part 2, London.

Law Society (1986) 'Lawyers and the Courts: Time for Some Changes', A Discussion Paper issued by the Law Society's Contentious Business Committee, London.

Leary, T. B. (1982) 'A Corporate Counsel's Perspective', *Antitrust Law Journal*, vol. 51, 447–50.

Leigh, L. H. (1980) *Economic Crime in Europe* (London: Macmillan).

Levy, B. H. (1961) *Corporation Lawyer: Saint or Sinner?* (Philadelphia: Chilton).

Lewis, P. (1982) 'Report of the Commission: Analysis and Change in Legal Services', in P. A. Thomas (ed.) (1982) *Law in the Balance*, 60–83.

Lippitt, G. L. (1982) *Organizational Renewal: A Holistic Approach to Organizational Development* (2nd ed. (New Jersey: Prentice-Hall).

Lord Chancellor's Department (1987) *Civil Justice Review: General Issues* (London).

Macaulay, S. (1963) 'Non-Contractual Relations in Business: A Preliminary Study', *American Sociological Review*, 28, 55–67.

Mackie, K. J. (1983) 'The Application of Learning Theory to Adult Teaching' in Normie, G. and Toye, M. *Learning About Learning: Selected Readings* (Milton Keynes: Open University Press), 21–8.

Mackie, K. J. (1983a) 'The Significance of the Work-place for Adult Education', *International Journal of Lifelong Education*, vol. 2, no. 2, 179–88.

Mackie, K. J. (1984) 'Three Faces of Democracy and Three Missing Persons: The Trade Union Act 1984', *Industrial Relations Journal*, vol. 15, Winter 1984, no. 4, 83–97.

Mackie, K. J. (1986) 'Commercial Arbitration and Dispute Resolution in Australia', Research Report to the British Academy.

Mackie, K. J. (1987) 'Lessons From Down-Under: conciliation and arbitration in Australia', *Industrial Relations Journal*, vol. 18, no. 2, 100–16.

Maddock, C. S. (1968), 'The Challenge to House Counsel', in *Le Juriste D'Entreprise* (Belgium: Université de Liège).

McBarnet, D. J. (1981) *Conviction: The Law, The State and the Construction of Justice* (London: Macmillan).

Mintzberg, H. (1973) *The Nature of Managerial Work* (London: Harper & Row).

Mungham, G. and Thomas, P. A. (1983) 'Solicitors and Clients: Altruism or Self-Interest', in Dingwall and Lewis, op. cit., 131–51.

Murphy, R. W. (1968) 'The Profile of a General Counsel, His Position and Function in an American Corporation', in *Le Juriste D'Entreprise* (Belgium: Université de Liège).

Murray, T., Dingwall, R. and Eekelaar, J. (1983) 'Professionals in Bureaucracies: Solicitors in Private Practice and local Government', in Dingwall and Lewis, op. cit., 195–220.

Napley, Sir D. (1983) 'The Growing Threat to the Independence of the Professions', *Law Society's Gazette*, 29 June, 1651–3.

Office of Fair Trading (1986) 'Restrictions On The Kind Of Organisation Through Which Members of Professions May Offer Their Services' (London).

Page, R. (1985) 'Compulsory Continuing Education', *Law Society Gazette*, vol. 82, 28, 2141–4.

Paterson, A. (1983) 'Becoming a Judge' in Dingwall and Lewis, op. cit., 263–85.

Patterson, B. H. (1971) 'A Legal Audit Questionnaire', *The Business Lawyer*, January, 983–96.

Pfeffer, J. and Salancik, G. R. (1978) *The External Control of Organizations: A Resource-Dependence Perspective* (New York: Harper & Row).

Podmore, D. (1980) *Solicitors and the Wider Community* (London: Heinemann).

Podmore, D. (1980a) 'Bucher & Strauss Revisited: The Case of the Solicitors' Profession', *British Journal of Law and Society*, vol. 7, no. 1, 1–21.

Porter, M. E. (1980) *Competitive Strategy: Techniques for Analysing Industries and Competitors* (New York: Free Press).

Preston, L. E. (1980) 'Corporate Power and Social Performance' in Siegfried, J. J. (ed.) *The Economics of Firm Size, Market Structure and Social Performance*, Proceedings of a Conference sponsored by the Bureau of Competition, Federal Trade Commission.

Pritchard, R. L. (1985) 'Corporate Legal Departments — Lasting Fashion or Passing Fad?' (Sydney, unpublished paper).

Rast, L. E. (1978) 'What the Chief Executive Looks for in his Corporate Law Department', *The Business Lawyer*, vol. 33, no. 2, 811–15.

Report of the Committee on Legal Education (1971), Cmnd. 4595 (London: HMSO).

Report to Parliament on the Subordinate Legislation (Deregulation) Bill 1983, (1984) Legal and Constitutional Committee, Parliament of Victoria, D.no.44/1982–84, September 1984.

Report of the Royal Commission on Legal Services (1979) Cmnd. 7648 (London: HMSO).

Reeves, P. (1986) *Are Two Legal Professions Necessary?* (London: Waterlow).

Reiss, A. J., Jr. (1984) 'Selecting Strategies of Social Control over Organizational Life', in Hawkins and Thomas, op. cit., ch. 2, 23–36.

Richards, D. (1986) 'Government by Order' in *Business Law Review*, vol. 7, no. 12, 329.

Rosen, R. E. (1984) *Lawyers in Corporate Decision-Making*, Dissertation (unpublished) (University of California-Berkeley).

Rosenthal, D. (1974) *Lawyer and Client: Who's in Charge?* (New Jersey: Transaction Books).

Ruder, D. S. (1968) 'A Suggestion for Increased Use of Corporate Legal Departments in Modern Corporations', in *Le Juriste D'Entreprise* (Belgium: Université de Liège).

Ruescheymeyer, D. (1973) *Lawyers and Their Society: A Comparative Study of the Legal Profession in Germany and in the United States* (Cambridge, Mass.: Harvard University Press).

Russell, B. S. 'The Company Lawyer's Relations with the Bar', in *Le Juriste D'Entreprise* (Belgium: Universite de Liège).

Sarnoff, P. (1970) *Careers in the Legal Profession* (New York: Julian Messner).

Schein, E. H. (1972) *Professional Education: Some New Directions* (New York: McGraw Hill).

Schon, D. A. (1983) *The Reflective Practitioner* (London: Temple Smith).

Schon, D. A. (1987) *Educating The Reflective Practitioner* (New York: Jossey Bass).

Sexton, M. and Maher, L. W. (1982) *The Legal Mystique: The Role of Lawyers in Australian Society* (Sydney: Angus & Robertson).

Sherr, A. (1986) *Client Interviewing for Lawyers* (London: Sweet & Maxwell).

Smigel, E. O. (1969) *The Wall Street Lawyer: Professional Organization Man?* (Indiana: Indiana University Press).

Smyser, J. M. 'In-House Corporate Counsel: The Erosion of Independence' in Nader, R. and Green, M. (eds) (1976) *Verdicts on Lawyers* (New York: Thomas Y. Crowell).

Snider, L. (1987) 'Towards a Political Economy of Reform, Regulation and Corporate Crime', *Law and Policy*, vol. 9, no. 1, 37–68.

Spangler, E. (1986) *Lawyers for Hire: Salaried Professionals at Work* (New Haven: Yale University Press).

Steinberg, M. I. (1983) *Corporate Internal Affairs: A Corporate and Securities Law Perspective* (Westport, Connecticut: Quorum Books).

Stichnoth, J. A. and Dolan, P. J. (1982) 'Management Strategies for Corporate Counsel', *Legal Economics*, 8, January-February 1982, 13–19.

Stone, C. D. (1975) *Where the Law Ends: The Social Control of Corporate Behavior* (New York: Harper Colophon).

Swaine, R. T. (1949) 'Impact of Big Business on the Profession: An Answer to the Critics of the Modern Bar', *American Bar Association Journal* 35, 89–92, 168–71.

Thomas, P. A. (ed.) (1982) *Law in the Balance: Legal Services in the 1980s* (London: Martin Robertson).

Thomas, P. and Mungham, G. (1983) 'Solicitors and Clients: Altruism or Self-Interest', in Dingwall and Lewis, op. cit., 131–51.

Todd, F. (ed.) (1987) *Planning Continuing Professional Development* (London: Croom Helm).

Tomasic, R. (1985) 'Cynicism and Ambivalence Towards Law and Legal Institutions in Australia', in Gibson and Baldwin, op. cit., ch. 3.

Tomasic, R. and Bullard, C. (1978) *Lawyers and their Work in New South Wales: Preliminary Report* (Sydney: Law Foundation of New South Wales).

Tomasic, R. and Feeley, M. M. (1982) *Neighborhood Justice: Assessment of an Emerging Idea* (New York: Longman).

Tough, A. (1979) *The Adult's Learning Projects* 2nd ed. (Toronto: Ontario Institute for Studies in Education).

Townsend, R. I., Jr. (1970) 'A Corporation Lawyer as "House Counsel" ', in B. Asbell, *What Laywers Really do: Six Lawyers Talk About Their Life and Work* (New York: Peter H. Wyden) 45–61.

Trist, E. L. and Beaver, H. (1964) *Social Research and a National Policy for Science* (London: Tavistock).

Twining, W. L. (1986) 'Taking Skills Seriously', *The Journal of Professional Legal Education*, vol. 4, 1.

Useem, M. (1980) 'The Corporate Community' in Hall and Qinn, op. cit.

Useem, M. (1984) *The Inner Circle: Large Corporations and the rise of Business Political Activity in the U. S. and U.K.* (New York: Oxford University Press).

Utton, M. A. (1986) *The Economics of Regulating Industry* (Oxford: Basil Blackwell).

Vickers, Sir G. (1983) *The Art of Judgment* 3rd ed. (London: Harper & Row).

Waterson, G. (1984) 'Continuing Professional Education: A Challenge for the Eighties?', *Journal of Further and Higher Education*, vol. 8, 60.

Westin, A. F. (1981) *Whistle-Blowing: Loyalty and Dissent in the Corporation* (New York: McGraw Hill).

Wilensky, H. L. (1964) 'The Professionalization of Everyone?', *American Journal of Sociology* 70, 142–6.

Wilson, C. deKay (1984) 'Managing for success at Skadden, Arps', *International Financial Law Review*, November 1984, 31–5.

Wilson, J. Q. (ed.) *The Politics of Regulation* (New York: Basic Books).

Zander, M. (1976) 'Independence of the legal profession — what does it mean?', *Law Society Gazette*, 73, 758–9.

Index